ATS-39　　ADMISSION TEST SERIES

This is your
PASSBOOK for...

California Proficiency Program (CPP)

Test Preparation Study Guide
Questions & Answers

COPYRIGHT NOTICE

This book is SOLELY intended for, is sold ONLY to, and its use is RESTRICTED to individual, bona fide applicants or candidates who qualify by virtue of having seriously filed applications for appropriate license, certificate, professional and/or promotional advancement, higher school matriculation, scholarship, or other legitimate requirements of education and/or governmental authorities.

This book is NOT intended for use, class instruction, tutoring, training, duplication, copying, reprinting, excerption, or adaptation, etc., by:

1) Other publishers
2) Proprietors and/or Instructors of "Coaching" and/or Preparatory Courses
3) Personnel and/or Training Divisions of commercial, industrial, and governmental organizations
4) Schools, colleges, or universities and/or their departments and staffs, including teachers and other personnel
5) Testing Agencies or Bureaus
6) Study groups which seek by the purchase of a single volume to copy and/or duplicate and/or adapt this material for use by the group as a whole without having purchased individual volumes for each of the members of the group
7) Et al.

Such persons would be in violation of appropriate Federal and State statutes.

PROVISION OF LICENSING AGREEMENTS – Recognized educational, commercial, industrial, and governmental institutions and organizations, and others legitimately engaged in educational pursuits, including training, testing, and measurement activities, may address request for a licensing agreement to the copyright owners, who will determine whether, and under what conditions, including fees and charges, the materials in this book may be used them. In other words, a licensing facility exists for the legitimate use of the material in this book on other than an individual basis. However, it is asseverated and affirmed here that the material in this book CANNOT be used without the receipt of the express permission of such a licensing agreement from the Publishers. Inquiries re licensing should be addressed to the company, attention rights and permissions department.

All rights reserved, including the right of reproduction in whole or in part, in any form or by any means, electronic or mechanical, including photocopying, recording, or by any information storage and retrieval system, without permission in writing from the Publisher.

Copyright © 2025 by
National Learning Corporation

212 Michael Drive, Syosset, NY 11791
(516) 921-8888 • www.passbooks.com
E-mail: info@passbooks.com

PASSBOOK® SERIES

THE *PASSBOOK® SERIES* has been created to prepare applicants and candidates for the ultimate academic battlefield – the examination room.

At some time in our lives, each and every one of us may be required to take an examination – for validation, matriculation, admission, qualification, registration, certification, or licensure.

Based on the assumption that every applicant or candidate has met the basic formal educational standards, has taken the required number of courses, and read the necessary texts, the *PASSBOOK® SERIES* furnishes the one special preparation which may assure passing with confidence, instead of failing with insecurity. Examination questions – together with answers – are furnished as the basic vehicle for study so that the mysteries of the examination and its compounding difficulties may be eliminated or diminished by a sure method.

This book is meant to help you pass your examination provided that you qualify and are serious in your objective.

The entire field is reviewed through the huge store of content information which is succinctly presented through a provocative and challenging approach – the question-and-answer method.

A climate of success is established by furnishing the correct answers at the end of each test.

You soon learn to recognize types of questions, forms of questions, and patterns of questioning. You may even begin to anticipate expected outcomes.

You perceive that many questions are repeated or adapted so that you can gain acute insights, which may enable you to score many sure points.

You learn how to confront new questions, or types of questions, and to attack them confidently and work out the correct answers.

You note objectives and emphases, and recognize pitfalls and dangers, so that you may make positive educational adjustments.

Moreover, you are kept fully informed in relation to new concepts, methods, practices, and directions in the field.

You discover that you are actually taking the examination all the time: you are preparing for the examination by "taking" an examination, not by reading extraneous and/or supererogatory textbooks.

In short, this PASSBOOK®, used directedly, should be an important factor in helping you to pass your test.

Test Specifications

The CHSPE consists of two test sections: English-language Arts and Mathematics.

English-language Arts Section

The English-language Arts section consists of two subtests: Language and Reading. Both subtests must be passed to pass the English-language Arts section.

Language Subtest

The Language subtest has one writing task and 48 multiple-choice questions. The writing task requires a persuasive essay. Persuasive writing requires the clear and logical presentation of reasons and details offered in support of a position in order to convince the reader to accept that position.

The multiple-choice questions combine mechanics and expression, as defined below, include some study skills items, and measure achievement in applying the principles that form effective writing.

A. Language Mechanics
Capitalization
    Distinguish correct capitalization
Usage
    Identify correctly applied grammar
Punctuation
    Distinguish correct punctuation

B. Language Expression
Sentence Structure
    Distinguish between clearly written sentences and sentences that contain errors in expression or construction
Prewriting
    Plan, organize, and improve writing samples
Content and Organization
    Determine appropriate editing of short paragraphs.

Reading Subtest

The Reading subtest has 30 vocabulary questions and 54 reading comprehension questions, all of which are multiple-choice.

The vocabulary questions assess synonyms, multiple-meaning words, and context clues as defined below.

A. Synonyms
Demonstrate the ability to recognize a synonym for a word used in context

B. Multiple-Meaning Words
Demonstrate the ability to determine the meaning of a given word with multiple meanings

C. Context Clues
Demonstrate the ability to use context clues to assign meaning to an unknown word

The reading comprehension questions test initial understanding, interpretation, critical analysis, and strategies using three types of text: literary (material typically read for enjoyment), informational (material typically found in textbooks and other sources of information), and functional (material typically encountered in everyday-life situations). The specific reading comprehension skills assessed are listed below.

A. Initial Understanding
Demonstrate the ability to comprehend explicitly stated relationships in a variety of reading selections.
- Determine explicit supporting details
- Determine explicit sequence or action
- Determine explicit explanation or cause

B. Interpretation
Demonstrate the ability to form an interpretation of a variety of reading selections based on explicit and implicit information in the selections.
- Determine implicit details, plot, sequence, or action
- Determine implicit causes for or effects of actions, events, or ideas
- Draw conclusions from details
- Extract implicit main idea or theme
- Determine problems and solutions in text
- Generalize beyond text
- Interpret character traits, motivation, or behavior
- Make predictions
- Determine important from less-important ideas
- Categorize, classify, compare, or contrast
- Provide support for conclusions or outcomes
- Apply ideas and information to new situations or problems

C. Critical Analysis
Demonstrate the ability to synthesize and evaluate explicit and implicit information in a variety of reading selections.
- Analyze author's purpose, assumptions, or viewpoint
- Analyze text structure or elements
- Distinguish fact from opinion
- Identify, differentiate, or analyze characteristics of genre
- Determine author's intended audience
- Discern author's voice
- Discern and interpret literary devices
- Evaluate sufficiency or consistency of information or text

D. Strategies
Demonstrate the ability to recognize and apply text factors and reading strategies in a variety of reading selections.
- Ask clarifying questions
- Determine background knowledge
- Select an appropriate reading strategy in a given situation
- Apply text structure to reading task
- Determine if needed information is within or out of text
- Determine unknown words from context
- Set purpose for reading

Mathematics Section

The Mathematics section has 50 multiple-choice questions that assess content in the following areas: number sense and operations; patterns, relationships, and algebra; data, statistics, and probability; and geometry and measurement. The questions also assess the mathematical processes of communication and representation, estimation, mathematical connections, and reasoning and problem solving. The skills and processes assessed are listed below.

A. Number Sense and Operations

Demonstrate understanding of the meaning and use of numbers, the various representations of numbers, number systems, and the relationships between and among numbers. Demonstrate understanding of the meaning of operations, the relationship between operations, and the practical settings in which a specific operation or set of operations is appropriate.

- Identify numbers expressed in scientific notation
- Identify factorial representation
- Identify the effects of an operation
- Compare and order real numbers
- Solve problems using estimation strategies
- Identify and use order of operations rules
- Simplify expressions containing exponents or radicals
- Solve problems involving absolute value
- Solve problems using nonroutine strategies

B. Patterns, Relationships, and Algebra

Describe, complete, continue, and demonstrate understanding of patterns involving numbers, symbols, and geometric figures. Patterns with numbers include those found in lists, function tables, ratios and proportions, and matrices. Demonstrate understanding of algebraic principles through interaction with expressions, equations, algebraic notation, and other representations of mathematical relationships.

- Identify slopes of lines given points, equations, or graphs
- Solve problems involving ratio or proportion
- Analyze characteristics of linear relationships
- Identify equations of linear functions given tables of values, points, or graphs
- Evaluate expressions
- Solve problems involving patterns
- Identify equations of quadratic functions given tables of values or graphs
- Identify graphs of inequalities
- Solve problems involving logical reasoning
- Solve linear, quadratic, or radical equations
- Solve systems of linear equations
- Translate problem situations into algebraic expressions and equations

C. Data, Statistics, and Probability

Describe, interpret, and make predictions based on the analysis of data presented in a variety of ways, including graphs, plots, tables, and lists. Demonstrate an understanding of probability concepts through interaction with simple events, compound events, and experimental probability.

- Analyze data and draw inferences from tables and graphs
- Make a prediction based on experimental or statistical data
- Determine combinations and permutations
- Determine and use measures of central tendency and dispersion
- Find the probability of a simple or compound event
- Solve problems involving probabilities

D. Geometry and Measurement

Demonstrate understanding of the characteristics and properties of plane and solid figures, coordinate geometry, and spatial reasoning. Demonstrate understanding of the meaning and use of various measurement systems, the tools of measurement, and the integral role of estimation in measurement.

- Identify and classify solid and plane figures
- Determine measurements indirectly from scale drawings
- Solve problems involving perimeter, circumference, area, or volume
- Solve problems using the Pythagorean theorem
- Identify geometric transformations
- Solve problems using properties of geometric figures
- Solve problems using spatial reasoning
- Solve problems involving similar figures

Processes

Communication and Representation

Demonstrate an understanding of the symbols and terms utilized in mathematics, and correctly interpret alternative representations of numbers, expressions, and data.

Estimation

Apply estimation strategies in problem solving and determine the reasonableness of results.

Mathematical Connections

Demonstrate an understanding of the interrelatedness of mathematical concepts, procedures, and processes both among different mathematical topics and with other content areas.

Reasoning and Problem Solving

Demonstrate the ability to apply inductive, deductive, or spatial reasoning and to make valid inferences and draw valid conclusions. Demonstrate the ability to apply strategies to solve conventional and nonroutine problems.

Sample Test Questions

English-language Arts Section
Language Subtest

Writing Task
The Language subtest of the English-language Arts section of the CHSPE includes one persuasive writing task. For the writing task you will be asked to write an essay to persuade a specified audience of your opinion about an issue. You will need to be specific and explain your reasons for your opinion.

Sample Writing Task

Some people believe that high school classes should not begin before 9:00 a.m. Do you agree **or** disagree? Write a letter to the editor of your local newspaper to **persuade** readers to accept your opinion on this issue. Be **specific** and **explain** your reasons. (Do <u>not</u> sign your letter.)

Essay Scoring Scale

5   **Essay addresses the writing task in an <u>effective</u> manner. The essay:**
- defends a clearly stated position with appropriate reasoning and specificity; is purposefully organized.
- effectively anticipates and addresses the readers' potential concerns.
- demonstrates control of a variety of sentence structures; uses precise word choice.
- is generally free of errors in grammar, usage, and/or conventions.

4   **Essay addresses the writing task in a <u>competent</u> manner. The essay:**
- defends a position with adequate reasoning and some degree of specificity; is organized.
- anticipates and addresses some of the readers' potential concerns.
- demonstrates control of sentence structure; uses generally appropriate word choice.
- may have a few minor errors in grammar, usage, and/or conventions.

3   **Essay addresses the writing task in a <u>basic</u> manner. The essay:**
- supports a position with some reasons and details; has some organization.
- anticipates and attempts to address some of the readers' potential concerns.
- demonstrates basic control of sentence structure and word choice.
- may have errors in grammar, usage, and/or conventions, but errors do not cause confusion.

2   **Essay addresses the writing task in a <u>limited</u> manner. The essay:**
- may not have a clear position; may provide limited reasons or irrelevant details; may be poorly organized.
- may make a limited attempt to anticipate and address the readers' potential concerns.
- exhibits inadequate control of sentence structure and word choice.
- may have serious and repeated errors in grammar, usage, and/or conventions that cause confusion.

1   **Essay may or may not address the writing task. The essay:**
- may have no position; provides few if any reasons or details.
- makes little or no attempt to anticipate and address the readers' potential concerns.
- exhibits little or no control of sentence structure.
- may have pervasive errors in grammar, usage, and/or conventions that cause significant confusion.

Writer's Checklist

☐ Did I write about the topic?

☐ Did I express my ideas in complete sentences?

☐ Did I give enough details to explain or support my ideas?

☐ Did I include only those details that are about my topic?

☐ Did I write my ideas in an order that is clear for the reader to follow?

☐ Did I write a topic sentence for each paragraph?

☐ Did I use a capital letter at the beginning of each sentence and for all other words that should be capitalized?

☐ Did I use the correct punctuation at the end of each sentence and within each sentence?

☐ Did I spell words correctly?

☐ Did I print or write clearly?

From the official announcement for educational purposes

Sample Essays

Below and on the next page are two sample essays in response to the sample writing task on the previous page. The first is an example of an essay at score point 4; the second is an example of an essay at score point 2. The commentary with each sample essay explains why the essay earned the score that it did.

Sample Essay — Score Point 4

The following essay earned a score of 4. The essay addresses the writing task in a competent manner.

Dear Editor:

Recently people have been discussing changing the hours of school, should schools begin at 8 am or after 9 am. I believe the early start is better for several reasons.

There are many advantages to starting school early. One of the most important reasons is for sports, and jobs. Students who play sports need to practice after school. If school begins later in the day, it will end later, and athletes will be practicing late into the afternoon, getting home after dark. Students who work in the afternoon will face the same problems and may have their hours cut if they can't get to work at an earlier time. Also, students often spend several hours a night online or text-messaging friends. If these activities are started later in the day students will be getting to bed even later than they do now.

Another reason for staying with the early start is that it prepares students to enter the work force. Very few jobs in the real world allow you to start work at 9 or later in the morning. Students need to be able to work in the early morning hours to be ready for college classes, the military, or a job.

I know that some people want to start school after 9 am and they do have a point. Recent studies have shown that teenagers are more alert in the afternoons than in the morning. These people argue that a late start will let students get more sleep and be more alert in school the next day. This arguement doesn't convince me, though, because teenagers will just stay up later if they know they can get up later. They will just stay up until 2 am and get up at 8 for the later start.

I believe that schools will do better to stay with 8 am starting times. Because so many students have jobs, play sports, or just like to hang out with their friends after school, it's better to get school over with early in the day. It's also better training for the future.

COMMENTARY

This essay establishes its position in the second sentence: *"I believe the early start is better for several reasons."* It supports its position in the following paragraph by citing the needs of both athletes and students who work as well as considering the socialization time that students spend on the phone and online. Paragraph three, while less well developed, also supports the writer's position by offering another reason for an early start: *"it prepares students to enter the work force."* The writer's reasoning is adequate although not well developed; it does include some degree of specificity, citing *"practicing late into the afternoon, getting home after dark."*

This essay also anticipates and addresses some of the readers' potential concerns or counter-arguments in paragraph four. Referring to *"studies [that show] that teenagers are more alert in the afternoons,"* the writer acknowledges that the late start does have some arguments in its favor. However, the writer finds this reasoning unpersuasive. While late start proponents might believe students would be able to get more sleep, the writer states that *"teenagers will just stay up later if they know they can get up later"* and offers an example: *"they will just stay up until 2 am and get up at 8."* The writer finishes the essay with a return to the initial statement of position and ends with a new idea: *"it's better to get school over with early in the day."*

This essay demonstrates control of sentence structure although there are some errors. The very first sentence is a run-on; there should be a semi-colon or a period between *"school"* and *"should."* Some commas are misused (paragraph two: *"for sports, and jobs"*) or omitted (*"day students"*), and there is one misspelled word: *"arguement"* (paragraph four). The word choice is generally appropriate, and while there are some awkwardly stated sentences (*"Recently people have been discussing changing the hours of school, should schools begin at 8 am or after 9 am."*), most sentences are under control and do not cause confusion. The writer is inconsistent in notation of time and part of day (sometimes *"8"* and sometimes *"8 am"*). These errors, however, do not cause confusion.

Overall, this is a solid 4 essay. It addresses the writing task in a competent manner, defining and defending its position with adequate reasoning and some specific examples, and it anticipates and addresses readers' concerns. It displays control of sentence structure, word choice, and the conventions of written English.

Sample Essay — Score Point 2

The following essay earned a score of 2. The essay addresses the writing task in a limited manner.

Note that with a writing score of 2, an examinee cannot pass the Language subtest. See "Score Combinations to Pass the Language Subtest" on page 18.

I do not believe that school classes should start before 9:00 am, I agree strongly that they should start afterwards. I agree with this statement for multiple reasons, reasons like that most kids do not like to wake up that early unless we are forced so then we are still sleepy and our minds do not work fully. More reasons are that if school could start after 9:00 more students would come to first and second period instead of sleeping in. If school was to start at a later time, students would be real happy and more awake and maybe try harder on work and in classes.

COMMENTARY

This essay is a limited response to the writing task. The writer does take a position; however, the support for that position is limited. The writer offers three general reasons: kids don't like to get up early, more students would come to first and second periods instead of sleeping in, and starting later would make students happy so they would try harder. The writer fails to extend or support those reasons with any specific details. In addition, the writer does not anticipate readers' concerns or counter-arguments in favor of the other position. A short series of sentences in general support of a simplistic central idea does not demonstrate competence in writing an organized persuasive essay.

In addition to the essay's lack of development, the writer exhibits inadequate control of sentence structure. The writer incorrectly joins two sentences with a comma ("*I do not believe that school classes should start before 9:00 am, I agree strongly ...*"). This is followed by a run-on sentence. However, this essay does not contain serious or repeated errors in usage or conventions. The essay's lack of development and support prevents it from receiving a higher score.

The writer could have improved the essay by incorporating specific examples, such as the effects of changing starting times on extracurricular activities, descriptions of student behavior in early morning classes, or specific personal experiences rather than general statements ("*most kids do not like to wake up that early ...*"). Also, the writer needs to have considered what arguments might be made for the early start: for example, getting out early in the day and having time for a job or to participate in sports. Supporting each of the ideas given with specific arguments and examples, as well as anticipating and addressing counter-arguments, could have moved this 2 essay into a higher score point.

Multiple-choice Questions

Read each sentence. Look at the underlined words in each one. There may be a mistake in punctuation, capitalization, or word usage. If you find a mistake, choose the answer that is the best way to write the underlined section of the sentence. If there is no mistake, choose *Correct as is*.

1. The club meeting will be held in the <u>debate teams practice</u> room.

    A. Debate teams practice
    B. debate teams Practice
    C. debate team's practice
    D. *Correct as is*

2. Sarah wanted to see the <u>concert she had been</u> looking forward to it for a long time.

    A. concert, she had been
    B. concert; she had been
    C. concert she has been
    D. *Correct as is*

Read the group of words in the box. There may be a mistake in the sentence structure. If you find a mistake, choose the answer that is written most clearly and correctly. If there is no mistake, choose *Correct as is*.

3. | Veronica left the room, turned right, and, without any hesitation, walked outside. |

    A. Leaving the room, turning right, Veronica walking outside without any hesitation.
    B. Veronica left the room and she turned right and walked outside without any hesitation.
    C. Veronica left the room turned right and walked outside without any hesitation.
    D. *Correct as is*

4. | There are extra chairs in that room that are not needed or necessary. |

    A. There are extra chairs in that room.
    B. There are extra and unnecessary chairs in that room.
    C. The extra chairs in that room are not needed or necessary.
    D. *Correct as is*

5. | Some tortoises living up to 100 years are among the world's oldest animals. |

    A. The world's oldest animals, some living up to 100 years are some tortoises.
    B. Some tortoises, among the world's oldest animals, are living up to 100 years.
    C. Living up to 100 years, some tortoises are among the world's oldest animals.
    D. *Correct as is*

Read the paragraph. Then read the questions that follow the paragraph. Choose the correct answer and mark your answer.

The Challenge

It started when she was in elementary school. Sonia knew that she wanted to be a champion synchronized swimmer. Today's competition would determine whether she would earn the opportunity to go to the national contest. She performed the required technical routines flawlessly and led the other swimmers going into the free competition, the portion of the program that counted most. This series of choreographed moves performed to music required a couple of qualities. For one particularly difficult element, Sonia had to remain upside down in the water for over half a minute. She could tell by the audience's thunderous applause when she emerged from the pool that the performance had gone well. Seconds later the judges confirmed it; Sonia was on her way to the national contest.

6. This series of choreographed moves performed to music required <u>a couple of qualities</u>?

   Good writers describe the subject using details. How can the underlined words be better written to include exact details?

   A. some abilities that she had to develop
   B. specific physical qualities
   C. special moves
   D. great strength and control

7. Which sentence would *not* belong in this paragraph?

   A. Sonia had worked hard for many years to get to this point.
   B. The routine had gone smoothly, and Sonia had done even better than she had anticipated.
   C. The cool water always felt wonderful to Sonia; she loved the smell of chlorine.
   D. Her dream, since childhood, was finally coming true.

8. Which of these would be the best topic sentence for this paragraph?

   A. A synchronized swimming team will be sent to the Olympics.
   B. Sonia got a new swimsuit and cap for the competition.
   C. Only a few extremely talented athletes win competitions.
   D. For almost as long as she could remember, Sonia had wanted to go to the Olympics.

Language Subtest Sample Items Answer Key

1. C	5. C
2. B	6. D
3. D	7. C
4. A	8. D

From the official announcement for educational purposes

Reading Subtest
Reading Comprehension

Read the passage. Then read each question about the passage. Decide which is the best answer to the question. Mark the answer you have chosen.

The Witness Tree
A Story from Kazakhstan

Two men came before a judge in his court. "Give me justice! My neighbor has robbed me!" said one man.

"He's lying," the other protested. "I've done nothing wrong."

"Let me hear what you both have to say," the judge said.

The first man began. "A while ago I went on a journey. I left my life savings – a pot of gold coins – with my neighbor, he promised to guard the money while I was away. When I returned, he denied that he had ever seen my gold coins. He says I gave him nothing!"

"My neighbor is lying!" the second man said. "I know nothing about any pot of gold coins. He never gave me anything!"

"Before you left, did you tell anyone about leaving the coins with your neighbor? Did anyone see you give them to him?" the judge asked the first man.

The man replied, "For secrecy, I told no one. No one saw us because I asked my neighbor to meet me at night by a tree in the forest. There, in the dark, I gave him the coins." The judge frowned. "It is best to have a human witness. Since there is none, we will have to ask the tree. Go to the forest. Ask the tree if it saw you give a pot of coins to your neighbor. My clerk will go with you to write down the tree's testimony."

The man and the clerk set off for the forest.

Meanwhile, the judge invited the neighbor to sit down. After a while he asked the neighbor, "Do you think they've reached the tree yet?"

The neighbor shook his head. "Not yet."

Time passed. The judge asked again, "Do you think they're there now?"

"No, not yet," the neighbor answered.

More time passed. The judge asked again, "Shouldn't they be there by now?"

The neighbor nodded. "Yes, they're probably there."

"Oh?" said the judge. "Didn't you say your neighbor never gave you anything? How do you know where he's going? How do you know how long it would take to arrive there if you've never been there? Bring back the gold you stole, or you'll be in serious trouble."

When the first man returned, the judge gave back his missing money.

"What did the tree say?" the judge asked.

"Nothing!" the bewildered man replied.

"But it revealed the truth anyway," said the judge.

---

1. What was the man asked to do with his neighbor's money?
   A. Protect it
   B. Bury it
   C. Spend it
   D. Divide it up

2. The judge invited the neighbor to sit and wait because the judge –
   A. knew the man was tired
   B. wanted to find out where the tree was
   C. had a plan to discover the truth
   D. wanted to talk to someone

3. People like the judge in this story can be described as –
   A. dishonest
   B. shrewd
   C. generous
   D. proud

4. The story tells the reader –
   A. how the neighbor was punished
   B. why the man had trusted his neighbor
   C. which man was lying
   D. how far the man and the clerk walked

5. A clue to predicting the outcome of the story occurs when the –
   A. neighbor denies that he robbed the first man
   B. judge is asked to settle the matter
   C. clerk goes with the man who was robbed
   D. judge says, "Oh?"

6. Why would the robber assume that no one would find out his secret?

   A. He thought that the judge was dishonest.
   B. He thought that he was smarter than the judge.
   C. He thought his neighbor would not be able to find the tree.
   D. He knew that trees cannot talk.

7. This story was probably told in order to –

   A. share a true experience
   B. help the reader settle disagreements
   C. help the reader become rich
   D. teach a lesson

Reading Vocabulary.

Choose the word or group of words that means the same, or about the same, as the underlined word. Then mark the space for the answer you have chosen.

8. <u>Amicable</u> means the same as –

   A. friendly
   B. anxious
   C. jealous
   D. patient

Read the sentence in the box. Then choose the answer in which the underlined word is used in the same way.

9. The cold air <u>mass</u> will move south from Canada.

   In which sentence does the word <u>mass</u> mean the same thing as in the sentence above?

   A. The storm warning of a blizzard caused <u>mass</u> concern.
   B. The oil <u>mass</u> spread quickly into the ocean.
   C. There was a <u>mass</u> of people gathering to watch the parade.
   D. The 100-member choir will <u>mass</u> in the auditorium on Saturday.

As you read each sentence, use the other words in the sentence to help you figure out what the underlined word means.

10. His reassuring words <u>mitigated</u> our fears. <u>Mitigated</u> means –

    A. reinforced
    B. added to
    C. caused
    D. eased

Reading Subtest Sample Items Answer Key

Reading Comprehension
1. A   5. D
2. C   6. B
3. B   7. D
4. C

Reading Vocabulary
8. A   10. D
9. B

From the official announcement for educational purposes

Mathematics Section

Read each question or problem carefully. Then answer the question or work the problem. Mark your answer.

1. The Arctic Ocean has a surface area of about 14 million square kilometers, approximately 9.8 million square kilometers of which is covered by a polar ice mass. What is the surface area of this polar ice mass written in standard form?

   A. 0.0000098 sq km
   B. 0.000098 sq km
   C. 9,800,000 sq km
   D. 98,000,000 sq km

2. Cyndi borrowed $390 from her parents when she went on the school ski trip. If she pays them 65% of her $40 baby-sitting fees each month, how many months will it take her to pay back the entire $390?

   A. 10
   B. 15
   C. 26
   D. 28

3. The total length of the world's major railroad routes is approximately 3¼ times the distance from Earth to the moon. This distance from Earth to the moon is close to 240,000 miles. Which measure is closest to the length of the world's major railroad routes?

   A. 7.8×10^3 mi.
   B. 7.8×10^4 mi.
   C. 7.8×10^5 mi.
   D. 7.8×10^6 mi.

4.

Number of Term	Term
1	8
2	4
3	2
...	...
n^{th}	$8(0.5)^{n-1}$

   What is the fifth term of the geometric sequence shown in the table above?

   A. 1.0
   B. 0.75
   C. 0.5
   D. 0.25

5. What value for x makes

   $$\frac{2}{x-1} = \frac{5}{x+2}$$ true?

   A. 3
   B. 1
   C. –1
   D. –3

6. A river surveyor was creating a map to show the elevation changes in a river. The line that he used to describe the changes has the equation shown below.

   $$2x + 3y = 6$$

   What is the slope of this line?

   A. $-\frac{3}{2}$
   B. $-\frac{2}{3}$
   C. $\frac{2}{3}$
   D. 2

7. An airplane is moving down a runway with constant acceleration. The graph below shows the relationship between d, the distance from the beginning of the runway, and t, the time after the airplane begins to move.

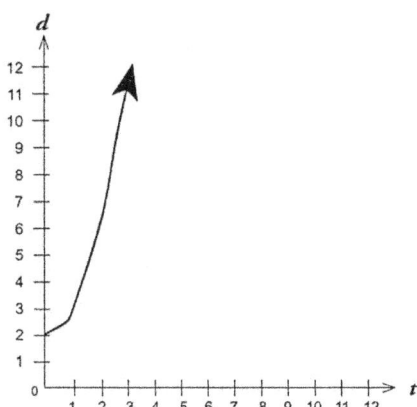

Which equation best represents this curve when $t \geq 0$?

A. $d = \dfrac{t^2}{2}$

B. $d = 2t^2$

C. $d = t^2 - 2$

D. $d = t^2 + 2$

8. A group of students is collecting money to fund a bicycle path. A total of 280 people have donated. The circle graph below shows the proportion of donors by the amounts given.

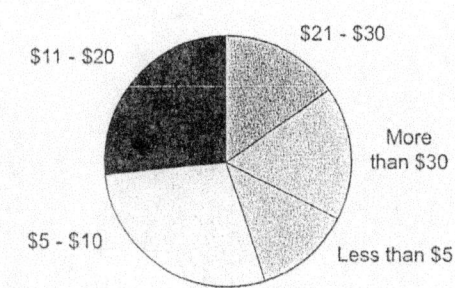

Which is the closest to the number of people who gave more than $20?

A. 56
B. 98
C. 168
D. 182

9. The table below shows the lengths of the major north-to-south routes in the United States.

Major United States Routes

Interstate Number	Length of Highway (to the nearest 10 miles)
I-65	890
I-55	940
I-75	1790
I-15	1440
I-5	1380
I-35	1830
I-95	1890

To the nearer 10 miles, what is the difference between the mean and median of these lengths?

A. 0
B. 10
C. 20
D. 30

10. Four of the islands of Japan account for about 96% of Japan's land area. The area of the 4 islands is shown in the bar graph below.

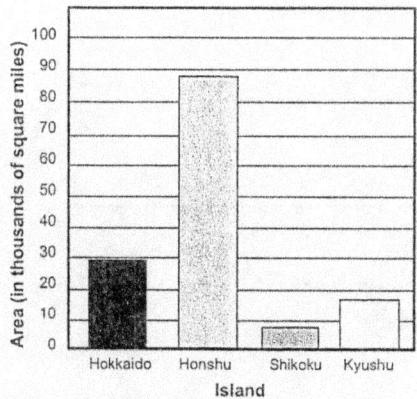

Which is closest to the total land area of Japan?

A. Between 90,000 and 100,000 square miles
B. Between 130,000 and 140,000 square miles
C. Between 140,000 and 150,000 square miles
D. Between 230,000 and 240,000 square miles

11. Mr. Wu's biology class is writing group reports about the Hawaiian Islands. He has a total of 10 groups. Mr. Wu will assign an island and a topic at random to each of the groups. No two group assignments will be the same.

    Five Islands: Hawaii, Maui, Lanai, Oahu, or Kauai

    Topics: Plant Life or Animal Life

    Linda and Kim are in different groups, but they both want to write about Kauai. What is the probability that both Linda's and Kim's groups will receive Kauai assignments?

    A. $\frac{1}{5}$

    B. $\frac{1}{45}$

    C. $\frac{1}{50}$

    D. $\frac{1}{90}$

12. Each day a freight train leaves Lake City and travels to Hilltown, Chester, and Freeburg. Then it returns to Lake City. The train's route forms a trapezoid with a right angle as shown below.

    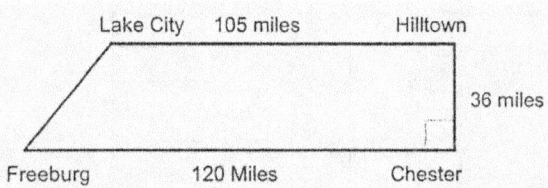

    Which is closest to the distance in miles from Freeburg to Lake City?

    A. 51
    B. 43.8
    C. 39
    D. 32.7

13. Cargo Ship A, carrying salmon from Alaskan waters, is traveling a linear path into port at Seattle. Cargo Ship B, from San Francisco, is traveling on a path parallel to the path of Cargo Ship A.

    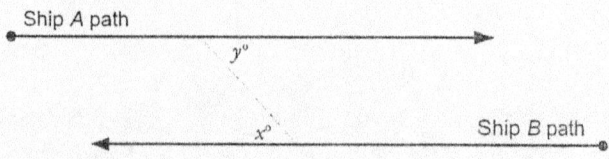

    If the value of x is 42, what is the value of y?

    A. 42
    B. 48
    C. 138
    D. 148

14. Elaine has two suitcases that are similar rectangular solids. The length of the second suitcase is twice the length of the first suitcase. If the first suitcase has a volume of 1568 cubic inches, what is the volume of the second suitcase in cubic inches?

    A. 3136
    B. 6272
    C. 9408
    D. 12,544

Mathematics Section Sample Items Answer Key

1. C	8. B
2. B	9. B
3. C	10. C
4. C	11. B
5. A	12. C
6. B	13. A
7. D	14. D

From the official announcement for educational purposes

HOW TO TAKE A TEST

I. YOU MUST PASS AN EXAMINATION

A. *WHAT EVERY CANDIDATE SHOULD KNOW*

Examination applicants often ask us for help in preparing for the written test. What can I study in advance? What kinds of questions will be asked? How will the test be given? How will the papers be graded?

As an applicant for a civil service examination, you may be wondering about some of these things. Our purpose here is to suggest effective methods of advance study and to describe civil service examinations.

Your chances for success on this examination can be increased if you know how to prepare. Those "pre-examination jitters" can be reduced if you know what to expect. You can even experience an adventure in good citizenship if you know why civil service exams are given.

B. *WHY ARE CIVIL SERVICE EXAMINATIONS GIVEN?*

Civil service examinations are important to you in two ways. As a citizen, you want public jobs filled by employees who know how to do their work. As a job seeker, you want a fair chance to compete for that job on an equal footing with other candidates. The best-known means of accomplishing this two-fold goal is the competitive examination.

Exams are widely publicized throughout the nation. They may be administered for jobs in federal, state, city, municipal, town or village governments or agencies.

Any citizen may apply, with some limitations, such as the age or residence of applicants. Your experience and education may be reviewed to see whether you meet the requirements for the particular examination. When these requirements exist, they are reasonable and applied consistently to all applicants. Thus, a competitive examination may cause you some uneasiness now, but it is your privilege and safeguard.

C. *HOW ARE CIVIL SERVICE EXAMS DEVELOPED?*

Examinations are carefully written by trained technicians who are specialists in the field known as "psychological measurement," in consultation with recognized authorities in the field of work that the test will cover. These experts recommend the subject matter areas or skills to be tested; only those knowledges or skills important to your success on the job are included. The most reliable books and source materials available are used as references. Together, the experts and technicians judge the difficulty level of the questions.

Test technicians know how to phrase questions so that the problem is clearly stated. Their ethics do not permit "trick" or "catch" questions. Questions may have been tried out on sample groups, or subjected to statistical analysis, to determine their usefulness.

Written tests are often used in combination with performance tests, ratings of training and experience, and oral interviews. All of these measures combine to form the best-known means of finding the right person for the right job.

II. HOW TO PASS THE WRITTEN TEST

A. NATURE OF THE EXAMINATION

To prepare intelligently for civil service examinations, you should know how they differ from school examinations you have taken. In school you were assigned certain definite pages to read or subjects to cover. The examination questions were quite detailed and usually emphasized memory. Civil service exams, on the other hand, try to discover your present ability to perform the duties of a position, plus your potentiality to learn these duties. In other words, a civil service exam attempts to predict how successful you will be. Questions cover such a broad area that they cannot be as minute and detailed as school exam questions.

In the public service similar kinds of work, or positions, are grouped together in one "class." This process is known as *position-classification*. All the positions in a class are paid according to the salary range for that class. One class title covers all of these positions, and they are all tested by the same examination.

B. FOUR BASIC STEPS

1) Study the announcement

How, then, can you know what subjects to study? Our best answer is: "Learn as much as possible about the class of positions for which you've applied." The exam will test the knowledge, skills and abilities needed to do the work.

Your most valuable source of information about the position you want is the official exam announcement. This announcement lists the training and experience qualifications. Check these standards and apply only if you come reasonably close to meeting them.

The brief description of the position in the examination announcement offers some clues to the subjects which will be tested. Think about the job itself. Review the duties in your mind. Can you perform them, or are there some in which you are rusty? Fill in the blank spots in your preparation.

Many jurisdictions preview the written test in the exam announcement by including a section called "Knowledge and Abilities Required," "Scope of the Examination," or some similar heading. Here you will find out specifically what fields will be tested.

2) Review your own background

Once you learn in general what the position is all about, and what you need to know to do the work, ask yourself which subjects you already know fairly well and which need improvement. You may wonder whether to concentrate on improving your strong areas or on building some background in your fields of weakness. When the announcement has specified "some knowledge" or "considerable knowledge," or has used adjectives like "beginning principles of…" or "advanced … methods," you can get a clue as to the number and difficulty of questions to be asked in any given field. More questions, and hence broader coverage, would be included for those subjects which are more important in the work. Now weigh your strengths and weaknesses against the job requirements and prepare accordingly.

3) Determine the level of the position

Another way to tell how intensively you should prepare is to understand the level of the job for which you are applying. Is it the entering level? In other words, is this the position in which beginners in a field of work are hired? Or is it an intermediate or advanced level? Sometimes this is indicated by such words as "Junior" or "Senior" in the class title. Other jurisdictions use Roman numerals to designate the level – Clerk I, Clerk II, for example. The word "Supervisor" sometimes appears in the title. If the level is not indicated by the title, check the description of duties. Will you be working under very close supervision, or will you have responsibility for independent decisions in this work?

4) Choose appropriate study materials

Now that you know the subjects to be examined and the relative amount of each subject to be covered, you can choose suitable study materials. For beginning level jobs, or even advanced ones, if you have a pronounced weakness in some aspect of your training, read a modern, standard textbook in that field. Be sure it is up to date and has general coverage. Such books are normally available at your library, and the librarian will be glad to help you locate one. For entry-level positions, questions of appropriate difficulty are chosen – neither highly advanced questions, nor those too simple. Such questions require careful thought but not advanced training.

If the position for which you are applying is technical or advanced, you will read more advanced, specialized material. If you are already familiar with the basic principles of your field, elementary textbooks would waste your time. Concentrate on advanced textbooks and technical periodicals. Think through the concepts and review difficult problems in your field.

These are all general sources. You can get more ideas on your own initiative, following these leads. For example, training manuals and publications of the government agency which employs workers in your field can be useful, particularly for technical and professional positions. A letter or visit to the government department involved may result in more specific study suggestions, and certainly will provide you with a more definite idea of the exact nature of the position you are seeking.

III. KINDS OF TESTS

Tests are used for purposes other than measuring knowledge and ability to perform specified duties. For some positions, it is equally important to test ability to make adjustments to new situations or to profit from training. In others, basic mental abilities not dependent on information are essential. Questions which test these things may not appear as pertinent to the duties of the position as those which test for knowledge and information. Yet they are often highly important parts of a fair examination. For very general questions, it is almost impossible to help you direct your study efforts. What we can do is to point out some of the more common of these general abilities needed in public service positions and describe some typical questions.

1) General information

Broad, general information has been found useful for predicting job success in some kinds of work. This is tested in a variety of ways, from vocabulary lists to questions about current events. Basic background in some field of work, such as sociology or economics, may be sampled in a group of questions. Often these are principles which have become familiar to most persons through exposure rather than through formal training. It is difficult to advise you how to study for these questions; being alert to the world around you is our best suggestion.

2) Verbal ability

An example of an ability needed in many positions is verbal or language ability. Verbal ability is, in brief, the ability to use and understand words. Vocabulary and grammar tests are typical measures of this ability. Reading comprehension or paragraph interpretation questions are common in many kinds of civil service tests. You are given a paragraph of written material and asked to find its central meaning.

3) Numerical ability

Number skills can be tested by the familiar arithmetic problem, by checking paired lists of numbers to see which are alike and which are different, or by interpreting charts and graphs. In the latter test, a graph may be printed in the test booklet which you are asked to use as the basis for answering questions.

4) Observation

A popular test for law-enforcement positions is the observation test. A picture is shown to you for several minutes, then taken away. Questions about the picture test your ability to observe both details and larger elements.

5) Following directions

In many positions in the public service, the employee must be able to carry out written instructions dependably and accurately. You may be given a chart with several columns, each column listing a variety of information. The questions require you to carry out directions involving the information given in the chart.

6) Skills and aptitudes

Performance tests effectively measure some manual skills and aptitudes. When the skill is one in which you are trained, such as typing or shorthand, you can practice. These tests are often very much like those given in business school or high school courses. For many of the other skills and aptitudes, however, no short-time preparation can be made. Skills and abilities natural to you or that you have developed throughout your lifetime are being tested.

Many of the general questions just described provide all the data needed to answer the questions and ask you to use your reasoning ability to find the answers. Your best preparation for these tests, as well as for tests of facts and ideas, is to be at your physical and mental best. You, no doubt, have your own methods of getting into an exam-taking mood and keeping "in shape." The next section lists some ideas on this subject.

IV. KINDS OF QUESTIONS

Only rarely is the "essay" question, which you answer in narrative form, used in civil service tests. Civil service tests are usually of the short-answer type. Full instructions for answering these questions will be given to you at the examination. But in case this is your first experience with short-answer questions and separate answer sheets, here is what you need to know:

1) Multiple-choice Questions

Most popular of the short-answer questions is the "multiple choice" or "best answer" question. It can be used, for example, to test for factual knowledge, ability to solve problems or judgment in meeting situations found at work.

A multiple-choice question is normally one of three types—
- It can begin with an incomplete statement followed by several possible endings. You are to find the one ending which *best* completes the statement, although some of the others may not be entirely wrong.
- It can also be a complete statement in the form of a question which is answered by choosing one of the statements listed.

- It can be in the form of a problem – again you select the best answer.

Here is an example of a multiple-choice question with a discussion which should give you some clues as to the method for choosing the right answer:

When an employee has a complaint about his assignment, the action which will *best* help him overcome his difficulty is to
- A. discuss his difficulty with his coworkers
- B. take the problem to the head of the organization
- C. take the problem to the person who gave him the assignment
- D. say nothing to anyone about his complaint

In answering this question, you should study each of the choices to find which is best. Consider choice "A" – Certainly an employee may discuss his complaint with fellow employees, but no change or improvement can result, and the complaint remains unresolved. Choice "B" is a poor choice since the head of the organization probably does not know what assignment you have been given, and taking your problem to him is known as "going over the head" of the supervisor. The supervisor, or person who made the assignment, is the person who can clarify it or correct any injustice. Choice "C" is, therefore, correct. To say nothing, as in choice "D," is unwise. Supervisors have and interest in knowing the problems employees are facing, and the employee is seeking a solution to his problem.

2) True/False Questions

The "true/false" or "right/wrong" form of question is sometimes used. Here a complete statement is given. Your job is to decide whether the statement is right or wrong.

SAMPLE: A roaming cell-phone call to a nearby city costs less than a non-roaming call to a distant city.

This statement is wrong, or false, since roaming calls are more expensive.

This is not a complete list of all possible question forms, although most of the others are variations of these common types. You will always get complete directions for answering questions. Be sure you understand *how* to mark your answers – ask questions until you do.

V. RECORDING YOUR ANSWERS

Computer terminals are used more and more today for many different kinds of exams.
For an examination with very few applicants, you may be told to record your answers in the test booklet itself. Separate answer sheets are much more common. If this separate answer sheet is to be scored by machine – and this is often the case – it is highly important that you mark your answers correctly in order to get credit.

An electronic scoring machine is often used in civil service offices because of the speed with which papers can be scored. Machine-scored answer sheets must be marked with a pencil, which will be given to you. This pencil has a high graphite content which responds to the electronic scoring machine. As a matter of fact, stray dots may register as answers, so do not let your pencil rest on the answer sheet while you are pondering the correct answer. Also, if your pencil lead breaks or is otherwise defective, ask for another.

Since the answer sheet will be dropped in a slot in the scoring machine, be careful not to bend the corners or get the paper crumpled.

The answer sheet normally has five vertical columns of numbers, with 30 numbers to a column. These numbers correspond to the question numbers in your test booklet. After each number, going across the page are four or five pairs of dotted lines. These short dotted lines have small letters or numbers above them. The first two pairs may also have a "T" or "F" above the letters. This indicates that the first two pairs only are to be used if the questions are of the true-false type. If the questions are multiple choice, disregard the "T" and "F" and pay attention only to the small letters or numbers.

Answer your questions in the manner of the sample that follows:

32. The largest city in the United States is
    A. Washington, D.C.
    B. New York City
    C. Chicago
    D. Detroit
    E. San Francisco

1) Choose the answer you think is best. (New York City is the largest, so "B" is correct.)
2) Find the row of dotted lines numbered the same as the question you are answering. (Find row number 32)
3) Find the pair of dotted lines corresponding to the answer. (Find the pair of lines under the mark "B.")
4) Make a solid black mark between the dotted lines.

VI. BEFORE THE TEST

Common sense will help you find procedures to follow to get ready for an examination. Too many of us, however, overlook these sensible measures. Indeed, nervousness and fatigue have been found to be the most serious reasons why applicants fail to do their best on civil service tests. Here is a list of reminders:

- Begin your preparation early – Don't wait until the last minute to go scurrying around for books and materials or to find out what the position is all about.
- Prepare continuously – An hour a night for a week is better than an all-night cram session. This has been definitely established. What is more, a night a week for a month will return better dividends than crowding your study into a shorter period of time.
- Locate the place of the exam – You have been sent a notice telling you when and where to report for the examination. If the location is in a different town or otherwise unfamiliar to you, it would be well to inquire the best route and learn something about the building.
- Relax the night before the test – Allow your mind to rest. Do not study at all that night. Plan some mild recreation or diversion; then go to bed early and get a good night's sleep.
- Get up early enough to make a leisurely trip to the place for the test – This way unforeseen events, traffic snarls, unfamiliar buildings, etc. will not upset you.
- Dress comfortably – A written test is not a fashion show. You will be known by number and not by name, so wear something comfortable.

- Leave excess paraphernalia at home – Shopping bags and odd bundles will get in your way. You need bring only the items mentioned in the official notice you received; usually everything you need is provided. Do not bring reference books to the exam. They will only confuse those last minutes and be taken away from you when in the test room.
- Arrive somewhat ahead of time – If because of transportation schedules you must get there very early, bring a newspaper or magazine to take your mind off yourself while waiting.
- Locate the examination room – When you have found the proper room, you will be directed to the seat or part of the room where you will sit. Sometimes you are given a sheet of instructions to read while you are waiting. Do not fill out any forms until you are told to do so; just read them and be prepared.
- Relax and prepare to listen to the instructions
- If you have any physical problem that may keep you from doing your best, be sure to tell the test administrator. If you are sick or in poor health, you really cannot do your best on the exam. You can come back and take the test some other time.

VII. AT THE TEST

The day of the test is here and you have the test booklet in your hand. The temptation to get going is very strong. Caution! There is more to success than knowing the right answers. You must know how to identify your papers and understand variations in the type of short-answer question used in this particular examination. Follow these suggestions for maximum results from your efforts:

1) Cooperate with the monitor

The test administrator has a duty to create a situation in which you can be as much at ease as possible. He will give instructions, tell you when to begin, check to see that you are marking your answer sheet correctly, and so on. He is not there to guard you, although he will see that your competitors do not take unfair advantage. He wants to help you do your best.

2) Listen to all instructions

Don't jump the gun! Wait until you understand all directions. In most civil service tests you get more time than you need to answer the questions. So don't be in a hurry. Read each word of instructions until you clearly understand the meaning. Study the examples, listen to all announcements and follow directions. Ask questions if you do not understand what to do.

3) Identify your papers

Civil service exams are usually identified by number only. You will be assigned a number; you must not put your name on your test papers. Be sure to copy your number correctly. Since more than one exam may be given, copy your exact examination title.

4) Plan your time

Unless you are told that a test is a "speed" or "rate of work" test, speed itself is usually not important. Time enough to answer all the questions will be provided, but this does not mean that you have all day. An overall time limit has been set. Divide the total time (in minutes) by the number of questions to determine the approximate time you have for each question.

5) Do not linger over difficult questions

If you come across a difficult question, mark it with a paper clip (useful to have along) and come back to it when you have been through the booklet. One caution if you do this – be sure to skip a number on your answer sheet as well. Check often to be sure that you have not lost your place and that you are marking in the row numbered the same as the question you are answering.

6) Read the questions

Be sure you know what the question asks! Many capable people are unsuccessful because they failed to *read* the questions correctly.

7) Answer all questions

Unless you have been instructed that a penalty will be deducted for incorrect answers, it is better to guess than to omit a question.

8) Speed tests

It is often better NOT to guess on speed tests. It has been found that on timed tests people are tempted to spend the last few seconds before time is called in marking answers at random – without even reading them – in the hope of picking up a few extra points. To discourage this practice, the instructions may warn you that your score will be "corrected" for guessing. That is, a penalty will be applied. The incorrect answers will be deducted from the correct ones, or some other penalty formula will be used.

9) Review your answers

If you finish before time is called, go back to the questions you guessed or omitted to give them further thought. Review other answers if you have time.

10) Return your test materials

If you are ready to leave before others have finished or time is called, take ALL your materials to the monitor and leave quietly. Never take any test material with you. The monitor can discover whose papers are not complete, and taking a test booklet may be grounds for disqualification.

VIII. EXAMINATION TECHNIQUES

1) Read the general instructions carefully. These are usually printed on the first page of the exam booklet. As a rule, these instructions refer to the timing of the examination; the fact that you should not start work until the signal and must stop work at a signal, etc. If there are any *special* instructions, such as a choice of questions to be answered, make sure that you note this instruction carefully.

2) When you are ready to start work on the examination, that is as soon as the signal has been given, read the instructions to each question booklet, underline any key words or phrases, such as *least, best, outline, describe* and the like. In this way you will tend to answer as requested rather than discover on reviewing your paper that you *listed without describing*, that you selected the *worst* choice rather than the *best* choice, etc.

3) If the examination is of the objective or multiple-choice type – that is, each question will also give a series of possible answers: A, B, C or D, and you are called upon to select the best answer and write the letter next to that answer on your answer paper – it is advisable to start answering each question in turn. There may be anywhere from 50 to 100 such questions in the three or four hours allotted and you can see how much time would be taken if you read through all the questions before beginning to answer any. Furthermore, if you come across a question or group of questions which you know would be difficult to answer, it would undoubtedly affect your handling of all the other questions.

4) If the examination is of the essay type and contains but a few questions, it is a moot point as to whether you should read all the questions before starting to answer any one. Of course, if you are given a choice – say five out of seven and the like – then it is essential to read all the questions so you can eliminate the two that are most difficult. If, however, you are asked to answer all the questions, there may be danger in trying to answer the easiest one first because you may find that you will spend too much time on it. The best technique is to answer the first question, then proceed to the second, etc.

5) Time your answers. Before the exam begins, write down the time it started, then add the time allowed for the examination and write down the time it must be completed, then divide the time available somewhat as follows:
    - If 3-1/2 hours are allowed, that would be 210 minutes. If you have 80 objective-type questions, that would be an average of 2-1/2 minutes per question. Allow yourself no more than 2 minutes per question, or a total of 160 minutes, which will permit about 50 minutes to review.
    - If for the time allotment of 210 minutes there are 7 essay questions to answer, that would average about 30 minutes a question. Give yourself only 25 minutes per question so that you have about 35 minutes to review.

6) The most important instruction is to *read each question* and make sure you know what is wanted. The second most important instruction is to *time yourself properly* so that you answer every question. The third most important instruction is to *answer every question*. Guess if you have to but include something for each question. Remember that you will receive no credit for a blank and will probably receive some credit if you write something in answer to an essay question. If you guess a letter – say "B" for a multiple-choice question – you may have guessed right. If you leave a blank as an answer to a multiple-choice question, the examiners may respect your feelings but it will not add a point to your score. Some exams may penalize you for wrong answers, so in such cases *only*, you may not want to guess unless you have some basis for your answer.

7) Suggestions
    a. Objective-type questions
        1. Examine the question booklet for proper sequence of pages and questions
        2. Read all instructions carefully
        3. Skip any question which seems too difficult; return to it after all other questions have been answered
        4. Apportion your time properly; do not spend too much time on any single question or group of questions

5. Note and underline key words – *all, most, fewest, least, best, worst, same, opposite,* etc.
6. Pay particular attention to negatives
7. Note unusual option, e.g., unduly long, short, complex, different or similar in content to the body of the question
8. Observe the use of "hedging" words – *probably, may, most likely,* etc.
9. Make sure that your answer is put next to the same number as the question
10. Do not second-guess unless you have good reason to believe the second answer is definitely more correct
11. Cross out original answer if you decide another answer is more accurate; do not erase until you are ready to hand your paper in
12. Answer all questions; guess unless instructed otherwise
13. Leave time for review

   b. Essay questions
1. Read each question carefully
2. Determine exactly what is wanted. Underline key words or phrases.
3. Decide on outline or paragraph answer
4. Include many different points and elements unless asked to develop any one or two points or elements
5. Show impartiality by giving pros and cons unless directed to select one side only
6. Make and write down any assumptions you find necessary to answer the questions
7. Watch your English, grammar, punctuation and choice of words
8. Time your answers; don't crowd material

8) Answering the essay question

Most essay questions can be answered by framing the specific response around several key words or ideas. Here are a few such key words or ideas:

M's: manpower, materials, methods, money, management
P's: purpose, program, policy, plan, procedure, practice, problems, pitfalls, personnel, public relations

   a. Six basic steps in handling problems:
1. Preliminary plan and background development
2. Collect information, data and facts
3. Analyze and interpret information, data and facts
4. Analyze and develop solutions as well as make recommendations
5. Prepare report and sell recommendations
6. Install recommendations and follow up effectiveness

   b. Pitfalls to avoid
1. *Taking things for granted* – A statement of the situation does not necessarily imply that each of the elements is necessarily true; for example, a complaint may be invalid and biased so that all that can be taken for granted is that a complaint has been registered

2. *Considering only one side of a situation* – Wherever possible, indicate several alternatives and then point out the reasons you selected the best one
3. *Failing to indicate follow up* – Whenever your answer indicates action on your part, make certain that you will take proper follow-up action to see how successful your recommendations, procedures or actions turn out to be
4. *Taking too long in answering any single question* – Remember to time your answers properly

IX. AFTER THE TEST

Scoring procedures differ in detail among civil service jurisdictions although the general principles are the same. Whether the papers are hand-scored or graded by machine we have described, they are nearly always graded by number. That is, the person who marks the paper knows only the number – never the name – of the applicant. Not until all the papers have been graded will they be matched with names. If other tests, such as training and experience or oral interview ratings have been given, scores will be combined. Different parts of the examination usually have different weights. For example, the written test might count 60 percent of the final grade, and a rating of training and experience 40 percent. In many jurisdictions, veterans will have a certain number of points added to their grades.

After the final grade has been determined, the names are placed in grade order and an eligible list is established. There are various methods for resolving ties between those who get the same final grade – probably the most common is to place first the name of the person whose application was received first. Job offers are made from the eligible list in the order the names appear on it. You will be notified of your grade and your rank as soon as all these computations have been made. This will be done as rapidly as possible.

People who are found to meet the requirements in the announcement are called "eligibles." Their names are put on a list of eligible candidates. An eligible's chances of getting a job depend on how high he stands on this list and how fast agencies are filling jobs from the list.

When a job is to be filled from a list of eligibles, the agency asks for the names of people on the list of eligibles for that job. When the civil service commission receives this request, it sends to the agency the names of the three people highest on this list. Or, if the job to be filled has specialized requirements, the office sends the agency the names of the top three persons who meet these requirements from the general list.

The appointing officer makes a choice from among the three people whose names were sent to him. If the selected person accepts the appointment, the names of the others are put back on the list to be considered for future openings.

That is the rule in hiring from all kinds of eligible lists, whether they are for typist, carpenter, chemist, or something else. For every vacancy, the appointing officer has his choice of any one of the top three eligibles on the list. This explains why the person whose name is on top of the list sometimes does not get an appointment when some of the persons lower on the list do. If the appointing officer chooses the second or third eligible, the No. 1 eligible does not get a job at once, but stays on the list until he is appointed or the list is terminated.

X. HOW TO PASS THE INTERVIEW TEST

The examination for which you applied requires an oral interview test. You have already taken the written test and you are now being called for the interview test – the final part of the formal examination.

You may think that it is not possible to prepare for an interview test and that there are no procedures to follow during an interview. Our purpose is to point out some things you can do in advance that will help you and some good rules to follow and pitfalls to avoid while you are being interviewed.

What is an interview supposed to test?

The written examination is designed to test the technical knowledge and competence of the candidate; the oral is designed to evaluate intangible qualities, not readily measured otherwise, and to establish a list showing the relative fitness of each candidate – as measured against his competitors – for the position sought. Scoring is not on the basis of "right" and "wrong," but on a sliding scale of values ranging from "not passable" to "outstanding." As a matter of fact, it is possible to achieve a relatively low score without a single "incorrect" answer because of evident weakness in the qualities being measured.

Occasionally, an examination may consist entirely of an oral test – either an individual or a group oral. In such cases, information is sought concerning the technical knowledges and abilities of the candidate, since there has been no written examination for this purpose. More commonly, however, an oral test is used to supplement a written examination.

Who conducts interviews?

The composition of oral boards varies among different jurisdictions. In nearly all, a representative of the personnel department serves as chairman. One of the members of the board may be a representative of the department in which the candidate would work. In some cases, "outside experts" are used, and, frequently, a businessman or some other representative of the general public is asked to serve. Labor and management or other special groups may be represented. The aim is to secure the services of experts in the appropriate field.

However the board is composed, it is a good idea (and not at all improper or unethical) to ascertain in advance of the interview who the members are and what groups they represent. When you are introduced to them, you will have some idea of their backgrounds and interests, and at least you will not stutter and stammer over their names.

What should be done before the interview?

While knowledge about the board members is useful and takes some of the surprise element out of the interview, there is other preparation which is more substantive. It *is* possible to prepare for an oral interview – in several ways:

1) Keep a copy of your application and review it carefully before the interview

This may be the only document before the oral board, and the starting point of the interview. Know what education and experience you have listed there, and the sequence and dates of all of it. Sometimes the board will ask you to review the highlights of your experience for them; you should not have to hem and haw doing it.

2) Study the class specification and the examination announcement

Usually, the oral board has one or both of these to guide them. The qualities, characteristics or knowledges required by the position sought are stated in these documents. They offer valuable clues as to the nature of the oral interview. For example, if the job involves supervisory responsibilities, the announcement will usually indicate that knowledge of modern supervisory methods and the qualifications of the candidate as a supervisor will be tested. If so, you can expect such questions, frequently in the form of a hypothetical situation which you are expected to solve. NEVER go into an oral without knowledge of the duties and responsibilities of the job you seek.

3) Think through each qualification required

Try to visualize the kind of questions you would ask if you were a board member. How well could you answer them? Try especially to appraise your own knowledge and background in each area, *measured against the job sought*, and identify any areas in which you are weak. Be critical and realistic – do not flatter yourself.

4) Do some general reading in areas in which you feel you may be weak

For example, if the job involves supervision and your past experience has NOT, some general reading in supervisory methods and practices, particularly in the field of human relations, might be useful. Do NOT study agency procedures or detailed manuals. The oral board will be testing your understanding and capacity, not your memory.

5) Get a good night's sleep and watch your general health and mental attitude

You will want a clear head at the interview. Take care of a cold or any other minor ailment, and of course, no hangovers.

What should be done on the day of the interview?

Now comes the day of the interview itself. Give yourself plenty of time to get there. Plan to arrive somewhat ahead of the scheduled time, particularly if your appointment is in the fore part of the day. If a previous candidate fails to appear, the board might be ready for you a bit early. By early afternoon an oral board is almost invariably behind schedule if there are many candidates, and you may have to wait. Take along a book or magazine to read, or your application to review, but leave any extraneous material in the waiting room when you go in for your interview. In any event, relax and compose yourself.

The matter of dress is important. The board is forming impressions about you – from your experience, your manners, your attitude, and your appearance. Give your personal appearance careful attention. Dress your best, but not your flashiest. Choose conservative, appropriate clothing, and be sure it is immaculate. This is a business interview, and your appearance should indicate that you regard it as such. Besides, being well groomed and properly dressed will help boost your confidence.

Sooner or later, someone will call your name and escort you into the interview room. *This is it.* From here on you are on your own. It is too late for any more preparation. But remember, you asked for this opportunity to prove your fitness, and you are here because your request was granted.

What happens when you go in?

The usual sequence of events will be as follows: The clerk (who is often the board stenographer) will introduce you to the chairman of the oral board, who will introduce you to the other members of the board. Acknowledge the introductions before you sit down. Do not be surprised if you find a microphone facing you or a stenotypist sitting by. Oral interviews are usually recorded in the event of an appeal or other review.

Usually the chairman of the board will open the interview by reviewing the highlights of your education and work experience from your application – primarily for the benefit of the other members of the board, as well as to get the material into the record. Do not interrupt or comment unless there is an error or significant misinterpretation; if that is the case, do not hesitate. But do not quibble about insignificant matters. Also, he will usually ask you some question about your education, experience or your present job – partly to get you to start talking and to establish the interviewing "rapport." He may start the actual questioning, or turn it over to one of the other members. Frequently, each member undertakes the questioning on a particular area, one in which he is perhaps most competent, so you can expect each member to participate in the examination. Because time is limited, you may also expect some rather abrupt switches in the direction the questioning takes, so do not be upset by it. Normally, a board member will not pursue a single line of questioning unless he discovers a particular strength or weakness.

After each member has participated, the chairman will usually ask whether any member has any further questions, then will ask you if you have anything you wish to add. Unless you are expecting this question, it may floor you. Worse, it may start you off on an extended, extemporaneous speech. The board is not usually seeking more information. The question is principally to offer you a last opportunity to present further qualifications or to indicate that you have nothing to add. So, if you feel that a significant qualification or characteristic has been overlooked, it is proper to point it out in a sentence or so. Do not compliment the board on the thoroughness of their examination – they have been sketchy, and you know it. If you wish, merely say, "No thank you, I have nothing further to add." This is a point where you can "talk yourself out" of a good impression or fail to present an important bit of information. Remember, *you close the interview yourself.*

The chairman will then say, "That is all, Mr. _____, thank you." Do not be startled; the interview is over, and quicker than you think. Thank him, gather your belongings and take your leave. Save your sigh of relief for the other side of the door.

How to put your best foot forward

Throughout this entire process, you may feel that the board individually and collectively is trying to pierce your defenses, seek out your hidden weaknesses and embarrass and confuse you. Actually, this is not true. They are obliged to make an appraisal of your qualifications for the job you are seeking, and they want to see you in your best light. Remember, they must interview all candidates and a non-cooperative candidate may become a failure in spite of their best efforts to bring out his qualifications. Here are 15 suggestions that will help you:

1) Be natural – Keep your attitude confident, not cocky

If you are not confident that you can do the job, do not expect the board to be. Do not apologize for your weaknesses, try to bring out your strong points. The board is interested in a positive, not negative, presentation. Cockiness will antagonize any board member and make him wonder if you are covering up a weakness by a false show of strength.

2) Get comfortable, but don't lounge or sprawl

Sit erectly but not stiffly. A careless posture may lead the board to conclude that you are careless in other things, or at least that you are not impressed by the importance of the occasion. Either conclusion is natural, even if incorrect. Do not fuss with your clothing, a pencil or an ashtray. Your hands may occasionally be useful to emphasize a point; do not let them become a point of distraction.

3) Do not wisecrack or make small talk

This is a serious situation, and your attitude should show that you consider it as such. Further, the time of the board is limited – they do not want to waste it, and neither should you.

4) Do not exaggerate your experience or abilities

In the first place, from information in the application or other interviews and sources, the board may know more about you than you think. Secondly, you probably will not get away with it. An experienced board is rather adept at spotting such a situation, so do not take the chance.

5) If you know a board member, do not make a point of it, yet do not hide it

Certainly you are not fooling him, and probably not the other members of the board. Do not try to take advantage of your acquaintanceship – it will probably do you little good.

6) Do not dominate the interview

Let the board do that. They will give you the clues – do not assume that you have to do all the talking. Realize that the board has a number of questions to ask you, and do not try to take up all the interview time by showing off your extensive knowledge of the answer to the first one.

7) Be attentive

You only have 20 minutes or so, and you should keep your attention at its sharpest throughout. When a member is addressing a problem or question to you, give him your undivided attention. Address your reply principally to him, but do not exclude the other board members.

8) Do not interrupt

A board member may be stating a problem for you to analyze. He will ask you a question when the time comes. Let him state the problem, and wait for the question.

9) Make sure you understand the question

Do not try to answer until you are sure what the question is. If it is not clear, restate it in your own words or ask the board member to clarify it for you. However, do not haggle about minor elements.

10) Reply promptly but not hastily

A common entry on oral board rating sheets is "candidate responded readily," or "candidate hesitated in replies." Respond as promptly and quickly as you can, but do not jump to a hasty, ill-considered answer.

11) Do not be peremptory in your answers

A brief answer is proper – but do not fire your answer back. That is a losing game from your point of view. The board member can probably ask questions much faster than you can answer them.

12) Do not try to create the answer you think the board member wants

He is interested in what kind of mind you have and how it works – not in playing games. Furthermore, he can usually spot this practice and will actually grade you down on it.

13) Do not switch sides in your reply merely to agree with a board member

Frequently, a member will take a contrary position merely to draw you out and to see if you are willing and able to defend your point of view. Do not start a debate, yet do not surrender a good position. If a position is worth taking, it is worth defending.

14) Do not be afraid to admit an error in judgment if you are shown to be wrong

The board knows that you are forced to reply without any opportunity for careful consideration. Your answer may be demonstrably wrong. If so, admit it and get on with the interview.

15) Do not dwell at length on your present job

The opening question may relate to your present assignment. Answer the question but do not go into an extended discussion. You are being examined for a *new* job, not your present one. As a matter of fact, try to phrase ALL your answers in terms of the job for which you are being examined.

Basis of Rating

Probably you will forget most of these "do's" and "don'ts" when you walk into the oral interview room. Even remembering them all will not ensure you a passing grade. Perhaps you did not have the qualifications in the first place. But remembering them will help you to put your best foot forward, without treading on the toes of the board members.

Rumor and popular opinion to the contrary notwithstanding, an oral board wants you to make the best appearance possible. They know you are under pressure – but they also want to see how you respond to it as a guide to what your reaction would be under the pressures of the job you seek. They will be influenced by the degree of poise you display, the personal traits you show and the manner in which you respond.

ABOUT THIS BOOK

This book contains tests divided into Examination Sections. Go through each test, answering every question in the margin. We have also attached a sample answer sheet at the back of the book that can be removed and used. At the end of each test look at the answer key and check your answers. On the ones you got wrong, look at the right answer choice and learn. Do not fill in the answers first. Do not memorize the questions and answers, but understand the answer and principles involved. On your test, the questions will likely be different from the samples. Questions are changed and new ones added. If you understand these past questions you should have success with any changes that arise. Tests may consist of several types of questions. We have additional books on each subject should more study be advisable or necessary for you. Finally, the more you study, the better prepared you will be. This book is intended to be the last thing you study before you walk into the examination room. Prior study of relevant texts is also recommended. NLC publishes some of these in our Fundamental Series. Knowledge and good sense are important factors in passing your exam. Good luck also helps. So now study this Passbook, absorb the material contained within and take that knowledge into the examination. Then do your best to pass that exam.

EXAMINATION SECTION

READING COMPREHENSION
UNDERSTANDING AND INTERPRETING WRITTEN MATERIAL

STRATEGIES

SURVEYING PASSAGES, SENTENCES AS CUES

While individual readers develop unique reading styles and skills, there are some known strategies which can assist any reader in improving his or her reading comprehension and performance on the reading subtest. These strategies include understanding how single paragraphs and entire passages are structured, how the ideas in them are ordered, and how the author of the passage has connected these ideas in a logical and sequential way for the reader.

The section that follows highlights the importance of reading a passage through once for meaning, and provides instruction on careful reading for context cues within the sentences before and after the missing word.

SURVEY THE ENTIRE PASSAGE

To get a sense of the topic and the organization of ideas in a passage, it is important to survey each passage initially in its entirety and to identify the main idea. (The first sentence of a paragraph usually states the main idea.) Do not try to fill in the blanks initially. The purpose or surveying a passage is to prepare for the more careful reading which will follow. You need a sense of the big picture before you start to fill in the details; for example, a quick survey of the passage on page 11 indicate that the topic is the early history of universities. The paragraphs are organized to provide information on the origin of the first universities, the associations formed by teachers and students, the early curriculum, and graduation requirements.

READ PRECEDING SENTENCES CAREFULLY

The missing words in a passage cannot be determined by reading and understanding only the sentences in which the deletions occur. Information from the sentences which precede or follow can provide important cues to determine the correct choice. For example, if you read the first sentence from the passage about universities which contains a blank, you will notice that all the alternatives make sense if this one sentence is read in isolation:

Nobody actually _____ them.
  A. started   B. guarded   C. blamed
  D. compared   E. remembered

The only way that you can make the correct word choice is to read the preceding sentences. In the excerpt below, notice that the first sentence tells the reader what the passage will be about: how universities developed. A key word in the first sentence is *emerged*, which is closely related in meaning to one of the five choices for the first blank. The second sentence explains the key word *emerged*, by pointing out that we have no historical record of a decree or a date indicating when the first university was established. Understanding the ideas in the first two sentences makes it possible to select the correct word for the blank. Look at the sentence with the deleted word in the context of the preceding sentences and think about why you are now able to make the correct choice.

The first universities emerged at the end of the 11th century and beginning of the 12th. These institutions were not founded on any particular date or created by any formal action. Nobody actually _____ them.
   A. started   B. guarded   C. blamed
   D. compared   E. remembered

Started is the best choice because it fits the main idea of the passage and is closely related to the key word *emerged*.

READ THE SENTENCE WHICH FOLLOWS TO VERIFY YOUR CHOICE

The sentences which follow the one from which a word has been deleted may also provide cues to the correct choice. For example, look at an excerpt from the passage about universities again, and consider how the sentence which follows the one with the blank helps to reinforce the choice of the word *started*.

The first universities emerged at the end of the 11th century and the beginning of the 12th. These institutions were not founded on any particular date or created by any formal action. Nobody actually _____ them. Instead, they developed gradually in places like Paris, Oxford, and Bologna, where scholars had long been teaching students.
   A. started   B. guarded   C. blamed
   D. compared   E. remembered

The words *developed gradually* mean the same as the key word *emerged*. The signal word *instead* helps to distinguish the difference between starting on a specific date as a result of some particular act or event and emerging over a period of time as a result of various factors.

Here is another example of how the sentence which follows the one from which a word is deleted might help you decide which of two good alternatives is the correct choice. This excerpt is from the practice passage about bridges (page 10).

Bridges are built to allow a continuous flow of highway and railway traffic across water lying in their paths. But engineers cannot forget that river traffic, too, is essential to our economy. The role of _____ is important. To keep these vessels moving freely, bridges are built big enough, when possible, to let them pass underneath.
   A. wind   B. boats   C. weight
   D. wires   E. experience

After the first two sentences, the reader may be uncertain about the direction the writer intended to take in the rest of the paragraph. If the writer intended to continue the paragraph with information concerning how engineers make choices about the relative importance and requirements of land traffic and rive traffic, *experience* might be the appropriate choice for the missing word. However, the sentence following the one in which the deletion occurs makes it clear that *boats* is the correct choice. It provides the synonym *vessels*, which in the noun phrase *these vessels* must refer back to the previous sentence or sentences. The phrase *to let them pass underneath* also helps make it clear that *boats* is the appropriate choice. *Them* refers back to *these vessels* which, in turn, refers back to *boats* when the word *boats* is placed in the previous sentence. Thus, the reader may use these cohesive ties (the pronoun referents) to verify the final choice.

Even when the text following a sentence with a deletion is not necessary to choose the best alternative, it may be helpful in other ways. Specifically, complete sentences provide important transitions into a related topic which is developed in the rest of the paragraph or in the next paragraph of the same passage. For example, the first paragraph in the passage about universities ends with a sentence which introduces the term *guilds*: *But, over time, they joined together to form guilds.* Prior to this sentence, information about the slow emergence of universities and about how independently scholars had acted was introduced. The next paragraph begins with two sentences about guilds in general. Someone who had not read the last sentence in the first paragraph might have missed the link between guilds and scholars and universities and, thus, might have been unnecessarily confused.

COHESIVE TIES AS CUES

Sentences in a paragraph may be linked together by several devices called cohesive ties. Attention to these ties may provide further cues about missing words. This section will describe the different types of cohesive ties and show how attention to them can help you to select the correct word.

PERSONAL PRONOUNS

Personal pronouns (e.g., he, she, they, it, its) are often used in adjoining sentences to refer back to an already mentioned person, place, thing, or idea. The word to which the pronoun refers is called the antecedent.

Tools used in farm work changed very slowly from ancient times to the eighteenth century, and the changes were minor. Since the eighteenth century *they* have changed quickly and dramatically.

The word *they* refers back to *tools* in the example above.

In the examination reading subtest, a deleted word sometimes occurs in a sentence in which the sentence subject is a pronoun that refers back to a previously mentioned noun. You must correctly identify the referent for the particular pronoun in order to interpret the sentence and select the correct answer. Here is an example from the passage about bridges.

An ingenious engineer designed the bridge so that it did not have to be raised above traffic. Instead it was _____.
  A. burned   B. emptied   C. secured
  D. shared   E. lowered

Q. What is the antecedent of *it* in both cases in the example?
A. The antecedent, of course, is *bridge*.

DEMONSTRATIVE PRONOUNS

Demonstrative pronouns (e.g., this, that, these) are also used to refer to a specific, previously mentioned noun. They may occur alone as noun replacements, or they may accompany and modify nouns.

I like jogging, swimming, and tennis. *These* are the only sports I enjoy.

In the sentence above, the word *these* is a replacement noun. However, demonstrative pronouns may also occur as adjectives modifying nouns.

I like jogging, swimming, and tennis. *These* sports are the only ones I enjoy.

The word *these* in the example above is an adjective modifier. The word *these* in each of the two previous examples refers to *jogging, swimming,* and *tennis*.

Here is an example from the passage about universities on page 11.

Undergraduates took classes in Greek philosophy, Latin grammar, arithmetic, music, and astronomy. These were the only _____ available.
  A. rooms   B. subjects   C. clothes
  D. pens   E. company

Q. Which word is a noun replacement?
A. The word *these* is the replacement for *Greek philosophy, Latin grammar, arithmetic, music,* and *astronomy.*

Here is another example from the same passage.

The concept of a fixed program of study leading to a degree first evolved in Medieval Europe. This _____ had not appeared before.
  A. idea   B. desk   C. library   D. capital

Q. What is the antecedent of *this*?
A. The antecedent is *the concept of a fixed program of study leading to a degree.*

COMPARATIVE ADJECTIVES AND ADVERBS

When comparative adjectives and adverbs (e.g., so, such, better, more) occur, they refer to something else in the passage, otherwise a comparison could not be made.

The hotels in the city were all full; so were the motels and boarding houses.

Q. To what in the first sentence does the word *so* refer?
A. So tells us to compare the *motels* and *boarding houses* to the *hotels in the city.*

Q. In what way are the *hotels, motels,* and *boarding houses* similar to each other?
A. The *hotels, motels,* and *boarding houses* are similar in that they were all *full*.

Look at an example from the passage about universities.

Guilds were groups of tradespeople, somewhat akin to modern trade unions. In the Middle Ages, all the crafts had such
  A. taxes   B. secrets   C. products
  D. problems   E. organizations

Q. To what in the first sentence does the word *such* refer?
A. *Such* refers to *groups of tradespeople*.

SUBSTITUTIONS

Substitution is another form of cohesive tie. A substitution occurs when one linguistic item (e.g., a noun) is replaced by another. Sometimes the substitution provides new or contrasting information. The substitution is not identical to the original, or antecedent, idea. A frequently occurring substitution involves the use of *one*. A noun substitution may involve another member of the same class as the original one.

My car is falling apart. I need a new one.

Q. What in the first sentence is replaced in the second sentence with *one*?
A. *One* is a substitute for the specific car mentioned in the first sentence. The contrast comes from the fact that the *new one* isn't the writer's current car.

The substitution may also pinpoint a specific member of a general class.

1. There are many unusual courses available at the university this summer. The *one* I am taking is called *Death and Dying*.
2. There are many unusual courses available at the university this summer. *Some* have never been offered before.

Q. In these examples, what is the general class in the first sentence that is replaced by *one* and by *some*?
A. In both cases the words *one* and *some* replace *many unusual* courses.

SYNONYMS

Synonyms are words that have similar meaning. In the examination reading subtest, a synonym of a deleted word is sometimes found in one of the sentences before and/or after the sentence with the deletion. Examine the following excerpt from the passage about bridges again.

But engineers cannot forget that river traffic, too, is essential to our economy. The role of _____ is important. To keep these vessels moving freely, bridges are built high enough, when possible, to let them pass underneath.
  A. wind   B. boats   C. weight
  D. wires   E. experience

Q. Can you identify synonyms in the sentences, before and after the sentence containing the deletion, which are cues to the correct deleted word?
A. If you identified the correct words, you probably noticed that *river traffic* is not exactly a synonym since it is a slightly more general term than the word *boats* (the correct choice). But the word *vessels* is a direct synonym. Demonstrative pronouns (this, that, these, those) are sometimes used as modifiers for synonymous nouns in sentences which follow those containing deletions. The word *these* in *these vessels* is the demonstrative pronoun (modifier) for the synonymous noun *vessels*.

ANTONYMS

Antonyms are words of opposite meaning. In the examination reading subtest passages, antonyms may be cues for missing words. A contrasting relationship, which calls for the use of an antonym, is often signaled by the connective words *instead, however, but*, etc. Look at an excerpt from the passage about bridges.

An ingenious engineer designed the bridges so that it did not have to be raised above traffic. Instead it was
 A. burned   B. emptied   C. secured
 D. shared   E. lowered

Q: Can you identify an antonym in the first sentence for one of the five alternatives?
A. The word *raised* is an antonym for the word *lowered*.

SUBORDINATE-SUBORDINATE WORDS

In the examination reading subtest, a passage sometimes contains a general term which provides a cue that a more specific term is the appropriate alternative. At other times, the passage may contain a specific term which provides cues that a general term is the appropriate alternative for a particular deletion. The general and more specific words are said to have superordinate-subordinate relationships.

Look at Example 1 below. The more specific word *boy* in the first sentence serves as the antecedent for the more general word *child* in the second sentence. In Example 2, the relationship is reversed. In both examples, the words *child* and *boy* reflect a superordinate-subordinate relationship.

1. The *boy* climbed the tree. Then the *child* fell.
2. The *child* climbed the tree. Then the *boy* fell.

In the practice passage about bridges on Page 11, the phrase *river traffic* is a general term that is superordinate to the alternative *boats* (Item 1). Later in the passage about bridges the following sentences also contain superordinate-subordinate words:

A lift bridge was desired, but there were wartime shortages of steel and machinery needed for the towers. It was hard to find enough _____.
 A. work   B. material   C. time
 D. power   E. space

Q. Can you identify two words in the first sentence that are specific examples for the correct response in the second sentence?
A. Of course, the words *steel* and *machinery* are the specific examples for the more general term *material*.

WORDS ASSOCIATED BY ENTAILMENT

Sometimes the concept described by one word within the context of the passage entails, or implies, the concept described by another word. For example, consider again Item 7 in the practice passage about bridges. Notice how the follow-up sentence to Item 7 provides a cue to the correct response.

An ingenious engineer designed the bridge so that it did not have to be raised above traffic. Instead it was _____. It could be submerged seven meters below the surface of the river.
  A. burned   B. emptied   C. secured
  D. shared   E. lowered

Q. What word in the sentence after the blank implies the concept of an alternative?
A. *Submerged* implies *lowered*. The concept of submerging something implies the idea of lowering the object beneath the surface of the water.

WORDS ASSOCIATED BY PART-WHOLE RELATIONSHIPS

Words may be related because they involve part of a whole and the whole itself; for example, *nose* and *face*. Words may also be related because they involve two parts of the same whole; for example, *radiator* and *muffler* both refer to parts of a car.

The captain of the ship was nervous. The storm was becoming worse and worse. The hardened man paced the _____.
  A. floor   B. hall   C. deck   D. court

Q. Which choice has a part-whole relationship with a word in the sentences above?
A. A *deck* is a part of a *ship*. Therefore, *deck* has a part-whole relationship with *ship*.

CONJUNCTIVE AND CONNECTIVE WORDS AND PHRASES

Conjunctions or connectives are words or phrases that connect parts of sentences or parts of a passage to each other. Their purpose is to help the reader understand the logical and conceptual relationships between ideas and events within a passage. Examples of these words and phrases include coordinate conjunctions (e.g., and, but, yet), subordinate conjunctions (e.g., because, although, since, after), and other connective words and phrases (e.g., too, also, on the other hand, as a result).

Listed below are types of logical relationships expressed by conjunctive, or connective words. Also listed are examples of words used to cue relationships to the reader.

Additive and comparative words and phrases: and, in addition to, too, also, furthermore, similarly.

Adversative and contrastive words and phrases: yet, though, only, but, however, instead, rather, on the other hand, conversely.

Causal words or phrases: so, therefore, because, as a result, if…then, unless, except, in that case, under the circumstances.

Temporal words and phrases: before, after, when, while, initially, lastly, finally, until.

<u>Examples</u>

1. I enjoy fast-paced sports like tennis and volleyball, but my brother prefers _____ sports.
   A. running   B. slower   C. team   D. active

   Q. What is the connective word that tells you to look for a contrast relationship between the two parts of the sentence?
   A. The connective word *but* signals that a contrast relationship exists between the two parts of the sentence.

   Q. Of the four options, what is the best choice for the blank?
   A. The word *slower* is the best response here.

2. The child stepped to close to the edge of the brook. As a result, he _____ in.
   A. fell   B. waded   C. ran   D. jumped

   Q. What is the connective phrase that links the two sentences?
   A. The connective phrase *as a result* links the two sentences.

   Q. Of the four relationships of words and phrases listed previously, what kind of relationship between the two sentences does the connective phrase in the example signal to the reader?
   A. The phrase *as a result* signals that a cause and effect relationship exists between the two sentences.

   Q. Identify the correct response which makes the second sentence reflect and cause and effect relationship.
   A. The correct response is *fell*.

Understanding connectives is very important to success on the examination reading subtest. Sentences with deletions are often very closely related to adjacent sentences in meaning, and the relationships often signaled by connective words or phrases. Here is an example from the practice passage about universities.

At first, these tutors had not been associated with one another. Rather, they had been _____. But, over time, they joined together to form guilds.
    A. curious   B. poor   C. religious
    D. ready   E. independent

Q. Identify the connective and contrastive words and phrases in the example.
A. *At first* and *over time* are connective phrases that set up temporal progression. *Rather* and *but* are contrastive items. The use of *rather* in the sentence with the deletion tells the reader that the missing word has to convey a meaning in contrast to *associated with one another*. (Notice also that *rather* occurs after a negative statement.) The use of *but* in the sentence after the one with the deletion indicates that the deleted word in the previous sentence has to reflect a meaning that contrasts with *joined together*. Thus, the reader is given two substantial cues to the meaning of the missing word. *Independent* is the only choice that meets the requirement for contrastive meaning.

SAMPLE QUESTIOINS

DIRECTIONS: There are two passages on the following pages. In each passage some words are missing. Wherever a word is missing, there is a blank line with a number on it. Below the passage you will find the same number and five words. Choose the word that makes the best sense in the blank. You may not be sure of the answer to a question until you read the sentences that come after the blank, so be sure to read enough to answer the questions. As you work on these passages, you will find that the second passage is harder to read than the first. Answer as many questions as you can.

    Bridges are built to allow a continuous flow of highway and railway traffic across water lying in their paths. But engineers cannot forget that river traffic, too, is essential to our economy. The role of __1__ is important. To keep these vessels moving freely, bridges are built high enough, when possible, to let them pass underneath. Sometimes, however, channels must accommodate very tall ships. It may be uneconomical to build a tall enough bridge. The __2__ would be too high. To save money, engineers build movable bridges.

    In the swing bridge, the middle part pivots or swings open. When the bridge is closed, this section joins the two ends of the bridge, blocking tall vessels. But this section __3__. When swung open, it is perpendicular to the ends of the bridge, creating two free channels for river traffic. With swing bridges channel width is limited by the bridge's piers. The largest swing bridge provides only a 75-meter channel. Such channels are sometimes __4__. In such cases, a bascule bridge may be built.

    Bascule bridges are drawbridges with two arms that swing upward. They provide an opening as wide as the span. They are also versatile. These bridges are not limited to being fully opened or fully closed. They can be __5__ in many ways. They can be fixed at different angles to accommodate different vessels.

    In vertical lift bridges, the center remains horizontal. Towers at both ends allow the center to be lifted like an elevator. One interesting variation of this kind of bridge was built during World War II. A lift bridge was desired, but there were wartime shortages of the steel and machinery needed for the towers. It was hard enough to find enough __6__. An ingenious engineer designed the bridge so that it did not have to be raised above traffic. Instead it was __7__. It could be submerged seven meters below the surface of the river. Ships sailed over it.

1.   A. wind   B. boats   C. experience   1.____
     D. wires   E. experience

2.   A. levels   B. cost   C. standards   2.____
     D. waves   E. deck

3.   A. stands   B. floods   C. wears   3.____
     D. turns   E. supports

4.   A. narrow   B. rough   C. long   4.____
     D. deep   E. straight

5.   A. crossed   B. approached   C. lighted   5.____
     D. planned   E. positioned

6.	A. work D. power	B. material E. space	C. time	6.____
7.	A. burned D. shared	B. emptied E. lowered	C. secured	7.____

The first universities emerged at the end of the 11th century and beginning of the 12th. These institutions were not founded on any particular date or created by any formal action. Nobody actually __8__ them. Instead, they developed gradually in places like Paris, Oxford, and Bologna, where scholars had long been teaching students. At first, these tutors had not been associated with one another. Rather, they had been __9__. But, over time, they joined together to form guilds.

Guilds were groups of tradespeople, somewhat akin to modern unions. In the Middle Ages, all the crafts had such __10__. The scholars' guilds built school buildings and evolved an administration which charged fees and set standards for the curriculum. It set prices for members' services and fixed requirements for entering the profession.

Professors were not the only schoolpeople forming associations. In Italy, students joined guilds to which teachers had to swear obedience. The students set strict rules, fining professors for beginning class a minute late. Teachers had to seek their students' permission to marry, and such permission was not always granted. Sometimes the students __11__. Even if they said yes, the teacher got only one day's honeymoon.

Undergraduates took classes in Greek philosophy, Latin grammar, arithmetic, music, and astronomy. These were the only __12__ available. More advanced study was possible in law, medicine, and theology, but one could not earn such postgraduate degrees quickly. It took a long time to __13__. Completing the requirements in theology, for example, took at least 13 years.

The concept of a fixed program of study leading to a degree first evolved in medieval Europe. This __14__ had not appeared before, in earlier academic settings, notions about *meeting requirements meeting requirements* and *graduating* had been absent. Since the middle ages, though, we have continued to view education as a set curriculum culminating in a degree.

8.	A. started D. compared	B. guarded E. remembered	C. blamed	8.____
9.	A. curious D. ready	B. poor E. independent	C. religious	9.____
10.	A. taxes D. problems	B. secrets E. organizations	C. products	10.____
11.	A. left D. paid	B. copied E. prepared	C. refused	11.____
12.	A. rooms D. pens	B. subjects E. markets	C. clothes	12.____
13.	A. add D. finish	B. answer E. travel	C. forget	13.____

14. A. idea   B. desk   C. library   14.____
    D. capital   E. company

KEY (CORRECT ANSWERS)

1.	B	6.	B	11.	C
2.	B	7.	E	12.	B
3.	D	8.	A	13.	D
4.	A	9.	E	14.	A
5.	E	10.	E		

READING COMPREHENSION
UNDERSTANDING AND INTERPRETING WRITTEN MATERIAL
EXAMINATION SECTION
TEST 1

DIRECTIONS: Each question or incomplete statement is followed by several suggested answers or completions. Select the one that BEST answers the question or completes the statement. *PRINT THE LETTER OF THE CORRECT ANSWER IN THE SPACE AT THE RIGHT.*

Question 1.
DIRECTIONS: Question 1 is to be answered on the basis of the following passage.

    Skiing has recently become one of the more popular sports in the United States. Because of its popularity, thousands of winter vacationers are flying north rather than south. In many areas, reservations are required months ahead of time.
    I discovered the accommodation shortage through an unfortunate experience. On a sunny Saturday morning, I set out from Denver for the beckoning slopes of Aspen, Colorado. After passing signs for other ski areas, I finally reached my destination. Naturally, I lost no time in heading for the nearest tow. After a stimulating afternoon of miscalculated stem turns, I was famished. Well, one thing led to another, and it must have been eight o'clock before I concerned myself with a bed for my bruised and aching bones.
    It took precisely one phone call to ascertain the lack of lodgings in the Aspen area. I had but one recourse. My auto and I started the treacherous jaunt over the pass and back towards Denver. Along the way, I went begging for a bed. Finally, a jolly tavernkeeper took pity, and for only thirty dollars a night allowed me the privilege of staying in a musty, dirty, bathless room above his tavern.

1. The author's problem would have been avoided if he had
   A. not tired himself out skiing
   B. taken a bus instead of driving
   C. arranged for food as soon as he arrived
   D. arranged for accommodations well ahead of his trip
   E. answer cannot be determined from the information given

1._____

Question 2.
DIRECTIONS: Question 2 is to be answered on the basis of the following passage.

    Helen Keller was born in 1880 in Tuscumbia, Alabama. When she was two years old, she lost her sight and hearing as the result of an illness. In 1886, she became the pupil of Anne Sullivan, who taught Helen to see with her fingertips, to *hear* with her feet and hands, and to communicate with other people. Miss Sullivan succeeded in arousing Helen's curiosity and interest by spelling the names of objects into her hand. At the end of three years, Helen had mastered the manual and the braille alphabet and could read and write.

2. When did Helen Keller lose her sight and hearing?

2._____

Question 3.
DIRECTIONS: Question 3 is to be answered on the basis of the following passage.

   Sammy got to school ten minutes after the school bell had rung. He was breathing hard and had a black eye. His face was dirty and scratched. One leg of his pants was torn.
   Tommy was late to school, too; however, he was only five minutes late. Like Sammy, he was breathing hard, but he was happy and smiling.

3.   Sammy and Tommy had been fighting.   3.____
     Who probably won?
       A. Sammy   B. Tommy
       C. Cannot tell from story   D. The teacher
       E. The school

Question 4.
DIRECTIONS: Question 4 is to be answered on the basis of the following passage.

   This is like a game to see if you can tell what the nonsense word in the paragraph stands for. The nonsense word is just a silly word for something that you know very well. Read the paragraph and see if you can tell what the underlined nonsense word stands for.
   You can wash your hands and face in zup. You can even take a bath in it. When people swim, they are in the zup. Everyone drinks zup.

4.   Zup is PROBABLY
       A. milk   B. pop   C. soap   D. water   E. soup

Question 5.
DIRECTIONS: Question 5 is to be answered on the basis of the following passage.

   After two weeks of unusually high-speed travel, we reached Xeno, a small planet whose population, though never before visited by Earthmen, was listed as *friendly* in the INTERSTELLAR GAZETTEER.
   On stepping lightly (after all, the gravity of Xeno is scarcely more than twice that of our own moon) from our spacecraft, we saw that *friendly* was an understatement. We were immediately surrounded by Frangibles of various colors, mostly pinkish or orange, who held out their *hands* to us. Imagine our surprise when their *hands* actually merged with ours as we tried to shake them!
   Then, before we could stop them (how could we have stopped them?), two particularly pink Frangibles simply stepped right into two eminent scientists among our party, who immediately lit up with the same pink glow. While occupied in this way, the scientists reported afterwards they suddenly discovered they *knew* a great deal about Frangibles and life on Xeno..
   Apparently, Frangibles could take themselves apart atomically and enter right into any other substance. They communicated by thought waves, occasionally merging *heads* for greater clarity. Two Frangibles who were in love with each other would spend most of their time merged into one; they were a bluish-green color unless they were having a love's quarrel, when they turned gray.

5. In order to find out about an object which interested him, what would a Frangible MOST likely do?   5.____
   A. Take it apart
   B. Enter into it
   C. Study it scientifically
   D. Ask earth scientists about it
   E. Wait to see if it would change color

Question 6.
DIRECTIONS: Question 6 is to be answered on the basis of the following passage.

This is like a game to see if you can tell what the nonsense word in the paragraph stands for. The nonsense word is just a silly word for something that you know very well. Read the paragraph and see if you can tell what the underlined nonsense word stands for.
Have you ever smelled a mart? They smell very good. Bees like marts. They come inn many colors. Marts grow in the earth, and they usually bloom in the spring.

6. Marts are PROBABLY
   A. bugs   B. flowers   C. perfume   D. pies   E. cherries

Question 7.
DIRECTIONS: Question 7 is to be answered on the basis of the following passage.

Christmas was only a few days away. The wind was strong and cold. The walks were covered with snow. The downtown streets were crowded with people. Their faces were hidden by many packages as they went in one store after another. They all tried to move faster as they looked at the clock.

7. When did the story PROBABLY happen?   7.____
   A. November 28   B. December 1   C. December 21
   D. December 25   E. December 2

Question 8.
DIRECTIONS: Question 8 is to be answered on the basis of the following passage.

THE WAYFARER

The Wayfarer,
Perceiving the pathway to truth,
Was struck with astonishment.
It was thickly grown with weeds.
Ha, he said,
I see that no one has passed here
In a long time.
Later he saw that each weed
Was a singular knife,
Well, he mumbled at last,
Doubtless there are other roads.

8. *I see that no one has passed here in a long time.*
    What do the above lines from the poem mean?
    A. The way of truth is popular.
    B. People are fascinated by the truth.
    C. Truth comes and goes like the wind.
    D. The truth is difficult to recognize.
    E. Few people are searching for the truth.

Question 9.
DIRECTIONS: Question 9 is to be answered on the basis of the following passage.

   Any attempt to label an entire generation is unrewarding, and yet the generation which went through the last war, or at least could get a drink easily once it was over, seems to possess a uniform, general quality which demands an adjective. It was John Kerouac, the author of a fine, neglected novel, THE TOWN AND THE CITY, who final came up with it. It was several years ago, when the face was harder to recognize, but he had a sharp, sympathetic eye, and one day he said, *You know, this is really a* beat *generation*. The origins of the word *beat* are obscure, but the meaning is only too clear to most Americans. More than mere weariness, it implies the feeling of having been used, of being raw. It involves a sort of nakedness of mind, and, ultimately of soul; a feeling of being reduced to the bedrock of consciousness. In short, it means being undramatically pushed up against the wall of oneself. A man is beat whenever he goes for broke and waters the sum of his resources on a single number; and the young generation has done that continually from early youth.

9. What does the writer suggest when he mentions a *fine, neglected novel*?
    A. Kerouac had the right idea about the war.
    B. Kerouac had a clear understanding of the new post-war generation.
    C. Kerouac had not received the recognition of THE TOWN AND THE CITY that was deserved.
    D. Kerouac had the wrong idea about the war.
    E. All of the above

Questions 10-11.
DIRECTIONS: Questions 10 and 11 are to be answered on the basis of the following passage.

   One spring, Farmer Brown had an unusually good field of wheat. Whenever he say any birds in this field, he got his gun and shot as many of them as he could. In the middle of the summer, he found that his wheat was being ruined by insects. With no birds to feed on them, the insects had multiplied very fast. What Farmer Brown did not understand was this: A bird is not simply an animal that eats food the farmer may want for himself. Instead, it is one of many links in the complex surroundings, or environment, in which we live.
   How much grain a farmer can raise on an acre of ground depends on many factors. All of these factors can be divided into two big groups. Such things as the richness of the soil, the amount of rainfall, the amount of sunlight, and the temperature belong together in one of these groups. This group may be called nonliving factors. The second group may be called living factors. The living factors in any plant's environment are animals and other plants. Wheat, for example, may be damaged by wheat rust, a tiny plant that feeds on wheat, or it may be eaten by plant-eating animals such as birds or grasshoppers…

It is easy to see that the relations of plants and animals to their environment are very complex, and that any change in the environment is likely to bring about a whole series of changes.

10. What does the passage suggest a good farmer should understand about nature? 10.____
    A. Insects are harmful to plants.
    B. Birds are not harmful to plants.
    C. Wheat may be damaged by both animals and other plants.
    D. The amount of wheat he can raise depends on two factors: birds and insects.
    E. A change in one factor of plants' surroundings may cause other factors to change.

11. What important idea about nature does the writer want us to understand? 11.____
    A. Farmer Brown was worried about the heavy rainfall.
    B. Nobody needs to have such destructive birds around.
    C. Farmer Brown did not want the temperature to change.
    D. All insects need not only wheat rust but grasshoppers.
    E. All living things are dependent on other living things.

Question 12.
DIRECTIONS: Question 12 is to be answered on the basis of the following passage.

For a 12-year-old, I've been around a lot because my father's in the Army. I have been to New York and to Paris. When I was nine, my parents took me to Rome. I didn't like Europe very much because the people don't speak the same language as I do. When I am older, my mother says I can travel by myself. I think I will like that. Ever since I was 13, I have wanted to go to Canada.

12. Why can't everything this person said be TRUE? 12.____
    A. 12-year-olds can't travel alone.
    B. No one can travel that much in 12 years.
    C. There is a conflict in the ages used in the passage.
    D. 9-year-olds can't travel alone.
    E. He is a liar.

Question 13.
DIRECTIONS: Question 13 is to be answered on the basis of the following passage.

Between April and October, the Persian Gulf is dotted with the small boats of pearl divers. Some seventy-five thousand of them are busy diving down and bringing up pearl-bearing oysters. These oysters are not the kind we eat. The edible oyster produces pearls of little or no value. You may have heard tales of divers who discovered pearls and sold them for great sums of money. These stories are entertaining but not accurate.

13. The Persian Gulf has many   13._____
    A. large boats of pearl divers
    B. pearl divers who eat oysters
    C. edible oysters that produce pearls
    D. non-edible oysters that produce pearls
    E. edible oysters that do not produce pearls

Question 14.
DIRECTIONS: Question 14 is to be answered on the basis of the following passage.

Art says that the polar ice cap is melting at the rate of 3% per year. Bert says that this isn't true because the polar ice cap is really melting at the rate of 7% per year.

14. We know for certain that   14._____
    A. Art is wrong.   B. Bert is wrong.
    C. they are both wrong.   D. they both might be right
    E. they can't both be right

Question 15.
DIRECTIONS: Question 15 is to be answered on the basis of the following passage.

FORTUNE AND MEN'S EYES
                                            Shakespeare

When, in disgrace with fortune and men's eyes,
I all alone beweep my outcast state,
And trouble deaf heaven with my bootless cries,
And look upon myself and curse my fate,
Wishing me like to one more rich in hope,
Featured like him, like him with friends possessed
Desiring this man's art, and that man's scope,
With what I most enjoy contented least;
Yet in these thoughts myself almost despising,
Haply I think on thee; and then my state,
Like to the lark at break of day arising
From sullen earth, sings hymns at heaven's gate;
For thy sweet love remembered, such wealth brings
That then I scorn to change my state with kings.

15. What saves this man from wishing to be different than he is?   15._____
    A. Such wealth brings   B. Hymns at heaven's gate
    C. The lark at break of day D. Thy sweet love remembered
    E. Change my state with kings

Question 16.
DIRECTIONS: Question 16 is to be answered on the basis of the following passage.

My name is Gregory Gotrocks, and I live in Peoria, Illinois. I sell tractors. In June 1952, the Gotrocks Tractor Company (my dad happens to be the president) sent me to Nepal-Tibet to check on our sales office there.

Business was slow, and I had a lot of time to kill. I decided to see Mt. Everest so that I could tell everyone back in Peoria that I had seen it.

It was beautiful; I was spellbound. I simply had to see what the view looked like from the top. So I started up the northwest slope. Everyone know that this is the best route to take. It took me three long hours to reach the top, but the climb was well worth it.

16. Gregory Gotrocks went to see Mt. Everest so that he could   16._____
    A. see some friends   B. sell some tractors
    C. take a picture of it   D. plant a flag at its base
    E. entertain his friends back home

Questions 17-18.
DIRECTIONS: Questions 17 and 18 are to be answered on the basis of the following passage.

Suburbanites are not irresponsible. Indeed, what is striking about the young couples' march along the abyss is the earnestness and precision with which they go about it. They are extremely budget-conscious. They can rattle off most of their monthly payments down to the last penny; one might say that even their impulse buying is deliberately planned. They are conscientious in meeting obligations and rarely do they fall delinquent in their accounts.

They are exponents of what could be called budgetism. This does not mean that they actually keep formal budgets—quite the contrary. The beauty of budgetism is that one doesn't have to keep a budget at all. It's done automatically. In the new middle-class rhythms of life, obligations are homogenized, for the overriding aim is to have oneself precommitted to regular, unvarying monthly payments on all the major items,

Americans used to be divided into three sizable groups: those who thought of money obligations in terms of the week, of the month, and of the year. Many people remain at both ends of the scale; but with the widening of the middle class, the mortgage payments are firmly geared to a thirty-day cycle, and any dissonant peaks and valleys are anathema. Just as young couples are now paying winter fuel bills in equal monthly fractions through the year, so they seek to spread out all the other heavy seasonal obligations they can anticipate. If vendors will not oblige by accepting equal monthly installments, the purchasers will smooth out the load themselves by floating loans.

It is, suburbanites cheerfully explain, a matter of psychology. They don't trust themselves. In self-entrapment is security. They try to budget so tightly that there is no unappropriated funds, for they know these would burn a hole in their pocket. Not merely out of greed for goods, then, do they commit themselves; it is protection they want, too. And though it would be extreme to say that they go into debt to be secure, carefully chartered debt does give them a certain peace of mind—and in suburbia this is more coveted than luxury itself.

17. What is the *abyss* along which the young couples are marching?   17._____
    A. Nuclear war   B. Unemployment
    C. Mental breakdown   D. Financial disaster
    E. Catastrophic illness

18. What conclusion does the author reach concerning carefully chartered debt   18._____
    among young couples in the United States today?
    It
    A. is a symbol of love   B. bring marital happiness
    C. helps them to feel secure D. enables them to acquire wealth
    E. provides them with material goods

Question 19.
DIRECTIONS: Question 19 is to be answered on the basis of the following passage. Read the verse and fill in the space at the right the object described in the verse.

You see me when I'm right or wrong;
My face I never hide.
My hands move slowly round and round
And o'er me minutes glide.

19. A. Book   B. Clock   C. Record   D. Table   E. Lock   19.____

Question 20-22.
DIRECTIONS: Questions 20 through 22 are to be answered on the basis of the following passage.

Until about thirty years ago, the village of Nayon seems to have been a self-sufficient agricultural community with a mixture of native and sixteenth century Spanish customs. Lands were abandoned when too badly eroded. The balance between population and resources allowed a minimum subsistence. A few traders exchanged goods between Quito and the villages in the tropical barrancas, all within a radius of ten miles. Houses had dirt floors, thatched roofs, and pole walls that were sometimes plastered with mud. Guinea pigs ran freely about each house and were the main meat source. Most of the population spoke no Spanish. Men wore long hair and concerned themselves chiefly with farming.

The completion of the Guayaquil-Quito railway in 1908 brought the first real contacts with industrial civilization to the high inter-Andean valley. From this event gradually flowed not only technological changes but new ideas and social institutions. Feudal social relationships no longer seemed right and immutable; medicine and public health improved; elementary education became more common; urban Quito began to expand; and finally, and perhaps least important so far, modern industries began to appear, although even now on a most modest scale.

In 1948-49, the date of our visit, only two men wore their hair long; and only to old-style houses remained. If guinea pigs were kept, they were penned; their flesh was now a luxury food, and beef the most common meat. Houses were of adobe or fired brick, usually with tile roofs, and often contained five or six rooms, some of which had plank or brick floors. Most of the population spoke Spanish. There was no resident priest, but an appointed government official and a policeman represented authority. A six-teacher school provided education. Clothing was becoming citified; for men it often included overalls for work and a tailored suit, white shirt, necktie, and felt hat for trips to Quito. Attendance at church was low, and many festivals had been abandoned. Volleyball or soccer was played weekly in the plaza by young men who sometimes wore shorts, blazers, and berets. There were few shops, for most purchases were made in Quito, and from there came most of the food, so that there was a far more varied diet than twenty-five years ago. There were piped water and sporadic health services; in addition, most families patronized Quito doctors in emergencies.

The crops and their uses had undergone change. Maize, or Indian corn, was still the primary crop, but very little was harvested as grain. Almost all was sold in Quito as green corn to eat boiled on the cob, and a considerable amount of the corn eaten as grain in Nayon was imported. Beans, which do poorly here, were grown on a small scale for household consumption. Though some squash was eaten, most was exported. Sweet potatoes, tomatoes, cabbage, onions, peppers, and, at lower elevations, sweet yucca, and arrowroot were grown extensively for export; indeed, so export-minded was the community that it was almost impossible to buy locally grown produce in the village. People couldn't be bothered with retail scales.

20. Why was there primitiveness and self-containment in Nayon before 1910? 20.____
    A. Social mores
    B. Cultural tradition
    C. Biological instincts
    D. Geographical factors
    E. Religious regulations

21. By 1948, the village of Nayon was 21.____
    A. a self-sufficient village
    B. out of touch with the outside world
    C. a small dependent portion of a larger economic unit
    D. a rapidly growing and sound social and cultural unit
    E. a metropolis

22. Why was Nayon originally separated from its neighbors? 22.____
    A. Rich arable land
    B. Long meandering streams
    C. Artificial political barriers
    D. Broad stretches of arid desert
    E. Deep rugged gorges traversed by rock trails

Question 23.
DIRECTIONS: Question 23 is to be answered on the basis of the following passage. Read the verse and fill in the space at the right the object described in the verse.

I have two eyes and when I'm worn
I give the wearer four.
I'm strong or weak or thick or thin
Need I say much more?

23. A. Clock   B. Eyeglasses   C. Piano   23.____
    D. Thermometer   E. I don't know

Question 24.
DIRECTIONS: Question 24 is to be answered on the basis of the following passage.

Scarlet fever begins with fever, chills, headache, and sore throat. A doctor diagnoses the illness as scarlet fever when a characteristic rash erupts on the skin. This rash appears on the neck and chest in three to five days after the onset of the illness and spreads rapidly over the body. Sometimes the skin on the palm of the hands and soles of the feet shreds in flakes.
Scarlet fever is usually treated with penicillin and, in severe cases, a convalescent serum. The disease may be accompanied by infections of the ear and throat, inflammation of the kidneys, pneumonia, and inflammation of the heart.

24. How does the author tell us that scarlet fever may be a serious disease? 24.____
    A. He tells how many people die of it.
    B. He tells that he once had the disease.
    C. He tells that hands and feet may fall off.

D. He tells how other infections may come with scarlet fever.
E. None of the above

Question 25.
DIRECTIONS: Question 25 is to be answered on the basis of the following passage. Read the verse and fill in the space at the right the object described in the verse.

I have no wings but often fly;
I come in colors many.
From varied nationalities
Respect I get a-plenty.

25. A. Deck of cards   B. Eyeglasses   C. Flag   25.____
    D. Needles   E. None of the above

KEY (CORRECT ANSWERS)

1.	D	11.	E
2.	B	12.	C
3.	B	13.	D
4.	D	14.	E
5.	B	15.	D
6.	B	16.	E
7.	C	17.	D
8.	E	18.	C
9.	C	19.	B
10.	E	20.	D

21. C
22. E
23. B
24. D
25. C

READING COMPREHENSION
UNDERSTANDING AND INTERPRETING WRITTEN MATERIAL
EXAMINATION SECTION
TEST 1

DIRECTIONS: Each question or incomplete statement is followed by several suggested answers or completions. Select the one that BEST answers the question or completes the statement. *PRINT THE LETTER OF THE CORRECT ANSWER IN THE SPACE AT THE RIGHT.*

1. The National Assessment of Educational Progress recently released the results of the first statistically valid national sampling of young adult reading skills in the United States. According to the survey, ninety-five percent of United States young adults (aged 21-25) can read at a fourth-grade level or better. This means they can read well enough to apply for a job, understand a movie guide or join the Army. This is a higher literacy rate than the eighty to eighty-five percent usually estimated for all adults. The study also found that ninety-nine percent can write their names, eighty percent can read a map or write a check for a bill, seventy percent can understand an appliance warranty or write a letter about a billing error, twenty-five percent can calculate the amount of a tip correctly, and fewer than ten percent can correctly figure the cost of a catalog or understand a complex bus schedule.
    Which statement about the study is BEST supported by the above passage?
    A. United States literacy rates among young adults are at an all-time high.
    B. Forty percent of young people in the United States cannot write a letter about a billing error.
    C. Twenty percent of United States teenagers cannot read a map,
    D. More than ninety percent of United States young adults cannot correctly calculate the cost of a catalog order.

    1.____

2. It is now widely recognized that salaries, benefits, and working conditions have more of an impact on job satisfaction than on motivation. If they aren't satisfactory, work performance and morale will suffer. But even when they are high, employees will not necessarily be motivated to work well. For example, THE WALL STREET JOURNAL recently reported that as many as forty or fifty percent of newly hired Wall Street lawyers (whose salaries start at upwards of $50,000) quit within the first three years, citing long hours, pressures, and monotony as the prime offenders. It seems there's just not enough of an intellectual challenge in their jobs. An up and coming money-market executive concluded: *Whether it was $1 million or $100 million, the procedure was the same. Except for the tension, a baboon could do my job.* When money and benefits are adequate, the most important additional determinants of job satisfaction are: more responsibility, a sense of achievement, recognition, and a chance to advance. All of these factors have a more significant influence on employee motivation and performance. As a footnote, several studies have found that the absence of these non-monetary factors can lead to serious stress-related illnesses.

    2.____

Which statement is BEST supported by the above passage?
A. A worker's motivation to perform well is most affected by salaries, benefits, and working conditions.
B. Low pay can lead to high levels of job stress.
C. Work performance will suffer if workers feel they are not paid well.
D. After satisfaction with pay and benefits, the next most important factor is more responsibility.

3. The establishment of joint labor-management production committees occurred in the United States during World War I and again during World War II. Their use was greatly encouraged by the National War Labor Board in World War I and the War Production Board in 1942. Because of the war, labor-management cooperation was especially desired to produce enough goods for the war effort, to reduce conflict, and to control inflation. The committees focused on how to achieve greater efficiency, and consulted on health and safety, training, absenteeism, and people issues in general. During the second world war, there were approximately five thousand labor-management committees in factories, affecting over six million workers. While research has found that only a few hundred committees made significant contributions to productivity, there were additional benefits in many cases. It became obvious to many that workers had ideas to contribute to the running of the organization, and that efficient enterprises could become even more so. Labor-management cooperation was also extended to industries that had never experienced it before. Directly after each war, however, few United States labor-management committees were in operation.
Which statement is BEST supported by the above passage?
A. The majority of United States labor-management committees during the second world war accomplished little.
B. A major goal of United States labor-management committees during the first and second world wars was to increase productivity.
C. There were more United States labor-management committees during the second world war than during the first world war.
D. There are few United States labor-management committees in operation today.

4. Studies have found that stress levels among employees who have a great deal of customer contact or a great deal of contact with the public can be very high. There are many reasons for this. Sometimes stress results when the employee is caught in the middle—an organization wants things done one way, but the customer wants them done another way. The situation becomes even worse for the employee's stress levels when he or she knows was to more effectively provide the service, but isn't allowed to, by the organization. An example is the bank teller who is required to ask a customer for two forms of identification before he or she can cash a check, even though the teller knows the customer well. If organizational mishaps occur or if there are problems with job design, the employee may be powerless to satisfy the customer, and also powerless to protect himself or herself from the customer's wrath. An example of this is the waitress who is forced to serve poorly prepared food. Studies have also found,

however, that if the organization and the employee design the positions and the service encounter well, and encourage the use of effective stress management techniques, stress can be reduced to levels that are well below average.
Which statement is BEST supported by the above passage?
- A. It is likely that knowledgeable employees will experience greater levels of job-related stress.
- B. The highest levels of occupational stress are found among those employees who have a great deal of customer contact.
- C. Organizations can contribute to the stress levels of their employees by poorly designing customer contact situations.
- D. Stress levels are generally higher in banks and restaurants.

5. It is estimated that approximately half of the United States population suffers from varying degrees of adrenal malfunction. When under stress for long periods of time, the adrenals produce extra cortisol and norepinephrine. By producing more hormones than they were designed to comfortably manufacture and secrete, the adrenals can *burn out* over time and then decrease their secretion. When this happens, the body loses its capacity to cope with stress, and the individual becomes sicker more easily and for longer periods of time. A result of adrenal malfunction may be a diminished output of cortisol. Symptoms of diminished cortisol output include any of the following: craving substances that will temporarily raise serum glucose levels such as caffeine, sweets, soda, juice, or tobacco; becoming dizzy when standing up too quickly; irritability; headaches; and erratic energy levels. Since cortisol is an anti-inflammatory hormone, a decreased output over extended periods of time can make one prone to inflammatory disease such ass arthritis, bursitis, colitis, and allergies. (Many food and pollen allergies disappear when adrenal function is restored to normal.) The patient will have no reserve energy, and infections can spread quickly. Excessive cortisol production, on the other hand, can decrease immunity, leading to frequent and prolonged illnesses.
Which statement is BEST supported by the above passage?
- A. Those who suffer from adrenal malfunction are most likely to be prone to inflammatory diseases such as arthritis and allergies.
- B. The majority of Americans suffer from varying degrees of adrenal malfunction.
- C. It is better for the health of the adrenals to drink juice instead of soda.
- D. Too much cortisol can inhibit the body's ability to resist disease.

6. Psychologist B.F. Skinner pointed out long ago that gambling is reinforced either by design or accidentally, by what he called a variable ratio schedule. A slot machine, for example, is cleverly designed to provide a payoff after it has been played a variable number of times. Although the person who plays it and wins while playing receives a great deal of monetary reinforcement, over the long run the machine will take in much more money than it pays out. Research on both animals and humans has consistently found that such variable reward schedules maintain a very high rate of repeat behavior, and that this behavior is particularly resistant to extinction.

Which statement is BEST supported by the above passage?
A. Gambling, because it is reinforced by the variable ratio schedule, is more difficult to eliminate than most addictions.
B. If someone is rewarded or wins consistently, even if it is not that often, he or she is likely to continue that behavior.
C. Playing slot machines is the safest form of gambling because they are designed so that eventually the player will indeed win.
D. A cat is likely to come when called if its owner has trained it correctly.

7. Paper entrepreneurialism is an offshoot of scientific management that has become so extreme that it has lost all connection to the actual workplace. It generates profits by cleverly manipulating rules and numbers that only in theory represent real products and real assets. At its worst, paper entrepreneurialism involves very little more than imposing losses on others for the sake of short-term profits. The others may be taxpayers, shareholders who end up indirectly subsidizing other shar holders, consumers, or investors. Paper entrepreneurialism has replaced product entrepreneurialism, is seriously threatening the United States economy, and is hurting our necessary attempts to transform the nation's industrial and productive economic base. An example is the United States company that complained loudly in 1979 that it did not have the $200 million needed to develop a video-cassette recorder, though demand for them had been very high. The company, however, did not hesitate to spend $1.2 billion that same year to buy a mediocre finance company. The video recorder market was handed over to other countries, who did not hesitate to manufacture them.

    Which statement is BEST supported by the above passage?
    A. Paper entrepreneurialism involves very little more than imposing losses on others for the sake of short-term profits.
    B. Shareholders are likely to benefit most from paper entrepreneurialism.
    C. Paper entrepreneurialism is hurting the United States economy.
    D. The United States could have made better video-cassette recorders than the Japanese but we ceded the market to them in 1979.

    7.____

8. The *prisoner's dilemma* is an almost 40-year-old game-theory model psychologists, biologists, economists, and political scientists use to try to understand the dynamics of competition and cooperation. Participants in the basic version of the experiment are told that they and their *accomplice* have been caught red-handed. Together, their best strategy is to cooperate by remaining silent. If they do this, each will get off with a 30-day sentence. But either person can do better for himself or herself. If you double-cross your partner, you will go scot free while he or she serves ten years. The problem is, if you each betray the other, you will both go to prison for eight years, not thirty days. No matter what your partner chooses, you are logically better off choosing betrayal. Unfortunately, your partner realizes this too, and so the odds are good that you will both get eight years. That's the dilemma. (The length of the prison sentences is always the same for each variation.) Participants at a recent symposium on behavioral economics at Harvard University discussed the many variations on the game that have been used

    8.____

over the years. In one standard version, subjects are paired with a supervisor who pays them a dollar for each point they score. Over the long run, both subjects will do best if they cooperate every time. Yet in each round, there is a great temptation to betray the other because no one knows what the other will do. The best overall strategy for this variation was found to be *tit for tat*, doing unto your opponent as he or she has just done unto you. It is a simple strategy, but very effective. The partner can easily recognize it and respond. It is retaliatory enough not to be easily exploited, but forgiving enough to allow a pattern of mutual cooperation to develop.
Which statement is BEST supported by the above passage?
- A. The best strategy for playing *prisoner's dilemma* is to cooperate and remain silent.
- B. If you double-cross your partner, and he or she does not double-cross you, your partner will receive a sentence of eight years.
- C. When playing *prisoner's dilemma*, it is best to double-cross your partner.
- D. If you double-cross your partner, and he or she double-crosses you, you will receive an eight-year sentence.

9. After many years of experience as the vice president and general manager of a large company, I feel that I know what I'm looking for in a good manager. First, the manager has to be comfortable with himself or herself, and not be arrogant or defensive. Secondly, he or she has to have a genuine interest in people. There are some managers who love ideas—and that's fine—but to be a manager, you must love people, and you must make a hobby of understanding them, believing in them and trusting them. Third, I look for a willingness and a facility to manage conflict. Gandhi defined conflict as a way of getting at the truth. Each person brings his or her own grain of truth and the conflict washes away the illusion and fantasy. Finally, a manager has to have a vision, and the ability and charisma to articulate it. A manager should be seen as a little bit crazy. Some eccentricity is an asset. People don't want to follow vanilla leaders. They want to follow chocolate-fudge-ripple leaders.
Which statement is BEST supported by the above passage?
- A. It is very important that a good manager spend time studying people.
- B. It is critical for good managers to love ideas.
- C. Managers should try to minimize or avoid conflict.
- D. Managers should be familiar with people's reactions to different flavors of ice cream.

10. Most societies maintain a certain set of values and assumptions that make their members feel either good or bad about themselves, and either better or worse than other people. In most developed countries, these values are based on the assumption that we are all free to be what we want to be, and that differences in income, work, and education are a result of our own efforts. This may make us believe that people with more income work that is more skilled, more education, and more power are somehow *better* people. We may view their achievements as proof that they have more intelligence, more motivation, and more initiative than those with lower status. The myth tells us that power, income, and education are freely and equally available to all, and that our

failure to achieve them is due to our own personal inadequacy. This simply is not the case.

The possessions we own may also seem to point to our real worth as individuals. The more we own, the more worthy of respect we may feel we are. Or, the acquisition of possessions may be a way of trying to fulfill ourselves, to make up for the loss of community and/or purpose. It is a futile pursuit because lost community and purpose can never be compensated for by better cars or fancier houses. And too often, when these things fail to satisfy, we believe it is only because we don't have enough money to buy better quality items, or more items. We feel bad that we haven't been successful enough to get all that we think we need. No matter how much we do have, goods never really satisfy for long. There is always something else to acquire, and true satisfaction eludes many, many of us.
Which statement is BEST supported by the above passage?
  A. The author would agree with the theory of *survival of the fittest*.
  B. The possessions an individual owns are not a proper measure of his or her real worth.
  C. Many countries make a sincere attempt to ensure equal access to quality education for their citizens.
  D. The effect a society's value system has on the lives of its members is greatly exaggerated.

11. *De nihilo nihil* is Latin for *nothing comes from nothing*. In the first century, the Roman poet Persius advised that if anything is to be produced of value, effort must be expended. He also said, *In nihilum nil posse revorti*—anything once produced cannot become nothing again. It is thought that Persius was parodying Lucretius, who expounded the 500-year-old physical theories of Epicurus. *De nihilo nihil* can also be used as a cynical comment, to negatively comment on something that is of poor quality produced by a person of little talent. The implication here is: *What can you expect from such a source?*
Which statement is BEST supported by the above passage?
  A. *In nihilum nil posse revorti* can be interpreted as meaning, *If anything is to be produced of value, then effort must be expended.*
  B. *De nihilo nihil* can be understood in two different ways,
  C. Lucretius was a great physicist.
  D. Persius felt that Epicurus put in little effort while developing his theories.

11.____

12. A Cornell University study has found that less than one percent of the billion pounds of pesticides used in this country annually strike their intended targets. The study found that the pesticides, which are somewhat haphazardly applied to 370 million acres, or about sixteen percent of the nation's total land area, end up polluting the environment and contaminating almost all 200,000 species of plants and animals, including humans. While the effect of indirect contamination on human cancer rates was not estimated, the study found that approximately 45,000 human pesticide poisonings occur annually, including about 3,000 cases admitted to hospitals and approximately 200 fatalities.

12.____

Which statement is BEST supported by the above passage?
- A. It is likely that indirect pesticide contamination affects human health.
- B. Pesticides are applied to over one-quarter of the total United States land area.
- C. If pesticides were applied more carefully, fewer pesticide-resistant strains of pests would develop.
- D. Human cancer rates in this country would drop considerably if pesticide use was cut in half.

13. The new conservative philosophy presents a unified, coherent approach to the world. It offers to explain much of our experience since the turbulent 1960s, and it shows what we've learned since about the dangers of indulgence and permissiveness. But it also warns that the world has become more ruthless, and that as individuals and as a nation, we must struggle for survival. It is necessary to impose responsibility and discipline in order to defeat those forces that threaten us. This lesson is dramatically clear, and can be applied to a wide range of issues.
    Which statement is BEST supported by the above passage?
    - A. The 1970s were a time of permissiveness and indulgence.
    - B. The new conservative philosophy may help in imposing discipline and a sense of responsibility in order to meet the difficult challenges facing this country.
    - C. The world faced greater challenges during the second world war than it faces at the present time.
    - D. More people identify themselves today as conservative in their political philosophy.

14. One of the most puzzling questions in management in recent years has been how usually honest, compassionate, intelligent managers can sometimes act in ways that are dishonest, uncaring, and unethical. How could top-level managers at the Manville Corporation, for example, suppress evidence for decades that proved beyond all doubt that asbestos inhalation was killing their own employees? What drove the managers of a Midwest bank to continue to act in a way that threatened to bankrupt the institution, ruin its reputation, and cost thousands of employees and investors their jobs and their savings? It's been estimated that about two out of three of America's five hundred largest corporations have been involved in some form of illegal behavior. There are, of course, some common rationalizations used to justify unethical conduct: believing that the activity is in the organization's or the individual's best interest, believing that the activity is not *really* immoral or illegal, believing that no one will ever know, or believing that the organization will sanction the behavior because it helps the organization. Ambition can distort one's sense of *duty*.
    Which statement is BEST supported by the above passage?
    - A. Top-level managers of corporations are currently involved in a plan to increase ethical behavior among their employees.
    - B. There are many good reasons why a manager may act unethically.
    - C. Some managers allow their ambitions to override their sense of ethics.
    - D. In order to successfully compete, some organizations may have to indulge in unethical or illegal behavior from time to time.

15. Some managers and supervisors believe that they are leaders because they occupy positions of responsibility and authority. But leadership is more than holding a position. It is often defined in management literature as *the ability to influence the opinions, attitudes and behaviors of others.* Obviously, there are some managers that would not qualify as leaders, and some leaders that are not *technically* managers. Research has found that many people overrate their own leadership abilities. In one recent study, seventy percent of those surveyed rated themselves in the top quartile in leadership abilities, and only two percent felt they were below average as leaders.
Which statement is BEST supported by the above passage?
   A. In a recent study, the majority of people surveyed rated themselves in the top twenty-five percent in leadership abilities.
   B. Ninety-eight percent of the people surveyed in a recent study had average or above-average leadership skills.
   C. In order to be a leader, one should hold a management position.
   D. Leadership is best defined as the ability to be liked by those one must lead.

15.____

KEY (CORRECT ANSWERS)

1.	D	6.	B	11.	B
2.	C	7.	C	12.	A
3.	B	8.	D	13.	B
4.	C	9.	A	14.	C
5.	D	10.	B	15.	A

READING COMPREHENSION
UNDERSTANDING AND INTERPRETING
WRITTEN MATERIAL

EXAMINATION SECTION

TEST 1

DIRECTIONS: Each question or incomplete statement is followed by several suggested answers or completions. Select the one that BEST answers the question or completes the statement. *PRINT THE LETTER OF THE CORRECT ANSWER IN THE SPACE AT THE RIGHT.*

In its current application to art, the term *"primitive"* is as vague and unspecific as the term "heathen" is in its application to religion. A heathen sect is simply one which is not affiliated with one or another of three or four organized systems of theology. Similarly, a primitive art is one which flourishes outside the small number of cultures which we have chosen to designate as civilizations. Such arts differ vastly and it is correspondingly difficult to generalize about them. Any statements which will hold true for such diverse aesthetic experiences as the pictographs of the Australians, the woven designs of the Peruvians, and the abstract sculptures of the African tribes must be of the broadest and simplest sort. Moreover, the problem is complicated by the meaning attached to the term "primitive" in its other uses. It stands for something simple, undeveloped, and, by implication, ancestral to more evolved forms. Its application to arts and cultures other than our own is an unfortunate heritage from the nineteenth-century scientists who laid the foundations of anthropology. Elated by the newly enunciated doctrines of evolution, these students saw all cultures as stages in a single line of development and assigned them to places in this series on the simple basis of the degree to which they differed from European culture, which was blandly assumed to be the final and perfect flower of the evolutionary process. This idea has long since been abandoned by anthropologists, but before its demise it diffused to other social sciences and became a part of the general body of popular misinformation. It still tinges a great deal of the thought and writing about the arts of non-European peoples and has been responsible for many misunderstandings.

1. The MAIN purpose of the passage is to
    A. explain the various definitions of the term "primitive"
    B. show that the term "primitive" can be applied validly to art
    C. compare the use of the term "primitive" to the use of the term "heathen"
    D. deprecate the use of the term "primitive" as applied to art
    E. show that "primitive" arts vary greatly among themselves

1.____

2. The nineteenth-century scientists believed that the theory of evolution
    A. could be applied to the development of culture
    B. was demonstrated in all social sciences
    C. was substantiated by the diversity of "primitive" art
    D. could be applied only to European culture
    E. disproved the idea that some arts are more "primitive" than others

2.____

3. With which of the following would the author agree?
   A. The term "primitive" is used only by the misinformed.
   B. "Primitive" arts may be as highly developed as "civilized" arts.
   C. The arts of a culture often indicated how advanced that culture was.
   D. Australian, Peruvian, and African tribal arts are much like the ancestral forms from which European art evolved.
   E. A simple culture is likely to have a simple art.

4. According to the author, many misunderstandings have been caused by the belief that
   A. most cultures are fundamentally different
   B. inferior works of art in any culture are "primitive" art
   C. "primitive" arts are diverse
   D. non-European arts are diverse
   E. European civilization is the final product of the evolutionary process

KEY (CORRECT ANSWERS)

1. D
2. A
3. B
4. E

TEST 2

DIRECTIONS: Each question or incomplete statement is followed by several suggested answers or completions. Select the one that BEST answers the question or completes the statement. *PRINT THE LETTER OF THE CORRECT ANSWER IN THE SPACE AT THE RIGHT.*

One of the ways the intellectual *avant-garde* affects the technical intelligentsia is through the medium of art, and art is, if only implicitly, a critique of experience. The turning upon itself of modern culture in the forms of the new visual art, the utilization of the detritus of daily experience to mock that experience, constitutes a mode of social criticism. Pop art, it is true, does not go beyond the surface of the visual and tactile experience of an industrial (and a commercialized) culture. Dwelling on the surface, it allows its consumers to mock the elements of their daily life, without abandoning it. Indeed, the consumption of art in the organized market for leisure serves at times to encapsulate the social criticism of the *avant-garde*. However, the recent engagement of writers, artists, and theater people in contemporary issues suggests that this sort of containment may have begun to reach its limits.

In an atmosphere in which the intellectually dominant group insists on the contradictions inherent in daily experience, the technical intelligentsia will find it difficult to remain unconscious of those contradictions. The technical intelligentsia have until now avoided contradictions by accepting large rewards for their expertise. As expertise becomes increasingly difficult to distinguish from ordinary service on the one hand, and merges on the other with the change of the social environment, the technical intelligentsia's psychic security may be jeopardized. Rendering of labor services casts it back into spiritual proletarianization; a challenge to the social control exercised by elites, who use the technical intelligentsia's labor power, pushes it forward to social criticism and revolutionary politics. That these are matters, for the moment, of primarily spiritual import does not diminish their ultimate political significance. A psychological precondition for radical action is usually far more important than an "objectively" revolutionary situation—whatever that may be.

The chances for a radicalization of the technical intelligentsia, thus extending the student revolt cannot be even approximated. I believe I have shown there is a chance.

1. It may be *inferred* that the technical intelligentsia are
   I. The executives and employers in society
   II. Critics of *avant-garde* art
   III. Highly skilled technical workers
   The CORRECT answer is:
   A. I only   B. I and III   C. I, II, and III
   D. III only   E. I and II

2. The engagement of the intellectual *avant-garde* in contemporary issues
   A. indicates that people tire of questioning the contradictions inherent in day-to-day living
   B. indicates that the technical intelligentsia are close to the point where they will rebel against the *avant-garde*
   C. could cause a challenge to the social control of the elites
   D. could cause the public to become more leisure-oriented
   E. could cause an increase in the consumption of art in the organized market for leisure services

3. The *possible* effect of the intellectual *avant-garde* on the technical intelligentsia is that
   A. the intellectual *avant-garde* makes the technical intelligentsia conscious of society's contradictions
   B. rapid curtailment of large rewards for expertise will result
   C. it may cause a strong likelihood of a radicalization of the technical intelligentsia
   D. the *avant-garde* will replace the employment of the technical intelligentsia in contemporary issues
   E. the rendering of labor services will be eliminated

4. If it is assumed that the technical intelligentsia becomes fully aware of the contradictions of modern life, it is the author's position that
   A. revolution will result
   B. the technical intelligentsia may refuse to perform manual labor
   C. the technical intelligentsia will be pushed forward to social criticism and revolutionary politics
   D. the technical intelligentsia will experience some psychic dislocation
   E. ordinary service will replace technical expertise

5. According to the author,
   A. the state of mind of a particular group may have more influence on its action than the effect of environmental factors
   B. the influence of art will often cause social upheaval
   C. matters of primarily spiritual import necessarily lack political significance
   D. the detritus of day-to-day living should be mocked by the intellectual *avant-garde*
   E. the technical intelligentsia can only protect their psychic security by self-expression through art

6. With which of the following would the author agree?
   I. As contradictions are less contained, the psychic security of all members of the working class would be jeopardized.
   II. The expertise of the technical intelligentsia evolved from the ownership and management of property.
   III. The technical intelligentsia is not accustomed to rendering labor services.
   The CORRECT answer is:
   A. I only   B. III only   C. I and III
   D. II only   E. None of the above

7. The MAIN purpose of the passage is to
   A. discuss the influence of the *avant-garde* art form on the expertise of the technical intelligentsia
   B. discuss the effect of the intellectual *avant-garde* on the working classes
   C. discuss the social significance of the technical intelligentsia
   D. discuss the possible effects of the de-encapsulation of *avant-garde* social criticism
   E. point out that before a change psychological preconditions are first established

KEY (CORRECT ANSWERS)

1. D   5. A
2. C   6. B
3. A   7. D
4. D

TEST 3

DIRECTIONS: Each question or incomplete statement is followed by several suggested answers or completions. Select the one that BEST answers the question or completes the statement. *PRINT THE LETTER OF THE CORRECT ANSWER IN THE SPACE AT THE RIGHT.*

Turbulent flow over a boundary is a complex phenomenon for which there is no really complete theory even in simple laboratory cases. Nevertheless, a great deal of experimental data has been collected on flows over solid surfaces, both in the laboratory and in nature, so that, from an engineering point of view at least, the situation is fairly well understood. The force exerted on a surface varies with the roughness of that surface and approximately with the square of the wind speed at some fixed height above it. A wind of 10 meters per second (about 20 knots, or 22 miles per hour) measured at a height of 10 meters will produce a force of some 30 tons per square kilometer on a field of mown grass or of about 70 tons per square kilometer on a ripe wheat field. On a really smooth surface, such as glass, the force is only about 10 tons per square kilometer.

When the wind blows over water, the whole thing is much more complicated. The roughness of the water is not a given characteristic of the surface but depends on the wind itself. Not only that, the elements that constitute the roughness—the waves—themselves move more or less in the direction of the wind. Recent evidence indicates that a large portion of the momentum transferred from the air into the water goes into waves rather than directly into making currents in the water; only as the waves break, or otherwise lose energy, does their momentum become available to generate currents, or produce Ekman layers. Waves carry a substantial amount of both energy and momentum (typically about as much as is carried by the wind in a layer about one wavelength thick), and so the wave-generation process is far from negligible. A violently wavy surface belies its appearance by acting, as far as the wind is concerned, as though it were very smooth. At 10 meters per second, recent measurements seem to agree, the force on the surface is quite a lot less than the force over mown grass and scarcely more than it is over glass; some observations in light winds of two or three meters per second indicate that the force on the wavy surface is less than it is on a surface as smooth as glass. In some way the motion of the waves seems to modify the airflow so that air slips over the surface even more freely than it would without the waves. This seems not to be the case at higher wind speeds, above about five meters per second, but the force remains strikingly low compared with that over other natural surfaces.

One serious deficiency is the fact that there are no direct observations at all in those important cases in which the wind speed is greater than about 12 meters per second and has had time and fetch (the distance over water) enough to raise substantial waves. The few indirect studies indicate that the apparent roughness of the surface increases somewhat under high-wind conditions, so that the force on the surface increases rather more rapidly than as the square of the wind speed.

Assuming that the force increases at least as the square of the wind speed, it is evident that high-wind conditions produce effects far more important than their frequency of occurrence would suggest. Five hours of 60-knot storm winds will put more momentum into the water than a week of 10-knot breezes. If it should be shown that, for high winds, the force on the surface increases appreciably more rapidly than as the square of the wind speed, then the transfer of momentum to the ocean will turn out to be dominated by what happens during the occasional storm rather than by the long-term average winds.

2 (#3)

1. According to the passage, several hours of storm winds (60 miles per hour) over the ocean would
   A. be similar to the force exerted by light winds for several hours over glass
   B. create an ocean roughness which reduces the force exerted by the high winds
   C. have proved to be more significant in creating ocean momentum than light winds
   D. create a force not greater than 6 times the force of a 10-mile-per-hour wind
   E. eventually affect ocean current

2. According to the passage, a rough-like ocean surface
   A. is independent of the force of the wind
   B. has the same force exerted against it by high and light winds
   C. is more likely to have been caused by a storm than by continuous light winds
   D. nearly always allows airflow to be modified so as to cause the force of the wind to be less than on glass
   E. is a condition under which the approximate square of wind speed can never be an accurate figure in measuring the wind force

3. The author indicates that, where a hurricane is followed by light winds of 10 meters per second or less,
   I. ocean current will be unaffected by the light winds
   II. ocean current will be more affected by the hurricane winds than the following light winds
   III. the force of the light winds on the ocean would be less than that exerted on a wheat field.
   The CORRECT combination is:
   A. I only   B. III only   C. II and III   D. I and III   E. II only

4. The MAIN purpose of the passage is to discuss
   A. oceanic momentum and current
   B. turbulent flow of wind over water
   C. wind blowing over water as related to causing tidal flow
   D. the significance of high wind conditions on ocean momentum
   E. experiments in wind force

5. The author would be incorrect in concluding that the transfer of momentum to the ocean is dominated by the occasional storm if
   A. air momentum went directly into making ocean current
   B. high speed winds slipped over waves as easily as low speed winds
   C. waves did not move in the direction of wind
   D. the force exerted on a wheat field was the same as on mown grass
   E. the force of wind under normal conditions increased as the square of wind speed

6. A wind of 10 meters per second measured at a height of 10 meters will produce a force close to 30 tons per square mile on which of the following?   6.____
   A. Unmown grass B. Mown grass C. Glass
   D. Water E. A football field

KEY (CORRECT ANSWERS)

1. E
2. C
3. C
4. B
5. B
6. A

TEST 4

DIRECTIONS: Each question or incomplete statement is followed by several suggested answers or completions. Select the one that BEST answers the question or completes the statement. *PRINT THE LETTER OF THE CORRECT ANSWER IN THE SPACE AT THE RIGHT.*

Political scientists, as practitioners of a negligibly formalized discipline, tend to be accommodating to formulations and suggested techniques developed in related behavioral sciences. They even tend, on occasion, to speak of psychology, sociology, and anthropology as "hard core sciences." Such a characterization seems hardly justified. The disposition to uncritically adopt into political science non-indigenous sociological and general systems concepts tends, at times, to involve little more than the adoption of a specific, and sometimes barbarous, academic vocabulary which is used to redescribe reasonably well-confirmed or intuitively-grasped low-order empirical generalizations.

At its worst, what results in such instances is a runic explanation, a redescription in a singular language style, i.e., no explanation at all. At their best, functional accounts as they are found in the contemporary literature provide explanation sketches, the type of elliptical explanation characteristic of historical and psychoanalytic accounts. For each such account there is an indeterminate number of equally plausible ones, the consequence of either the complexity of the subject matter, differing perspectives, conceptual vagueness, the variety of sometimes mutually exclusive empirical or quasi-empirical generalizations employed, or syntactical obscurity, or all of them together.

Functional explanations have been most reliable in biology and physiology (where they originated) and in the analysis of servo mechanical and cybernetic systems (to which they have been effectively extended). In these areas we possess a well-standardized body of lawlike generalizations. Neither sociology nor political science has as yet the same resource of well-confirmed lawlike statements. Certainly sociology has few more than political science. What passes for functional explanation in sociology is all too frequently parasitic upon suggestive analogy and metaphor, trafficking on our familiarity with goal-directed systems.

What is advanced as "theory" in sociology is frequently a non-theoretic effort at classification or "codification," the search for an analytic conceptual schema which provides a typology or a classificatory system serviceable for convenient storage and ready retrieval of independently established empirical regularities. That such a schema takes on a hierarchic and deductive character, imparting to the collection of propositions a *prima facie* theoretical appearance, may mean no more than that the terms employed in the high-order propositions are so vague that they can accommodate almost any inference and consequently can be made to any conceivable state of affairs.

1. The author *implies* that, when the political scientist is at his best, his explanations   1.____
   A. are essentially a retelling of events
   B. only then form the basis of an organized discipline
   C. plausibly account for past occurrences
   D. are prophetic of future events
   E. are confirmed principles forming part of the political scientist's theory

2. With which of the following would the author probably agree?
   I. Because of an abundance of reasonable explanations for past conduct, there is the possibility of contending schools within the field of political science developing.
   II. Political science is largely devoid of predictive power.
   III. Political science has very few verified axioms.
   The CORRECT answer is:
   A. III only   B. I and III   C. I and II   D. I, II, III   E. I only

3. The passage *implies* that many sociological theories
   A. are capable of being widely applied to various situations
   B. do not even appear to be superficially theoretical in appearance
   C. contrast with those of political science in that there are many more confirmed lawlike statements
   D. are derived from deep analysis and exhaustive research
   E. appear theoretical but are really very well proved

4. The author's thesis would be UNSUPPORTABLE if
   A. the theories of the political scientist possessed predictive power
   B. political science did not consist of redescription
   C. political scientists were not restricted to "hard core sciences"
   D. political science consisted of a body of theories capable of application to any situation
   E. none of the above

5. The author believe that sociology as a "hard core science," contains reliable and functional explanations
   A. is never more than a compilation of conceptual schema
   B. is in nearly every respect unlike political science
   C. is a discipline which allows for varied inferences to be drawn from its general propositions
   D. is a science indigenous *prima facie* theoretical appearance containing very little codification posing as theory

KEY (CORRECT ANSWERS)

1. C
2. D
3. A
4. A
5. D

TEST 5

DIRECTIONS: Each question or incomplete statement is followed by several suggested answers or completions. Select the one that BEST answers the question or completes the statement. *PRINT THE LETTER OF THE CORRECT ANSWER IN THE SPACE AT THE RIGHT.*

James' own prefaces to his works were devoted to structural composition and analytics and his approach in those prefaces has only recently begun to be understood. One of his contemporary critics, with the purest intention to blame, wrote what might be recognized today as sophisticated praise when he spoke of the later James as "an impassioned geometer" and remarked that "what interested him was not the figures but their relations, the relations which alone make pawns significant." James's explanations of his works often are so bereft of interpretation as to make some of our own austere defenses against interpretation seem almost embarrassingly rich with psychological meanings. They offer, with a kind of brazen unselfconsciousness, an astonishingly artificial, even mechanical view of novelistic invention. It's not merely that James asserts the importance of technique; more radically, he tends to discuss character and situation almost entirely as functions of technical ingenuities. The very elements in a Jamesian story which may strike us as requiring the most explanation are presented by James either as a *solution* to a problem of compositional harmony or else as the *donnee* about which it would be irrelevant to ask any questions at all.

James should constantly be referred to as a model of structuralist criticism. He consistently redirects our attention from the referential aspect of a work of art (its extensions into "reality") to its own structural coherence as the principal source of inspiration.

What is most interesting about James's structurally functional view of character is that a certain devaluation of what we ordinarily think of as psychological interest is perfectly consistent with an attempt to portray reality. It's as if he came to feel that a kind of autonomous geometric pattern, in which the parts appeal for their value to nothing but their contributive place in the essentially abstract pattern, is the artist's most successful representation of life. Thus, he could perhaps even think that verisimilitude—a word he liked—has less to do with the probability of the events the novelist describes than with those processes, deeply characteristic of life, by which he creates sense and coherence from any event. The only faithful picture of life in art is not in the choice of a significant subject (James always argues against the pseudo realistic prejudice), but rather in the illustration of sense- or design-making processes. James proves the novel's connection with life by deprecating its derivation from life; and it's when he is most abstractly articulating the growth of a structure that James is almost most successfully defending the mimetic function of art (and of criticism). His deceptively banal position that only execution matters means most profoundly that verisimilitude, properly considered, is the grace and the truth of a formal unity.

1. The author suggests that James, in explanations of his own art,   1.____
    A. was not bound by formalistic strictures but concentrated on verisimilitude
    B. was deeply psychological and concentrated on personal insight
    C. felt that his art had a one-to-one connection with reality
    D. was basically mechanical and concentrated on geometrical form
    E. was event-and-character-oriented rather than technique-oriented

2. The passage indicates that James's method of approaching reality was
   A. that objective reality did not exist and was patterned only by the mind
   B. that formalism and pattern were excellent means of approaching reality
   C. not to concentrate on specific events but rather on character development
   D. that the only objective reality is the psychological processes of the mind
   E. that in reality events occur which are not structured but rather as random occurrences

3. The MAIN purpose of the paragraph is to
   A. indicate that James's own approach to his work is only now beginning to be understood
   B. deprecate the geometrical approach towards the novel
   C. question whether James's novels were related to reality
   D. indicate that James felt that society itself could be seen as a geometric structure
   E. discuss James's explanation of his works

4. In discussing his own works, James
   I. talks of people and events as a function of technique to the exclusion of all else
   II. is quick to emphasize the referential aspect of the work
   III. felt that verisimilitude could be derived not from character but rather from the ordering of event
   The CORRECT answer is:
   A. I only   B. II only   C. III only   D. I and III   E. I and II

5. The author
   A. *approves* of James's explanations of his work but *disapproves* his lack of discussion into the psychological makings of his characters
   B. *disapproves* of James's explanation of his own work and his lack of discussion into the psychological makings of his characters
   C. *approves* of James's explanations of his works in terms of structure as being well-rated to life
   D. *disapproves* of James's explanation of his works in terms of structure as lacking verisimilitude
   E. *approves* of James's explanation of his works because of the significance of the subjects chosen

6. The following is NOT true of James's explanation of his own works: He
   A. did not explain intriguing elements of a story except as part of a geometric whole
   B. felt the artist could represent life by its patterns rather than its events
   C. defended the imitative function of art by detailing the growth of a structure
   D. attempted to give the reader insight into the psychology of his characters by insuring that his explanation followed a strict geometrical pattern
   E. was able to devalue psychological interest and yet be consistent with an attempt to truly represent life

7. James believed it to be *essential* to
   A. carefully choose a subject which would lend itself to processes by which sense and cohesion is achieved
   B. defend the mimetic function of art by emphasizing verisimilitude
   C. emphasize the manner in which different facets of a story could fit together
   D. explain character in order to achieve literary harmony
   E. be artificial and unconcerned with representing life

7.____

KEY (CORRECT ANSWERS)

1. D
2. B
3. E
4. C
5. C
6. D
7. C

TEST 6

DIRECTIONS: Each question or incomplete statement is followed by several suggested answers or completions. Select the one that BEST answers the question or completes the statement. *PRINT THE LETTER OF THE CORRECT ANSWER IN THE SPACE AT THE RIGHT.*

    The popular image of the city as it is now is a place of decay, crime, of fouled streets, and of people who are poor or foreign or odd. But what is the image of the city of the future? In the plans for the huge redevelopment projects to come, we are being shown a new image of the city. Gone are the dirt and the noise—and the variety and the excitement and the spirit. That it is an ideal makes it all the worse; these bleak new utopias are not bleak because they have to be; they are the concrete manifestation—and how literally—of a deep, and at times arrogant, misunderstanding of the function of the city.
    Being made up of human beings, the city is, of course, a wonderfully resilient institution. Already it has reasserted itself as an industrial and business center. Not so many years ago, there was much talk of decentralizing to campus-like offices, and a wholesale exodus of business to the countryside seemed imminent. But a business pastoral is something of a contradiction in terms, and for the simple reason that the city is the center of things because it is a center, the suburban heresy never came off. Many industrial campuses have been built, but the overwhelming proportion of new office building has been taking place in the big cities. But the rebuilding of downtown is not enough; a city deserted at night by its leading citizens is only half a city. If it is to continue as the dominant cultural force in American life, the city must have a core of people to support its theatres and museums, its shops and its restaurants—even a Bohemia of sorts can be of help. For it is the people who like living in the city who make it an attraction to the visitors who don't. It is the city dwellers who support its style; without them there is nothing to come downtown to.
    The cities have a magnificent opportunity. There are definite signs of a small but significant move back from suburbia. There is also evidence that many people who will be moving to suburbia would prefer to stay in the city—and it would not take too much more in amenities to make them stay. But the cities seem on the verge of muffing their opportunity and muffing it for generations to come. In a striking failure to apply marketing principles and an even more striking failure of aesthetics, the cities are freezing on a design for living ideally calculated to keep everybody in suburbia. These vast, barracks-like superblocks are not designed for people who like cities, but for people who have no other choice. A few imaginative architects and planners have shown that redeveloped blocks don't have to be repellent to make money, but so far their ideas have had little effect. The institutional approach is dominant, and, unless the assumptions embalmed in it are re-examined, the city is going to be turned into a gigantic bore.

1. The author would NOT be pleased with
    A. a crowded, varied, stimulating city
    B. the dedication of new funds to the reconstruction of the cities
    C. a more detailed understanding of the poor
    D. the elimination of assumptions which do not reflect the function of the city
    E. the adoption of a laissez-faire attitude by those in charge of redevelopment

1.____

2. "The rebuilding of downtown" (1st sentence, 3rd paragraph) refers to
   A. huge redevelopment projects to come
   B. the application of marketing and aesthetic principles to rejuvenating the city
   C. keeping the city as the center of business
   D. attracting a core of people to support the city's functions
   E. the doing away with barracks-like structures

3. According to the author the city, in order to better itself, *must*
   A. increase its downtown population
   B. attract an interested core of people to support its cultural institutions
   C. adhere to an institutional approach rather than be satisfied with the status quo
   D. erect campus-like business complexes
   E. establish an ideal for orderly future growth

4. The MAIN purpose of the passage is to
   A. show that the present people inhabiting the city do not make the city viable
   B. discuss the types of construction which should and should not take place in the city's future
   C. indicate that imaginative architects and planners have shown that redeveloped areas don't have to be ugly to make money
   D. discuss the human element in the city
   E. point out the lack of understanding by many city planners of the city's functions

5. The author's thesis would be LESS supportable if
   I. city planners presently understood that stereotyped reconstruction is doomed to ultimate failure
   II. the institutional approach referred to in the passage was based upon assumptions which took into account the function of the city
   III. there were signs that a shift back to the city from suburbia were occurring
   The CORRECT answer is:
   A. II only   B. II and III   C. I and II   D. I only   E. III only

KEY (CORRECT ANSWERS)

1. D
2. C
3. B
4. E
5. C

TEST 7

DIRECTIONS: Each question or incomplete statement is followed by several suggested answers or completions. Select the one that BEST answers the question or completes the statement. *PRINT THE LETTER OF THE CORRECT ANSWER IN THE SPACE AT THE RIGHT.*

In estimating the child's conceptions of the world, the first question is to decide whether external reality is as external and objective for the child as it is for adults. In other words, can the child distinguish the self from the external world? So long as the child supposes that everyone necessarily thinks like himself, he will not spontaneously seek to convince others, nor to accept common truths, nor, above all, to prove or test his opinions. If his logic lacks exactitude and objectivity, it is because the social impulses of mature years are counteracted by an innate egocentricity. In studying the child's thought, not in this case in relation to others but to things, one is faced at the outset with the analogous problem of the child's capacity to dissociate thought from self in order to form an objective conception of reality.

The child, like the uncultured adult, appears exclusively concerned with things. He is indifferent to the life of thought and the originality of individual points of view escape him. His earliest interests, his first games, his drawings are all concerned solely with the imitation of what is. In short, the child's thought has every appearance of being exclusively realistic.

But realism is of two types, or, rather, objectivity must be distinguished from realism. Objectivity consists in so fully realizing the countless intrusions of the self in everyday thought and the countless illusions which result—illusions of sense, language, point of view, value, etc.—that the preliminary step to every judgment is the effort to exclude the intrusive self. Realism, on the contrary, consists in ignoring the existence of self and thence regarding one's own perspective as immediately objective and absolute. Realism is thus anthropocentric illusion, finality—in short, all those illusions which teem in the history of science. So long as thought has not become conscious of self, it is a prey to perpetual confusions between objective and subjective, between the real and the ostensible; it values the entire content of consciousness on a single lane in which ostensible realities and the unconscious interventions of the self are inextricably mixed. It is thus not futile, but, on the contrary, indispensable to establish clearly and before all else the boundary the child draws between the self and the external world.

1. The result of a child's not learning that others think differently than he does is that
   A. the child will not be able to function as an adult
   B. when the child has matured, he will be innately egocentric
   C. when the child has matured, his reasoning will be poor
   D. upon maturity, the child will not be able to distinguish thought from objects
   E. upon maturity, the child will not be able to make non-ego-influenced value

2. Objectivity is the ability to
   A. distinguish ego from the external world
   B. dissociate oneself from others
   C. realize that others have a different point of view
   D. dissociate ego from thought

3. When thought is not conscious of self,
   A. one is able to draw the correct conclusions from his perceptions
   B. the apparent may not be distinguishable from the actual
   C. conscious thought may not be distinguishable from the unconscious
   D. the ego may influence the actual
   E. ontogeny recapitulates phylogony

4. The MAIN purpose of the passage is to
   A. argue that the child should be made to realize that others may not think like he does
   B. estimate the child's conception of the world
   C. explain the importance of distinguishing the mind from external objects
   D. emphasize the importance of non-ego-influenced perspective
   E. show how the child establishes the boundary between himself and the external world

5. The author *implies* that, if an adult is to think logically,
   A. his reasoning, as he matures, must be tempered by other viewpoints
   B. he must be able to distinguish one physical object from another
   C. he must be exclusively concerned with thought instead of things
   D. he must be able to perceive reality without the intrusions of the self
   E. he must not value the content of consciousness on a single plain

6. Realism, according to the passage, is
   A. the realization of the countless intrusions of the self
   B. final and complete objectivity
   C. a desire to be truly objective and absolute
   D. the ability to be perceptive and discerning
   E. none of the above

7. The child who is exclusively concerned with things
   A. thinks only objectivity
   B. is concerned with imitating the things he sees
   C. must learn to distinguish between realism and anthropomorphism
   D. has no innate ability
   E. will, through interaction with others, often prove his opinions

KEY (CORRECT ANSWERS)

1. C   5. A
2. E   6. E
3. B   7. B
4. D

TEST 8

DIRECTIONS: Each question or incomplete statement is followed by several suggested answers or completions. Select the one that BEST answers the question or completes the statement. *PRINT THE LETTER OF THE CORRECT ANSWER IN THE SPACE AT THE RIGHT.*

Democracy is not logically antipathetic to most doctrines of natural rights, fundamental or higher law, individual rights, or any similar ideals—but merely asks citizens to take note of the fact that the preservation of these rights rests with the majority, in political processes, and does not depend upon a legal or constitutional Maginot line. Democracy may, then, be supported by believers in individual rights providing they believe that rights—or any transcendental ends—are likely to be better safeguarded under such a system. Support for democracy on such instrumental ground may, of course, lead to the dilemma of loyalty to the system vs. loyalty to a natural right—but the same kind of dilemma may arise for anyone, over any prized value, and in any political system, and is insoluble in advance.

There is unanimous agreement that—as a matter of fact and law, not of conjecture—no single right can be realized, except at the expense of other rights and claims. For that reason their absolute status, in some philosophic sense, is of little political relevance. Political policies involve much more than very generable principles or rights. The main error of the older natural rights school was not that it had an absolute right, but that it had too many absolute rights. There must be compromise, and, as any compromise destroys the claim to absoluteness, the natural outcome of experience was the repudiation of all of them. And now the name of "natural right" can only creep into sight with the reassuring placard, "changing content guaranteed." Nor is it at all easy to see how many doctrine of inalienable, natural, individual rights can be reconciled with a political doctrine of common consent—except in an anarchist society, or one of saints. Every natural right ever put forward, and the lists are elusive and capricious, is every day invaded by governments, in the public interest and with widespread public approval.

To talk of relatively attainable justice or rights in politics is not to plump for a moral relativism—in the sense that all values are equally good. But while values may be objective, the specific value judgments and policies are inevitably relative to a context, and is only when a judgment divorces context from general principle that it looks like moral relativism. Neither, of course, does the fact of moral diversity invalidate all moral rules.

Any political system, then, deals only with relatively attainable rights, as with relative justice and freedoms. Hence, we may differ in given instances on specific policies, despite agreement on broad basic principles such as a right or a moral "ought"; and, per contra, we may agree on specific policies while differing on fundamental principles or long-range objectives or natural rights. Politics and through politics, law and policies, give these rights—and moral principles—their substance and limits. There is no getting away from the political nature of this or any other prescriptive ideal in a free society.

1. With which of the following would the author *agree*? 1._____
   A. Natural and individual rights can exist at all only under a democracy.
   B. While natural rights may exist, they are only relatively attainable.
   C. Civil disobedience has no place in a democracy where natural rights have no philosophic relevance.
   D. Utilitarianism, which draws its criteria from the happiness and welfare of individuals, cannot logically be a goal of a democratic state.
   E. Some natural rights should never be compromised for the sake of political policy.

2. It can be *inferred* that a democratic form of government
   A. can be supported by natural rightists as the best pragmatic method of achieving their aims
   B. is a form of government wherein fundamental or higher law is irrelevant
   C. will inn time repudiate all inalienable rights
   D. forces a rejection of moral absolutism
   E. will soon exist in undeveloped areas of the world

3. The MAIN purpose of the passage is to
   A. discuss natural rights doctrine
   B. compare and contrast democracy to individual rights
   C. discuss the reconciliation of a doctrine of inalienable natural rights with a political system
   D. discuss the safeguarding of natural rights in a democratic society
   E. indicate that moral relativism is antipathetic to democracy

4. The author indicates that natural rights
   I. are sometimes difficult to define
   II. are easily definable but at times unreconcilable with a system of government predicated upon majority rule
   III. form a basis for moral relativism
   The CORRECT answer is:
   A. I only   B. II only   C. I and II   D. III only   E. II and III

5. The fact that any political system deals with relatively attainable rights
   A. shows that all values are equally good or bad
   B. is cause for divorcing political reality from moral rules
   C. shows that the list of natural rights is elusive and capricious
   D. is inconsistent with the author's thesis
   E. does not necessarily mean that natural rights do not exist

6. The passage indicates that an important conflict which can exist in a democracy is the rights of competing groups, i.e., labor versus management
   A. adherence to the democratic process versus non-democratic actions by government
   B. difficulty in choosing between two effective compromises
   C. adherence to the democratic process versus the desire to support a specific right
   D. difficulty in reconciling conflict by natural rights

KEY (CORRECT ANSWERS)

1. B   4. A
2. A   5. E
3. C   6. D

READING COMPREHENSION
UNDERSTANDING AND INTERPRETING WRITTEN MATERIAL
EXAMINATION SECTION
TEST 1

DIRECTIONS: Each question or incomplete statement is followed by several suggested answers or completions. Select the one that BEST answers the question or completes the statement. *PRINT THE LETTER OF THE CORRECT ANSWER IN THE SPACE AT THE RIGHT.*

1. Most managers make the mistake of using absolutes as signals of trouble or its absence. A quality problem emerges—that means trouble; a test is passed—we have no problems. Outside of routine organizations, there are always going to be such signals of trouble or success, but they are not very meaningful. Many times everything looks good, but the roof is about to cave in because something no one thought about and for which there is no rule, procedure, or test has been neglected. The specifics of such problems cannot be predicted, but they are often signaled in advance by changes in the organizational system: Managers spend less time on the project; minor problems proliferate; friction in the relationships between adjacent work groups or departments increases; verbal progress reports become overly glib, or overly reticent; change occur in the rate at which certain events happen, not in whether or not they happen. And they are monitored by random probes into the organization—seeing how things are going.
   According to the above paragraph,
   A. managers do not spend enough time managing
   B. managers have a tendency to become overly glib when writing reports
   C. managers should be aware that problems that exist in the organization may not exhibit predictable signals of trouble
   D. managers should attempt to alleviate friction in the relationship between adjacent work groups by monitoring random probes into the organization's problems

   1.____

2. *Lack of challenge* and *excessive zeal* are opposite villains. You cannot do your best on a problem unless you are motivated. Professional problem solvers learn to be motivated somewhat by money and future work that may come their way if they succeed. However, challenge must be present for at least some of the time, or the process ceases to be rewarding. On the other hand, an excessive motivation to succeed, especially to succeed quickly, can inhibit the creative process. The tortoise-and-the-hare phenomenon is often apparent in problem solving. The person who thinks up the simple elegant solution, although he or she may take longer in doing so, often wins. As in the race, the tortoise depends upon an inconsistent performance from the rabbit. And if the rabbit spends so little time on conceptualization that the rabbit merely chooses the first answers that occur, such inconsistency is almost guaranteed.

   2.____

According to the above paragraph,
- A. excessive motivation to succeed can be harmful in problem solving
- B. it is best to spend a long time on solving problems
- C. motivation is the most important component in problem solving
- D. choosing the first solution that occurs is a valid method of problem solving

3. Virginia Woolf's approach to the question of women and fiction, about which she wrote extensively, polemically, and in a profoundly feminist way, was grounded in a general theory of literature. She argued that the writer was the product of her or his historical circumstances and that material conditions were of crucial importance. Secondly, she claimed that these material circumstances had a profound effect on the psychological aspects of writing, and that they could be seen to influence the nature of the creative work itself. According to this paragraph,
   - A. the material conditions and historical circumstances in which male and female writers find themselves greatly influence their work
   - B. a woman must have an independent income to succeed as a writer
   - C. Virginia Woolf preferred the writings of female authors, as their experiences more clearly reflected hers
   - D. male writers are less likely than women writers to be influenced by material circumstances

3.____

4. A young person's first manager is likely to be the most influential person in his or her career. If this manager is unable or unwilling to develop the skills the young employee needs to perform effectively, the latter will set lower personal standards than he or she is capable of achieving, that person's self-image will be impaired, and he or she will develop negative attitudes toward the job, the employer—in all probability—his or her career. Since the chances of building a successful career with the employer will decline rapidly, he or she will leave, if that person has high aspirations, in hope of finding a better opportunity. If, on the other hand, the manager helps the employee to achieve maximum potential, he or she will build a foundation for a successful career.
   According to the above paragraph,
   - A. If an employee has negative attitudes towards his or her job, the manager is to blame
   - B. managers of young people often have a great influence upon their careers
   - C. good employees will leave a job they like if they are not given a chance to develop their skills
   - D. managers should develop the full potential of their young employees

4.____

5. The reason for these difference is not that the Greeks had a superior sense of form or an inferior imagination or joy in life, but that they thought differently. Perhaps an illustration will make this clear. With the historical plays of Shakespeare in mind, let the reader contemplate the only extant Greek play on a historical subject, the Persians of Aeschylus, a play written less than ten years after the event which it deals with, and performed before the Athenian people who had played so notable a part in the struggle—incidentally,

5.____

immediately below the Acropolis which the Persians had sacked and defiled. Any Elizabethan dramatist would have given us a panorama of the whole war, its moments of despair, hope, and triumph; we should see on the stage the leaders who planned and some of the soldiers who won the victory. In the Persians we see nothing of the sort. The scene is laid in the Persian capital, one action is seen only through Persian eyes, the course of the war is simplified so much that the naval battle of Artemisium is not mentioned, nor even the heroic defense of Thermopylae, and not a single Greek is mentioned by name. The contrast could hardly be more complete.
Which sentence is BEST supported by the above paragraph?
   A. Greek plays are more interesting than Elizabethan plays.
   B. Elizabethan dramatists were more talented than Greek dramatists.
   C. If early Greek dramatists had the same historical material as Shakespeare had, the final form the Greek work would take would be very different from the Elizabethan work.
   D. Greeks were historically more inaccurate than Elizabethans.

6. The problem with present planning systems, public or private, is that accountability is weak. Private planning systems in the global corporations operate on a set of narrow incentives that frustrate sensible public policies such as full employment, environmental protection, and price stability. Public planning is Olympian and confused because there is neither a clear consensus on social values nor political priorities. To accomplish anything, explicit choices must be made, but these choices can be made effectively only with the active participation of the people most directly involved. This, not nostalgia for small-town times gone forever, is the reason that devolution of political power to local communities is a political necessity. The power to plan locally is a precondition for sensible integration of cities, regions, and countries into the world economy.
According to the author,
   A. people most directly affected by issues should participate in deciding those issues
   B. private planning systems are preferable to public planning systems
   C. there is no good system of government
   D. county governments are more effective than state governments

6.____

Questions 7-11.

DIRECTIONS: Questions 7 through 11 are to be answered SOLELY on the basis of the following passage.

The ideal relationship for the interview is one of mutual confidence. To try to pretend, to put on a front of cordiality and friendship is extremely unwise for the interviewer because he will certainly convey, by subtle means, his real feelings. It is the interviewer's responsibility to take the lead in establishing a relationship of mutual confidence.

As the interviewer, you should help the interviewee to feel at ease and ready to talk. One of the best ways to do this is to be at ease yourself. If you are, it will probably be evident; if you are not, it will almost certainly be apparent to the interviewee. Begin the interview with topics for discussion which are easy to talk about and non-menacing. This interchange can be like the conversation of people when they are waiting for a bus, at the ballgame, or discussing the weather. However, do not prolong this warm-up too long since the interviewee knows as well as you do that these are not the things he came to discuss. Delaying too long in betting down too business may suggest to him that you are reluctant to deal with the topic.

Once you get onto the main topics, do all that you can to get the interviewee to talk freely with a little prodding from you as possible. This will probably require that you give him some idea of the area and of ways of looking at it. Avoid, however, prejudicing or coloring his remarks by what you say; especially, do not in any way indicate that there are certain things you want to hear, others which you do not want to hear. It is essential that he feel free to express his own ideas unhampered by your ideas, your values and preconceptions.

Do not appear to dominate the interview, nor have even the suggestion of a patronizing attitude. Ask some questions which will enable the interviewee to take pride in his knowledge. Take the attitude that the interviewee sincerely wants the interview to achieve its purpose. This creates a warm, permissive atmosphere that is most important in all interviews.

7. Of the following, the BEST title for the above passage is
   A. PERMISSIVENESS IN INTERVIEWING
   B. INTERVIEW TECHNIQUES
   C. THE FACTOR OF PRETENSE IN THE INTERVIEW
   D. THE CORDIAL INTERVIEW

8. Which of the following recommendations on the conduct of an interview is made by the above passage?
   A. Conduct the interview as if it were an interchange between people discussing the weather.
   B. The interview should be conducted in a highly impersonal manner.
   C. Allow enough time for the interview so that the interviewee does not feel rushed.
   D. Start the interview with topics which are not threatening to the interviewee.

9. The above passage indicates that the interviewer should
   A. feel free to express his opinions
   B. patronize the interviewee and display a permissive attitude
   C. permit the interviewee to give the needed information in his own fashion
   D. provide for privacy when conducting the interview

10. The meaning of the word *unhampered*, as it is used in the last sentence of the fourth paragraph of the above passage, is MOST NEARLY
    A. unheeded   B. unobstructed   C. hindered   D. aided

11. It can be INFERRED from the above passage that
    A. interviewers, while generally mature, lack confidence
    B. certain methods in interviewing are more successful than others in obtaining information
    C. there is usually a reluctance on the part of interviewers to deal with unpleasant topics
    D. it is best for the interviewer not to waiver from the use of hard and fast rules when dealing with clients

Questions 12-19.

DIRECTIONS: Questions 12 through 19 are to be answered SOLELY on the basis of the following passage.

Disabled cars pose a great danger to bridge traffic at any time, but during rush hours it is especially important that such vehicles be promptly detected and removed. The term *disable car* is an all-inclusive label referring to cars stalled due to a flat tire, mechanical failure, an accident, or locked bumpers. Flat tires are the most common reason why cars become disabled. The presence of disabled vehicles caused 68% of all traffic accidents last year. Of these, 75% were serious enough to require hospitalization of at least one of the vehicle's occupants.

The basic problem in the removal of disabled vehicles is detection of the car. Several methods have been proposed to aid detection. At a 1980 meeting of traffic experts and engineers, the idea of sinking electronic eyes into roadways was first suggested. Such *eyes* let officers know when traffic falls below normal speed and becomes congested. The basic argument against this approach is the high cost of installation of these eyes. One Midwestern state has, since 1978, employed closed circuit television to detect the existence and locations of stalled vehicles. When stalled vehicles are seen on the closed circuit television screen, the information is immediately communicated by radio to units stationed along the roadway, thus enabling the prompt removal of these obstructions to traffic. However, many cities lack the necessary manpower and equipment to use this approach. For the past five years, several east-coast cities have used the method known as *safety chains*, consisting of mobile units which represent the links at the *safety chain*. These mobile units are stationed as posts one or two miles apart along roadways to detect disabled cars. Standard procedure is for the units in the *safety chain* to have roof blinker lights turned on to full rotation. The officer, upon spotting a disabled car, at once assumes a post that gives him the most control in directing traffic around the obstruction. Only after gaining such control does he investigate and decide what action should be taken.

12. From the above passage, The PERCENTAGE of accidents caused by disabled cars in which hospitalization was required by at least one of the occupants of a vehicle last year was
    A. 17%   B. 51%   C. 68%   D. 75%

13. According to the above passage, vehicles are MOST frequently disabled because of
    A. flat tires   B. locked bumpers
    C. brake failure   D. overheated motors

14. According to the above passage, in the electronic eye method of detection, the *eyes* are placed
    A. on lights along the roadway
    B. on patrol cars stationed along the roadway
    C. in booths spaced two miles apart
    D. into the roadway

15. According to the above passage, the factor COMMON to both the *safety chain* method and the *closed circuit television* method of detecting disabled vehicles is that both
    A. require the use of *electronic eyes*
    B. may be used where there is a shortage of officers
    C. employ units that are stationed along the highway
    D. require the use of trucks to move the heavy equipment used

16. The one of the following which is NOT discussed in the above passage as a method that may be used to detect disabled vehicles is
    A. closed circuit television   B. radar
    C. electronic eyes   D. safety chains

17. One DRAWBACK mentioned by the above passage to the use of the closed circuit television method for detection of disabled cars is that this technique
    A. cannot be used during bad weather
    B. does not provide for actual removal of the cars
    C. must be operated by a highly skilled staff of traffic engineers
    D. requires a large amount of manpower and equipment

18. The NEWEST of the methods discussed in the above passage for detection of disabled vehicles is
    A. electronic eyes   B. the mobile unit
    C. the safety chain   D. closed circuit television

19. When the *safety chain* method is being used, an officer who spots a disabled vehicle should FIRST
    A. turn off his roof blinker lights
    B. direct traffic around the disabled vehicle
    C. send a ratio message to the nearest mobile unit
    D. conduct an investigation

20. The universe is 15 billion years old, and the geological underpinnings of the earth were formed long before the first sea creature slithered out of the slime. But it is only in the last 6,000 years or so that men have descended into mines to chop and scratch at the earth's crust. Human history is, as Carl Sagan has put it, the equivalent of a few seconds in the 15 billion year life of the earth. What alarms those who keep track of the earth's crust is that since 1950 human beings have managed to consume more minerals than were mined in all previous history, a splurge of a millisecond in geologic time that cannot be long repeated without using up the finite riches of the earth.
    Of the following, the MAIN idea of this paragraph is:
    A. There is true cause for concern at the escalating consumption of the earth's minerals in recent years.
    B. Human history is the equivalent of a few seconds in the 15 billion year life of the earth
    C. The earth will soon run out of vital mineral resources

21. The authors of the Economic Report of the President are collectively aware, despite their vision of the asset-rich household, of the real economy in which millions of Americans live. There are glimpses, throughout the Report, of the underworld in which about 23 million people do not have public or private health insurance; in which the number of people receiving unemployment compensation was 41 percent of the total unemployed, in which the average dole for the compensated unemployed is about one-half of take-home pay. The authors understand, for example, that a worker may become physically disabled and that individuals generally do not like the risk of losing their ability to earn income. But such realities justify no more than the most limited interference in the (imperfect) market for disability insurance. There is only, as far as I can tell, one moment of genuine emotion in the entire Report when the authors' passions are stirred beyond market principles. They are discussing the leasing provisions of the 1981 Tax Act (conditions which so reduce tax revenues that they are apparently opposed in their present form by the Business Roundtable, the American Business Conference, and the National Association of Manufacturers).

    In the dark days before the 1981 ACT, according to the Report, (*firms with temporary tax losses* (a condition especially characteristic of new enterprises) were often unable to take advantage of investment tax incentives. The reason was that temporarily unprofitable companies had no taxable income against which to apply the investment tax deduction. It was a piteous contingency for the truly needy entrepreneur. But all was made right with the Tax Act. Social Security for the disabled incompetent corporation: the compassionate soul of Reagan's new economy.

    According to the above passage,
    A. the National Association of Manufacturers and those companies that are temporarily unprofitable oppose the leasing provisions of the 1981 Tax Act
    B. the authors of the Report are willing to ignore market principles in order to assist corporations unable to take advantage of tax incentives
    C. the authors of the Report feel the National Association of Manufacturers and the Business Roundtable are wrong in opposing the leasing provisions of the 1981 Tax Act
    D. the authors of the Report have more compassion for incompetent corporations than for disabled workers

22. Much of the lore of management in the West regards ambiguity as a symptom of a variety of organizational ills whose cure is larger doses of rationality, specificity, and decisiveness. But is ambiguity sometimes desirable? Ambiguity may be thought of as a shroud of the unknown surrounding certain events. The Japanese have a word for it, *ma*, for which there is no English translation. The word is valuable because it gives an explicit place to the unknowable aspect of things. In English, we may refer to an empty space between the chair and the table; the Japanese don't say the space is empty but *full of nothing*. However amusing the illustration, it goes to the core of the issue. Westerners speak of what is unknown primarily in reference to what is known (like the space between the chair and the table, while most eastern languages give honor to the unknown in its own right.

Of course, there are many situations that a manager finds himself in where being explicit and decisive is not only helpful but necessary. There is considerable advantage, however, in having a dual frame of reference—recognizing the value of both the clear and the ambiguous. The point to bear in mind is that in certain situations, ambiguity may serve better than absolute clarity.
Which sentence is BEST supported by the above passage?
- A. We should cultivate the art of being ambiguous.
- B. Ambiguity may sometimes be an effective managerial tool,
- C. Westerners do not have a dual frame of reference.
- D. It is important to recognize the ambiguous aspects of all situations.

23. Everyone ought to accustom himself to grasp in his thought at the same time facts that are at once so few and so simple, that he shall never believe that he has knowledge of anything which he does not mentally behold with a distinctiveness equal to that of the objects which he knows most distinctly of all. It is true that some people are born with a much greater aptitude for such discernment than others, but the mind can be made much more expert at such work by art and exercise. But there is one fact which I should here emphasize above all others; and that is everyone should firmly persuade himself that none of the sciences, however abstruse, is to be deduced from lofty and obscure matters, but that they all proceed only from what is easy and more readily understood.
According to the author,
- A. people should concentrate primarily on simple facts
- B. intellectually gifted people have a great advantage over others
- C. even difficult material and theories proceed from what is readily understood
- D. if a scientist cannot grasp a simple theory, he or she is destined to fail

24. Goethe's casual observations about language contain a profound truth. Every word in every language is a part of a system of thinking unlike any other. Speakers of different languages live in different worlds; or rather, they live in the same world but can't help looking at it in different ways. Words stand for patterns of experience. As one generation hand its language down to the next, it also hands down a fixed pattern of thinking, seeing, and feeling. When we go from one language to another, nothing stays put; different peoples carry different nerve patterns in their brains, and there's no point where they fully match.
According to the above passage,
- A. language differences and their ramifications are a major cause of tensions between nations
- B. it is not a good use of one's time to read novels that have been translated from another language because of the tremendous differences in interpretation
- C. differences in languages reflect the different experiences of people the world over
- D. language students should be especially careful to retain awareness of the subtleties of their native language

Questions 25-27.

DIRECTIONS: Questions 25 through 27 are to be answered SOLELY on the basis of the following passage.

The context of all education is twofold—individual and social. Its business is to make us more and more ourselves, too cultivate in each of us our own distinctive genius, however modest it may be, while showing us how this genius may be reconciled with the needs and claims of the society of which we are a part. Thought it is not education's aim to cultivate eccentrics, that society is richest, most flexible, and most humane that best uses and most tolerates eccentricity. Conformity beyond a point breeds sterile minds and, therefore, a sterile society.
The function of secondary—and still more of higher education is to affect the environment. Teachers are not, and should not be, social reformers. But they should be the catalytic agents by means of which young minds are influenced to desire and execute reform. To aspire to better things is a logical and desirable part of mental and spiritual growth.

25. Of the following, the MOST suitable title for the above passage is 25.____
    A. EDUCATION'S FUNCTION IN CREATING INDIVIDUAL DIFFERENCES
    B. THE NEED FOR EDUCATION TO ACQUAINT US WITH OUR SOCIAL ENVIRONMENT
    C. THE RESPONSIBILITY OF EDUCATION TOWARD THE INDIVIDUAL AND SOCIETY
    D. THE ROLE OF EDUCATION IN EXPLAINIING THE NEEDS OF SOCIETY

26. On the basis of the above passage, it may be inferred that 26.____
    A. conformity is one of the forerunners of totalitarianism
    B. education should be designed to create at least a modest amount of genius in everyone
    C. tolerance of individual differences tends to give society opportunities for improvement
    D. reforms are usually initiated by people who are somewhat eccentric

27. On the basis of the above passage, it may be inferred that 27.____
    A. genius is likely to be accompanied by a desire for social reform
    B. nonconformity is an indication of the inquiring mind
    C. people who are not high school or college graduates are not able to affect the environment
    D. teachers may or may not be social reformers

Questions 28-30.

DIRECTIONS: Questions 28 through 30 are to be answered SOLELY on the basis of the following passage.

Disregard for odds and complete confidence in one's self have produced many of our great successes. But every young man who wants to go into business for himself should appraise himself as a candidate for the one percent to survive. What has he to offer that is new or better? Has he special talents, special know-how, a new invention or service, or more capital than the average competitor? Has he the most important qualification of all, a willingness to work harder than anyone else? A man who is working for himself without limitation of hours or personal sacrifice can run circles around any operation that relies on paid help. But he must forget the eight-hour day, the forty-hour week, and the annual vacation. When he stops work, his income stops unless he hires a substitute. Most small operations have their busiest day on Saturday, and the owner uses Sunday to catch up on his correspondence, bookkeeping, inventorying, and maintenance chores. The successful self-employed man invariably works harder and worries more than the man on a salary. His wife and children make corresponding sacrifices of family unity and continuity; they never know whether their man will be home or in a mood to enjoy family activities.

28. The title that BEST expresses the ideas of the above passage is 28.____
    A. OVERCOMING OBSTACLES
    B. RUNNING ONE'S OWN BUSINESS
    C. HOW TO BECOME A SUCCESS
    D. WHY SMALL BUSINESSES FAIL

29. The above passage suggests that 29.____
    A. small businesses are the ones that last
    B. salaried workers are untrustworthy
    C. a willingness to work will overcome loss of income
    D. working for one's self may lead to success

30. The author of the above passage would MOST likely believe in 30.____
    A. individual initiative   B. socialism
    C. corporations   D. government aid to small business

KEY (CORRECT ANSWERS)

1.	C	11.	B	21.	D
2.	A	12.	B	22.	B
3.	A	13.	A	23.	C
4.	B	14.	D	24.	C
5.	C	15.	C	25.	C
6.	A	16.	B	26.	D
7.	B	17.	D	27.	D
8.	D	18.	A	28.	B
9.	C	19.	B	29.	D
10.	B	20.	A	30.	A

READING COMPREHENSION
UNDERSTANDING AND INTERPRETING WRITTEN MATERIAL
EXAMINATION SECTION
TEST 1

DIRECTIONS: Each question or incomplete statement is followed by several suggested answers or completions. Select the one that BEST answers the question or completes the statement. *PRINT THE LETTER OF THE CORRECT ANSWER IN THE SPACE AT THE RIGHT.*

1. The question *Who shall now teach Hegel?* is shorthand for the question *Who is going to teach this genre—all the so-called Continental philosophers?* The obvious answer to this question is *Whoever cares to study them*. This is also the right answer, but we can only accept it whole heartedly if we clear away a set of factitious questions. On such question is: *Are these Continental philosophers really philosophers?* Analytic philosophers, because they identify philosophical ability with argumentative skill and notice that there is nothing they would consider an argument in the bulk of Heidegger or Foucault, suggest that these must be people who tried to be philosophers and failed-incompetent philosophers. This is as silly as saying that Plato was an incompetent sophist, or that a hedgehog is an incompetent fox. Hegel knew what he thought about philosophers who imitated the method and style of mathematics. He thought they were incompetent. These reciprocal charges of incompetence do nobody any good. We should just drop the questions of what philosophy really is or who really counts as a philosopher.
Which sentence is BEST supported by the above paragraph?
   A. The study of Hegel's philosophy is less popular now than in the past.
   B. Philosophers must stop questioning the competence of other philosophers.
   C. Philosophers should try to be as tolerant as Foucault and Heidegger.
   D. Analytic philosophers tend to be more argumentative than other philosophers.

2. It is an interesting question: the ease with which organizations of different kinds at different stages in their history can continue to function with ineffectual leadership at the top, or even function without a clear system of authority. Certainly, the success of some experiments in worker self-management shows that bosses are not always necessary, as some contemporary Marxists argue. Indeed, sometimes the function of those at the top is merely to symbolize organizational accountability, especially in dealing with outside authorities, but not to guide the actions of those within the organization. A vice president of a large insurance company remarked to us that *Presidents are powerless; no one needs them. They should all be sent off to do public relations for the company.* While this is clearly a self-serving statement from someone next in line to command, it does give meaning to the expression *being kicked upstairs.* According to the author,

A. organizations function very smoothly without bosses
B. the function of those at the top is sometimes only to symbolize organizational accountability
C. company presidents are often inept at guiding the actions of those within the organization
D. presidents of companies have less power than one might assume they have

3. The goal of a problem is a terminal expression one wishes to cause to exist in the world of the problem. There are two types of goals: specified goal expressions in proof problems and incompletely specified goal expressions in find problems. For example, consider the problem of finding the value of X, given the expression 4X+5 = 17. In this problem, one can regard the goal expression as being of the form X = _____, the goal expression. The goal expression in a find problem of this type is incompletely specified. If the goal expression were specified completely—for example, X = 3—then the problem would be a proof problem, with only the sequence of operations to be determined in order to solve the problem. Of course, if one were not guaranteed that the goal expression X = 3 was true, then the terminal goal expression should really be considered to be incompletely specified—something like the statement X = 3 (true or false).
According to the preceding paragraph,
A. the goal of the equation 4X+5 = 17 is true, not false
B. if the goal expression was specified as being equal to 3, the problem 4X+5 = 17 would be a proof problem
C. if the sequence of operations of the problem given in the paragraph is predetermined, the goal of the problem becomes one of terminal expression, or the number 17
D. X cannot be found unless X is converted into a proof problem

3.____

4. We have human psychology and animal psychology, but no plant psychology. Why? Because we believe that plants have no perceptions or intentions. Some plants exhibit *behavior* and have been credited with *habits*. If you stroke the midrib of the compound leaf of a sensitive plant, the leaflets close. The sunflower changes with the diurnal changes in the source of light. The lowest animals have not much more complicated forms of behavior. The sea anemone traps and digests the small creatures that the water brings to it; the pitcher plant does the same thing and even more, for it presents a cup of liquid that attracts insects, instead of letting the surrounding medium drift them into its trap. Here as everywhere in nature where the great, general classes of living things diverge, the lines between them are not perfectly clear. A sponge is an animal; the pitcher plant is a flowering plant, but it comes nearer to *feeding itself* than the animal. Yet the fact is that we credit all animals, and only the animals, with some degree of feeling.
Of the following, the MAIN idea expressed in the above paragraph is:
A. The classification of plants has been based on beliefs about their capacity to perceive and feel
B. Many plants are more evolved than species considered animals

4.____

C. The lines that divide the classes of living things are never clear.
D. The abilities and qualities of plants are undervalued.

5. Quantitative indexes are not necessarily adequate measures of true economic significance or influence. But even the raw quantitative data speak loudly of the importance of the new transnationalized economy. The United Nations estimated value added in this new sector of the world economy at $500 billion in 2001, mounting to one-fifth of total GNP of the non-socialist world and exceeding the GNP of any one other country except the United States. Furthermore, all observers agree that the share of this sector in the world economy is growing rapidly. At least since 1980, its annual rate of growth has been high and remarkably steady at 10 percent compared to 4 percent for noninternationalized output in the Western developed countries.
One spokesman for the new system franklin envisages that within a generation some 400 to 500 multinational corporations will own close to two-thirds of the world's fixed assets.
According to the author, all of the following are true EXCEPT
   A. Quantitative indexes are not necessarily adequate measures of actual economic influence.
   B. The transnational sector of the world economy is growing rapidly.
   C. Since 1980, the rate of growth of transnationals has been 10% compared to 4% for internationalized output in the Western developed countries.
   D. Continued growth for multinational corporations is likely.

5.____

6. A bill may be sent to the Governor when it has passed both houses. During the session, he is given ten days to act on bills that reach his desk. Bills sent to him within ten days of the end of the session must be acted on within 30 days after the last day of the session. If the Governor takes no action on a ten day bill, it automatically becomes a law. If he disapproves or vetoes a ten day bill, it can become law only if it is re-passed by two-thirds vote in each house. If he fails to act on a 30 day bill, the bill is said to have received a *pocket veto*. It is customary for the Governor to act, however, on all bills submitted to him, and give his reason in writing for approving or disapproving important legislation.
According to the above paragraph, all of the following are true EXCEPT:
   A. Bills sent to the Governor in the last ten days of the session must be acted on within thirty days after the last day of the session,
   B. If the Governor takes no action on a 10 day bill, it is said to have received a *pocket veto*.
   C. It is customary for the Governor to act on all bills submitted to him.
   D. If the Governor vetoes a ten day bill, it can become law only if passed by a two-thirds vote of the Legislature.

6.____

7. It is particularly when I see a child going through the mechanical process of manipulating numbers without any intuitive sense of what it is all about that I recall the lines of Lewis Carroll: *Reeling and Writhing, of course, to begin with...and then the different branches of Arithmetic-Ambition, Distraction, Uglification, and Derision.* Or, as Max Beberman has put it, much more gently: *Somewhat related to the notion of discovery in teaching is our insistence that*

7.____

the student become aware of a concept before a name has been assigned to the concept. I am quite aware that the issue of intuitive understanding is a very live one among teachers of mathematics, and even a casual reading of the yearbook of the National Council of Teachers of Mathematics makes it clear that they are also very mindful of the gap that exists between proclaiming the importance of such understanding and actually producing it in the classroom.
The MAIN idea expressed in the above paragraph is:
- A. Math teachers are concerned about the difficulties inherent in producing an understanding of mathematics in their students.
- B. It is important that an intuitive sense in approaching math problems be developed, rather than relying on rote, mechanical learning.
- C. Mathematics, by its very nature, encourages rote, mechanical learning.
- D. Lewis Carroll was absolutely correct in his assessment of the true nature of mathematics.

8. Heisenberg's *Principle of Uncertainty*, which states that events at the atomic level cannot be observed with certainty, can be compared to this: In the world of everyday experience, we can observe any phenomenon and measure its properties without influencing the phenomenon in question to any significant extent. To be sure, if we try to measure the temperature of a demitasse with a bathtub thermometer, the instrument will absorb so much heat from the coffee that it will change the coffee's temperature substantially. But with a small chemical thermometer, we may get a sufficiently accurate reading. We can measure the temperature of a living cell with a miniature thermometer, which has almost negligible heat capacity. But in the atomic world, we can never overlook the disturbance caused by the introduction of the measuring apparatus.
Which sentence is BEST supported by the above paragraph?
- A. There is little we do not alter by the mere act of observation.
- B. It is always a good idea to use the smallest measuring device possible.
- C. Chemical thermometers are more accurate than bathtub thermometers.
- D. It is not possible to observe events at the atomic level and be sure that the same events would occur if we were not observing them.

9. It is a myth that American workers are pricing themselves out of the market, relative to workers in other industrialized countries of the world. The wages of American manufacturing workers increased at a slower rate in the 1990s than those of workers in other major western countries. In terms of American dollars, between 1990 and 2000, hourly compensation increased 489 percent in Japan and 464 percent in Germany, compared to 128 percent in the United States. Even though these countries experienced faster productivity growth, their unit labor costs still rose faster than in the United States, according to the Bureau of Labor Statistics. During the 1990s, unit labor costs rose 192 percent in Japan, 252 percent in Germany, and only 78 percent in the United States.
According to the above passage,
- A. unit labor costs in the 1990s were higher in Japan than they were in Germany or the United States
- B. the wages of American workers need to be increased to be consistent with other countries

8.____

9.____

C. American worker are more productive than Japanese or German workers
D. the wages of American workers in manufacturing increased at a slower rate in the 1990s than the wages of workers in Japan or Germany

10. No people have invented more ways to enjoy life than the Chinese, perhaps to balance floods, famines, warlords, and other ills of fate. The clang of gongs, clashing cymbals, and beating of drums sound through their long history. No month is without fairs and theatricals when streets are hung with fantasies of painted lanterns and crowded with *carriages that flow like water, horses like roaming dragons.* Night skies are illumined by firecrackers—a Chinese invention—bursting in the form of flowerpots, peonies, fiery devils. The ways of pleasure are myriad. Music plays in the air through bamboo whistles of different pitch tied to the wings of circling pigeons. To skim a frozen lake in an ice sleigh with a group of friends on a day when the sun is warm is rapture, like *moving in a cup of jade.* What more delightful than the ancient festival called *Half an Immortal,* when everyone from palace officials to the common man took a ride on a swing? When high in the air, one felt like an Immortal, when back to earth once again human—no more than to be for an instant a god.
According to the above passage,
   A. if the Chinese hadn't had so many misfortunes, they wouldn't have created so many pleasurable past times
   B. the Chinese invented flowerpots
   C. every month the Chinese have fairs and theatricals
   D. pigeons are required to play the game *Half an Immortal*

10.____

11. In our century, instead, poor Diphilus is lost in the crowd of his peers. We flood one another. No one recognizes him as he loads his basket in the supermarket. What grevious fits of melancholy have I not suffered in one of our larger urban bookstores, gazing at the hundreds, thousands, tens of thousands of books on shelve and tables? And what are they to the hundreds of thousands, the millions that stand in our research libraries? More books than Noah saw raindrops. How many readers will read a given one of them—mine, yours—in their lifetimes? And how will it be in the distant future? Incomprehensible masses of books, Pelion upon Ossa, hordes of books, each piteously calling for attention, respect, love, in competition with the vast disgorgements of the past and with one another in the present. Neither is it at all helpful that books can even now be reduced to the size of a postage stamp. Avanti! Place the Bible on a pinhead! Crowding more books into small spaces does not cram more books into our heads. Here I come to the sticking point that unnerves the modern Diphilus. The number of books a person can read in a given time is, roughly speaking, a historical constant. It does not change significantly even when the number of books available for reading does. Constants are pitted against variables to confound both writer and reader.
Of the following, the MAIN idea in this passage is:
   A. It is difficult to attain immortality because so many books are being published.
   B. Too many books are being published, so fewer people are reading them.

11.____

C. Because so many books are being published, the quality of the writing is poorer.
D. Because so many books are available, but only a fixed amount of time to read them, frustration results for both the reader and the writer.

12. Until recently, consciousness of sexual harassment has been low. But workers have become aware of it as more women have arrived at levels of authority in the workplace, feminist groups have focused attention on rape and other violence against women, and students have felt freer to report perceived abuse by professors. In the last 5 years, studies have shown that sexual misconduct at the workplace is a big problem. For example, in a recently published survey of federal employees, 42% of 694,000 women and 15% of 1,168,000 men said they had experienced some form of harassment. According to the author,   12._____
    A. the awareness of sexual harassment at the workplace is increasing
    B. the incidence of harassment is higher in universities than workplaces
    C. sexual harassment is much more commonly experienced by women than men
    D. it is rare for men to experience sexual harassment

Questions 13-17.

DIRECTIONS: Questions 13 through 17 are to be answered SOLELY on the basis of the following paragraph.

Since discounts are in common use in the commercial world and apply to purchases made by government agencies as well as business firms, it is essential that individuals in both public and private employment who prepare bills, check invoices, prepare payment vouchers, or write checks to pay bills have an understanding of the terms used. These include cash or time discount, trade discount, and discount series. A cash or time discount offers a reduction in price to the buyer for the prompt payment of the bill and is usually expressed as a percentage with a time requirement, stated in days, within which the bill must be paid in order to earn the discount. An example would be 3/10, meaning a 3% discount may be applied to the bill if the payment is forwarded to the vendor within 10 days. On an invoice, the cash discount terms are usually followed by the net terms, which is the time in days allowed for ordinary payment of the bill. Thus, 3/10, Net 30 means that full payment is expected in thirty days if the cash discount of 3% is not taken for having paid the bill within ten days. When the expression Terms Net Cash is listed on a bill, it means that no deduction for early payment is allowed. A trade discount is normally applied to list prices by a manufacturer to show the actual price to retailers so that they may know their cost and determine markups that will allow them to operate competitively and at a profit. A trade discount is applied by the seller to the list price and is independent of a cash or time discount. Discounts may also be used by manufacturers to adjust prices charged to retailers without changing list prices. This is usually done by series discounting and is expressed as a series of percentages. To compute a series discount, such as 40%, 20%, 10%, first apply the 40% discount to the list price, then apply the 20% discount to the remainder, and finally apply the 10% discount to the second remainder.

13. According to the above paragraph, trade discounts are 13.____
    A. applied by the buyer
    B. independent of cash discounts
    C. restricted to cash sales
    D. used to secure rapid payment of bills

14. According to the above paragraph, if the sales terms 5/10, Net 60 appear on a 14.____
    bill in the amount of $100 dated December 5 and the buyer submits his
    payment on December 15, his PROPER payment should be
    A. $60   B. $90   C. $95   D. $100

15. According to the above paragraph, if a manufacturer gives a trade discount of 15.____
    40% for an item with a list price of $250 and the terms are Net Cash, the price
    a retail merchant is required to pay for this item is
    A. $250   B. $210   C. $150   D. $100

16. According to the above paragraph, a series discount of 25%, 20%, 10% applied 16.____
    to a list price of $200 results in an ACTUAL price to the buyer of
    A. $88   B. $90   C. $108   D. $110

17. According to the above paragraph, if a manufacturer gives a trade discount 17.____
    of 50% and the terms are 6/10, Net 30, the cost to a retail merchant of an item
    with a list price of $500 and for which he takes the time discount, is
    A. $220   B. $235   C. $240   D. $250

Questions 18-22.

DIRECTIONS: Questions 18 through 22 are to be answered SOLELY on the basis of the following paragraph.

The city may issue its own bonds or it may purchase bonds as an investment. Bonds may be issued in various denominations, and the face value of the bond is its par value. Before purchasing a bond, the investor desires to know the rate of income that the investment will yield. In computing the yield on a bond, it is assumed that the investor will keep the bond until the date of maturity, except for callable bonds which are not considered in this paragraph. To compute exact yield is a complicated mathematical problem, and scientifically prepared tables are generally used to avoid such computation. However, the approximate yield can be computed much more easily. In computing approximate yield, the accrued interest on the date of purchase should be ignored, because the buyer who pays accrued interest to the seller receives it again at the next interest date. Bonds bought at a premium (which cost more) yield a lower rate of income than the same bonds bought at par (face value), and bonds bought at a discount (which cost less) yield a higher rate of income than the same bonds bought at par.

18. An investor bought a $10,000 city bond paying 6% interest. 18.____
    Which of the following purchase prices would indicate that the bond was
    bought at a PREMIUM?
    A. $9,000   B. $9,400   C. $10,000   D. $10,600

19. During the year, a particular $10,000 bond paying 74% sold at fluctuating prices.
Which of the following prices would indicate that the bond was bought at a DISCOUNT?
   A. $9,800   B. $10,000   C. $10,200   D. $10,750

20. A certain group of bonds was sold in denominations of $5,000, $10,000, $20,000 and $50,000.
In the following list of four purchase prices, which one is MOST likely to represent a bond sold at par value?
   A. $10,500   B. $20,000   C. $22,000   D. $49,000

21. When computing the approximate yield on a bond, it is DESIRABLE to
   A. assume the bond was purchased at par
   B. consult scientifically prepared tables
   C. ignore accrued interest on the date of purchase
   D. wait until the bond reaches maturity

22. Which of the following is MOST likely to be an exception to the information provided in the above paragraph? Bonds
   A. purchased at a premium   B. sold at par
   C. sold before maturity   D. which are callable

Questions 23-25

DIRECTIONS: Questions 23 through 25 are to be answered SOLELY on the basis of the following paragraph.

There is one bad habit of drivers that often causes chain collisions at traffic lights. It is the habit of keeping one foot poised over the accelerator pedal, ready to step on the gas the instant the light turns green. A driver who is watching the light, instead of watching the cars in front of him, may *jump the gun* and bump the car in front of him, and this car in turn may bump the next car. If a driver is resting his foot on the accelerator, his foot will be slammed down when he bumps into the car ahead. This makes the collision worse and makes it very likely that cars further ahead in the line are going to get involved in a series of violent bumps.

23. Which of the following conclusions can MOST reasonably drawn from the information given in the above paragraph?
   A. American drivers have a great many bad driving habits.
   B. Drivers should step on the gas as soon as the light turns green.
   C. A driver with poor driving habits should be arrested and fined.
   D. A driver should not rest his foot on the accelerator when the car is stopped for a traffic light.

24. From the information given in the above paragraph, a reader should be able to tell that a chain collision may be defined as a collision
   A. caused by bad driving habits at traffic lights
   B. in which one car hits another, this second car hits a third car, and so on

C. caused by drivers who fail to use their accelerators
D. that takes place at an intersection where there is a traffic light

25. The above passage states that a driver who watches the light instead of paying attention to traffic may 25.____
    A. be involved in an accident
    B. end up in jail
    C. lose his license
    D. develop bad driving habits

KEY (CORRECT ANSWERS)

1. B
2. B
3. B
4. A
5. C

6. B
7. B
8. D
9. D
10. C

11. D
12. A
13. B
14. C
15. C

16. C
17. B
18. D
19. A
20. B

21. C
22. D
23. D
24. B
25. A

TEST 2

DIRECTIONS: Each question or incomplete statement is followed by several suggested answers or completions. Select the one that BEST answers the question or completes the statement. *PRINT THE LETTER OF THE CORRECT ANSWER IN THE SPACE AT THE RIGHT.*

Questions 1-4.

DIRECTIONS: Each of the statements in this section is followed by several labeled choices. In the space at the right, write the letter of the sentence which means MOST NEARLY what is stated or implied in the passage.

1. It may be said that the problem in adult education seems to be not the piling up of facts but practice in thinking.
   This statement means MOST NEARLY that
   A. educational methods for adults and young people should differ
   B. adults seem to think more than young people
   C. a well-educated adult is one who thinks but does not have a store of information
   D. adult education should stress ability to think

2. Last year approximately 19,000 fatal accidents were sustained in industry. There were approximately 130 non-fatal injuries to each fatal injury.
   According to the above statement, the number of non-fatal accidents was
   A. 146,000   B. 190,000   C. 1,150,000   D. 2,500,000

3. No employer expects his stenographer to be a walking encyclopedia, but it is not unreasonable for him to expect her to know where to look for necessary information on a variety of topics.
   The above statement means MOST NEARLY that the stenographer should
   A. be a college graduate
   B. be familiar with standard office reference books
   C. keep a scrapbook of all interesting happenings
   D. go to the library regularly

4. For the United States, Canada has become the most important country in the world, yet there are few countries about which Americans know less. Canada is the third largest country in the world; only Russia and China are larger. The area of Canada is more than a quarter of the whole British Empire.
   According to the above statement, the
   A. British Empire is smaller than Russia or China
   B. territory of China is greater than that of Canada
   C. Americans know more about Canada than they do about China or Russia
   D. Canadian population is more than one-quarter the population of the British Empire

Questions 5-8.

DIRECTIONS: Questions 5 through 8 are to be answered SOLELY on the basis of the following paragraph.

    A few people who live in old tenements have had the bad habit of throwing garbage out of their windows, especially if there is an empty lot near their building. Sometimes the garbage is food; sometimes the garbage is half-empty soda cans. Sometimes the garbage is a little bit of both mixed together. These people just don't care about keeping the lot clean.

5. The above paragraph states that throwing garbage out of windows is a
   A. bad habit
   B. dangerous thing to do
   C. good thing to do
   D. good way to feed rats

6. According to the above paragraph, an empty lot next to an old tenement is sometimes used as a place to
   A. hold local gang meetings
   B. play ball
   C. throw garbage
   D. walk dogs

7. According to the above paragraph, which of the following throw garbage out of their windows?
   A. Nobody
   B. Everybody
   C. Most people
   D. Some people

8. According to the above paragraph, the kinds of garbage thrown out of windows are
   A. candy and cigarette butts
   B. food and half-empty soda cans
   C. fruit and vegetables
   D. rice and bread

Questions 9-12.

DIRECTIONS: Questions 9 through 12 are to be answered SOLELY on the basis of the following paragraph.

    The game that is recognized all over the world as an all-American game is the game of baseball. As a matter of fact, baseball heroes like Joe DiMaggio, Willie Mays, and Babe Ruth were as famous in their day as movie stars Robert Redford, Paul Newman, and Clint Eastwood are now. All these men have had the experience of being mobbed by fans whenever they put in an appearance anywhere in the world. Such unusual popularity makes it possible for stars like these to earn at least as much money off the job as on the job. It didn't take manufacturers and advertising men long to discover that their sales of shaving lotion, for instance, increased when they got famous stars to advertise their product for them on radio and television.

9. According to the above paragraph, baseball is known everywhere as a(n) _____ game.
   A. all-American   B. fast   C. unusual   D. tough

10. According to the above paragraph, being so well known means that it is possible for people like Willie Mays and Babe Ruth to
    A. ask for anything and get it
    B. make as much money off the job as on it
    C. travel anywhere free of charge
    D. watch any game free of charge

10.____

11. According to the above paragraph, which of the following are known all over the world?
    A. Baseball heroes
    B. Advertising men
    C. Manufacturers
    D. Basketball heroes

11.____

12. According to the above paragraph, it is possible to sell much more shaving lotion on television and radio if
    A. the commercials are in color instead of black and white
    B. you can get a prize with each bottle of shaving lotion
    C. the shaving lotion makes you smell nicer than usual
    D. the shaving lotion is advertised by famous stars

12.____

Questions 13-15.

DIRECTIONS: Questions 13 through 15 are to be answered SOLELY on the basis of the following passage.

That music gives pleasure is axiomatic. Because this is so, the pleasures of music may seem a rather elementary subject for discussion. Yet the source of that pleasure, our musical instinct, is not at all elementary. It is, in fact, one of the prime puzzles of consciousness. Why is it that we are able to make sense out of these nerve signals so that we emerge from engulfment in the orderly presentation of sound stimuli as if we had lived through an image of life?

If music has impact for the mere listener, it follows that it will have much greater impact for those who sing it or play it themselves with proficiency. Any educated person in Elizabethan times was expected to read musical notation and take part in a madrigalsing. Passive listeners, numbered in the millions, are a comparatively recent innovation.

Everyone is aware that so-called serious music has made great strikes in general public acceptance in recent years, but the term itself still connotes something forbidding and hermetic to the mass audience. They attribute to the professional musician a kind of initiation into secrets that are forever hidden from the outsider. Nothing could be more misleading. We all listen to music, professionals, and non-professionals alike in the same sort of way, in a dumb sort of way, really, because simple or sophisticated music attracts all of us in the first instance, on the primordial level of sheer rhythmic and sonic appeal. Musicians are flattered, no doubt, by the deferential attitude of the layman in regard to what he imagines to be our secret understanding of music. But in all honesty, we musicians know that in the main we listen basically as others do, because music hits us with an immediacy that we recognize in the reactions of the most simple minded of music listeners.

13. A suitable title for the above passage would be
    A. HOW TO LISTEN TO MUSIC
    B. LEARNING MUSIC APPRECIATION
    C. THE PLEASURES OF MUSIC
    D. THE WORLD OF THE MUSICIAN

    13.____

14. The author implies that the passive listener is one who
    A. cannot read or play music
    B. does not appreciate serious music
    C. does not keep time to the music by hand or toe tapping
    D. will not attend a concert if he has to pay for the privilege

    14.____

15. The author of the above passage is apparently inconsistent when he discusses
    A. the distinction between the listener who pays for the privilege and the one who does not
    B. the historical development of musical forms
    C. the pleasures derived from music by the musician
    D. why it is that we listen to music

    15.____

Questions 16-18.

DIRECTIONS: Questions 16 through 18 are to be answered SOLELY on the basis of the following passage.

Who are the clerisy? They are people who like to read books. The use of a word so unusual, so out of fashion, can only be excused on the ground that it has no familiar synonym. The word is little known because what it describes has disappeared, though I do not believe is gone forever. The clerisy are those who read for pleasure, but not for idleness; who read for pastime, but not to kill time; who love books, but do not live by books.

Let us consider the actual business of reading—the interpretive act of getting the words off the age and into your head in the most effective way. The most effective way is not the quickest way of reading; and for those who think that speed is the greatest good, there are plenty of manuals on how to read a book which profess to tell how to strip off the husk and guzzle the milk, like a chimp attacking a coconut. Who among today's readers would whisk through a poem, eyes aflicker, and say that he had read it? The answer to that last question must unfortunately be: far too many. For reading is not respected for the art it is.

Doubtless there are philosophical terms for the attitude of mind of which nasty reading is one manifestation, but here let us call it end-gaining, for its victims put ends before means; they value not reading, but having read. In this, the end-gainers make mischief and spoil all they do; end-gaining is one of the curses of our nervously tense, intellectually flabby civilization. In reading, as in all arts, it is the means, and not the end, which gives delight and brings the true reward. Not straining forward toward the completion, but the pleasure of every page as it comes, is the secret of reading. We must desire to read a book, rather than to have read it. This change in attitude, so simple to describe, is by no means simple to achieve,, if one has lived the life of an end-gainer.

16. A suitable title for the above passage would be
    A. READING FOR ENLIGHTENMENT
    B. THE ART OF RAPID READING
    C. THE WELL-EDUCATED READER
    D. VALUES IN READING

16.____

17. The author does NOT believe that most people read because they
    A. are bored
    B. have nothing better to do
    C. love books
    D. wish to say that they have read certain books

17.____

18. The change in attitude to which the author refers in the last sentence of the above passage implies a change from
    A. dawdling while reading so that the reader can read a greater number of books
    B. reading light fiction to reading serious fiction and non-fiction
    C. reading works which do not amuse the reader
    D. skimming through a book to reading it with care

18.____

Questions 19-22.

DIRECTIONS: Questions 19 through 22 are to be answered SOLELY on the basis of the following passage.

Violence is not new to literature. The writings of Shakespeare and Cervantes are full of it. But those classic writers did not condone violence. They viewed it as a just retribution for sins against the divine order or as a sacrifice sanctioned by heroism. What is peculiar to the modern literature is violence for the sake of violence. Perhaps our reverence for life has been dulled by mass slaughter, though mass slaughter has not been exceptional in the history of mankind. What is exceptional is the boredom that now alternates with war. The basic emotion in peacetime has become a horror of emptiness: a fear of being alone, of having nothing to do, a neurosis whose symptoms are restlessness, an unmotivated and undirected rage, sinking at times into vapid listlessness. This neurotic syndrome is intensified by the prevailing sense of insecurity. The threat of atomic war has corrupted our faith in life itself.

This universal neurosis has developed with the progress of technology. It is the neurosis of men whose chief expenditure of energy is to pull a lever or push a button, of men who have ceased to make things with their hands. Such inactivity applies not only to muscles and nerves but to the creative processes that once engaged the mind. If one could contrast visually, by time-and-motion studies, the daily actions of an eighteenth-century carpenter with a twentieth-century machinist, the latter would appear as a <u>confined, repetitive clot</u>, the former as a free and even fantastic pattern. But the most significant contrast could not be visualized—the contrast between a mind suspended aimlessly above an autonomous movement and a mind consciously bent on the shaping of a material substance according to the persistent evidence of the senses.

6 (#2)

19. A suitable title for the above passage would be
    A. INCREASING PRODUCTION BY MEANS OF SYSTEMATIZATION
    B. LACK OF A SENSE OF CREATIVENESS AND ITS CONSEQUENCE
    C. TECHNOLOGICAL ACHIEVEMENT IN MODERN SOCIETY
    D. WHAT CAN BE DONE ABOUT SENSELESS VIOLENCE

20. According to the author, Shakespeare treated violence as a
    A. basically sinful act not in keeping with religious thinking
    B. just punishment of transgressors against moral law
    C. means of achieving dramatic excitement
    D. solution to a problem provided no other solution was available

21. According to the author, boredom may lead to
    A. a greater interest in leisure-time activities
    B. chronic fatigue
    C. senseless anger
    D. the acceptance of a job which does not provide a sense of creativity

22. The underlined phrase refers to the
    A. hand movements made by the carpenter
    B. hand movements made by the machinist
    C. relative ignorance of the carpenter
    D. relative ignorance of the machinist

23. The concentration of women and female-headed families in the city is both cause and consequence of the city's fiscal woes. Women live in cities because it is easier and cheaper for them to do so, but because fewer women are employed, and those that are receive lower pay than men, they do not make the same contribution to the tax base that an equivalent population of men would. Concomitantly, they are more dependent on public resources, such as transportation and housing. For these reasons alone, urban finances would be improved by increasing women's employment opportunities and pay. Yet nothing in our current urban policy is specifically geared to improving women's financial resources. There are some proposed incentives to create more jobs, but not necessarily ones that would utilize the skills women currently have. The most innovative proposal was a tax credit for new hires from certain groups with particularly high unemployment rates. None of the seven targeted groups were women.
    Which sentence is BEST supported by the above paragraph?
    A. Innovative programs are rapidly improving conditions for seven targeted groups with traditionally high unemployment rates.
    B. The contribution of women to a city's tax base reflects their superior economic position.
    C. Improving the economic position of women who live in cities would help the financial conditions of the cities themselves.
    D. Most women in this country live in large cities.

24. None of this would be worth saying if Descartes had been right in positing a one-to-one correspondence between stimuli and sensations. But we know that nothing of the sort exists. The perception of a given color can be evoked by an infinite number of differently combined wavelengths. Conversely, a given stimulus can evoke a variety of sensations, the image of a duck in one recipient, the image of a rabbit in another. Nor are responses like these entirely innate. One can learn to discriminate colors or patterns which were indistinguishable prior to training. To an extent still unknown, the production of data from stimuli is a learned procedure. After the learning process, the same stimulus evokes a different datum. I conclude that, though data are the minimal elements of our individual experience, they need be shared responses to a given stimulus only within the membership of a relatively homogeneous community: educational, scientific, or linguistic.
Which sentence is BEST supported by the above paragraph?
   A. One stimulus can give rise to a number of different sensations.
   B. There is a one-to-one correspondence between stimuli and sensations.
   C. It is not possible to produce data from stimuli by using a learned procedure.
   D. It is not necessary for a group to be relatively homogeneous in order to share responses to stimuli.

25. Workers who want to move in the direction of participative structures will need to confront the issues of power and control. The process of change needs to be mutually shared by all involved, or the outcome will not be a really participative model. The demand for a structural redistribution of power is not sufficient to address the problem of change toward a humanistic, as against a technological, workplace. If we are to change our institutional arrangements from hierarchy to participation, particularly in our workplaces, we will need to look to transformations in ourselves as well. As long as we are imbued with the legitimacy of hierarchical authority, with the sovereignty of the status quo, we will never be able to generate the new and original forms that we seek. This means if we are to be equal to the task of reorganizing our workplaces, we need to think about how we can reeducate ourselves and become aware of our assumptions about the nature of our social life together. Unless the issue is approached in terms of these complexities, I fear that all the worker participation and quality of work life efforts will fail.
According to the above paragraph, which of the following is NOT true?
   A. Self-education concerning social roles must go hand in hand with workplace reorganization.
   B. The structural changing of the workplace, alone, will not bring about the necessary changes in the quality of work life.
   C. Individuals can easily overcome their attitudes towards hierarchical authority.
   D. Changing the quality of work life will require the participation of all involved.

KEY (CORRECT ANSWERS)

1.	D	11.	A
2.	D	12.	D
3.	B	13.	C
4.	B	14.	A
5.	A	15.	C
6.	C	16.	D
7.	D	17.	C
8.	B	18.	D
9.	A	19.	B
10.	B	20.	B

21. C
22. B
23. C
24. A
25. C

ENGLISH EXPRESSION
CHOICE OF EXPRESSION
COMMENTARY

One special form of the English Expression multiple-choice question in current use requires the candidate to select from among five (5) versions of a particular part of a sentence (or of an entire sentence), the one version that expresses the idea of the sentence most clearly, effectively, and accurately. Thus, the candidate is required not only to recognize errors, but also to choose the best way of phrasing a particular part of the sentence.

This is a test of choice of expression, which assays the candidate's ability to express himself correctly and effectively, including his sensitivity to the subtleties and nuances of the language.

SAMPLE QUESTIONS

DIRECTIONS: In each of the following sentences, some part of the sentence or the entire sentence is underlined. The underlined part presents a problem in the appropriate use of language. Beneath each sentence you will find five ways of writing the underlined part. The first of these indicates no change (that is, it repeats the original), but the other four are all different. If you think the original sentence is better than any of the suggested changes, you should choose answer A; otherwise you should mark one of the other choices. Select the BEST answer and print the letter in the space at the right.

This is a test of correctness and effectiveness of expression. In choosing answers, follow the requirements of standard written English; that is, pay attention to acceptable usage in grammar, diction (choice of words), sentence construction, and punctuation. Choose the answer that produces the most effective sentence—clear and exact, without awkwardness or ambiguity. Do not make a choice that changes the meaning of the original sentence.

SAMPLE QUESTION 1

Although these states now trade actively with the West, and although they are willing to exchange technological information, their arts and thoughts and social structure <u>remains substantially similar to what it has always been</u>.
  A. remains substantially similar to what it has always been
  B. remain substantially unchanged
  C. remains substantially unchanged
  D. remain substantially similar to what they have always been
  E. remain substantially without being changed

The purpose of questions of this type is to determine the candidate's ability to select the clearest and most effective means of expressing what the statement attempts to say. In this example, the phrasing in the statement, which is repeated in A, presents a problem of agreement between a subject and its verb (<u>their arts and thought and social structure</u> and <u>remains</u>), a problem of agreement between a pronoun and its antecedent (<u>their arts and thought and social structure</u> and <u>it</u>), an a problem of precise and concise phrasing (<u>remains</u>

substantially similar to what it has always been for remains substantially unchanged). Each of the four remaining choices in some way corrects one or more of the faults in the sentence, but only one deals with all three problems satisfactorily. Although C presents a more careful and concise wording of the phrasing of the statement and, in the process, eliminates the problem of agreement between pronoun and antecedent, it fails to correct the problem of agreement between the subject and its verb. In D, the subject agrees with its verb and the pronoun agrees with its antecedent, but the phrasing is not so accurate as it should be. The same difficulty persists in E. Only in B are all the problems presented corrected satisfactory. The question is not difficult.

SAMPLE QUESTION 2

Her latest novel is the largest in scope, the most accomplished in technique, and it is more significant in theme than anything she has written.
  A. it is more significant in theme than anything
  B. It is most significant in theme of anything
  C. more significant in theme than anything
  D. the most significant in theme than anything
  E. the most significant in theme of anything

This question is of greater difficulty than the preceding one. The problem posed in the sentence and repeated in A is essentially one of parallelism; Does the underlined portion of the sentence follow the pattern established by the first two elements of the series (the largest...the most accomplished)? It does not, for it introduces a pronoun and verb (it is) that the second term of the series indicates should be omitted and a degree of comparison (more significant) that is not in keeping with the superlatives used earlier in the sentence. B uses the superlative degree of significant but retains the unnecessary it is; C removes the it is, but retains the faulty comparative form of the adjective. D corrects both errors in parallelism, but introduces an error in idiom (the most...than). Only E corrects all the problems without introducing another fault.

SAMPLE QUESTION 3

Desiring to insure the continuity of their knowledge, magical lore is transmitted by the chiefs to their descendants.
  A. magical lore is transmitted by the chiefs
  B. transmission of magical lore is made by the chiefs
  C. the chiefs' magical lore is transmitted
  D. the chiefs transmit magical lore
  E. the chiefs make transmission of magical lore
The CORRECT answer is D.

SAMPLE QUESTION 4

As Malcolm walks quickly and confident into the purser's office, the rest of the crew wondered whether he would be charged with the theft.
  A. As Malcolm walks quickly and confident
  B. As Malcolm was walking quick and confident
  C. As Malcom walked quickly and confident

D. As Malcolm walked quickly and confidently
E. As Malcolm walks quickly and confidently
The CORRECT answer is D.

SAMPLE QUESTION 5

The chairman, <u>granted the power to assign any duties to whoever he</u> wished, was still unable to prevent bickering.
A. granted the power to assign any duties to whoever he wished
B. granting the power to assign any duties to whoever he wished
C. being granted the power to assign any duties to whoever he wished
D. having been granted the power to assign any duties to whosoever he wished
E. granted the power to assign any duties to whomever he wished
The CORRECT answer is E.

SAMPLE QUESTION 6

Certainly, well-seasoned products are more expensive, <u>but those kinds prove chaper</u> in the end.
A. but those kinds prove cheaper
B. but these kinds prove cheaper
C. but that kind proves cheaper
D. but those kind prove cheaper
E. but this kind proves cheaper
The CORRECT answer is A.

SAMPLE QUESTION 7

"We shall not," he shouted, "whatever the <u>difficulties." "lose faith in the success of our plan!!"</u>
A. difficulties," "lose faith in the success of our plan!"
B. difficulties, "lose faith in the success of our plan"!
C. "difficulties, lose faith in the success of our plan!"
D. difficulties, lose faith in the success of our plan"!
E. difficulties, lose faith in the success of our plan!"

SAMPLE QUESTION 8

<u>Climb up the tree</u>, the lush foliage obscured the chattering monkeys.
A. Climbing up the tree
B. Having climbed up the tree
C. Clambering up the tree
D. After we had climbed up the tree
E. As we climbed up the tree
The CORRECT answer is E.

EXAMINATION SECTION
TEST 1

DIRECTIONS: See DIRECTIONS for Sample Questions on Page 1. *PRINT THE LETTER OF THE CORRECT ANSWER IN THE SPACE AT THE RIGHT.*

1. At the opening of the story, Charles Gilbert <u>has just come</u> to make his home with his two unmarried aunts.
    A. No change
    B. hadn't hardly come
    C. has just came
    D. had just come
    E. has hardly came

    1.____

2. The sisters, who are no longer young, <u>are use to living</u> quiet lives.
    A. No change
    B. are used to live
    C. are use'd to living
    D. are used to living
    E. are use to live

    2.____

3. They <u>willingly except</u> the child.
    A. No change
    B. willingly eccepted
    C. willingly accepted
    D. willingly acepted
    E. willingly accept

    3.____

4. As the months pass, Charles' presence <u>affects many changes</u> in their household.
    A. No change
    B. affect many changes
    C. effects many changes
    D. effect many changes
    E. affected many changes

    4.____

5. These changes <u>is not all together</u> to their liking.
    A. No change
    B. is not altogether
    C. are not all together
    D. are not altogether
    E. is not alltogether

    5.____

6. In fact, they have some difficulty in adapting <u>theirselves</u> to these changes
    A. No change
    B. in adopting theirselves
    C. in adopting themselves
    D. in adapting theirselves
    E. in adapting themselves

    6.____

7. That is the man <u>whom I believe</u> was the driver of the car.
    A. No change
    B. who I believed
    C. whom I believed
    D. who to believe
    E. who I believe

    7.____

8. John's climb to fame was more rapid <u>than his brother's</u>.
    A. No change
    B. than his brother
    C. than that of his brother's
    D. than for his brother
    E. than the brother

    8.____

83

9. We knew that he had formerly swam on an Olympic team. 9._____
   A. No change
   B. has formerly swum
   C. did formerly swum
   D. had formerly swum
   E. has formerly swam

10. Not one of us loyal supporters ever get a pass to a game. 10._____
    A. No change
    B. ever did got a pass
    C. ever has get a pass
    D. ever had get a pass
    E. ever gets a pass

11. He was complemented on having done a fine job. 11._____
    A. No change
    B. was compliminted
    C. was compleminted
    D. was complimented
    E. did get complimented

12. This play is different from the one we had seen last night. 12._____
    A. No change
    B. have seen
    C. had saw
    D. have saw
    E. saw

13. A row of trees was planted in front of the house. 13._____
    A. No change
    B. was to be planted
    C. were planted
    D. were to be planted
    E. are planted

14. The house looked its age in spite of our attempts to beautify it. 14._____
    A. No change
    B. looks its age
    C. looked its' age
    D. looked it's age
    E. looked it age

15. I do not know what to council in this case. 15._____
    A. No change
    B. where to council
    C. when to councel
    D. what to counsel
    E. what to counsil

16. She is more capable than any other girl in the office. 16._____
    A. No change
    B. than any girl
    C. than any other girls
    D. than other girl
    E. than other girls

17. At the picnic the young children behaved very good. 17._____
    A. No change
    B. behave very good
    C. behaved better
    D. behave very well
    E. behaved very well

18. I resolved to go irregardless of the consequences. 18._____
    A. No change
    B. to depart irregardless of
    C. to go regarding of
    D. to go regardingly of
    E. to go regardless of

3 (#1)

19. The new movie has a number of actors <u>which have been famous</u> on Broadway.
    A. No change
    B. which had been famous
    C. who had been famous
    D. that are famous
    E. who have been famous

20. I am certain that these books <u>are not our's</u>.
    A. No change
    B. have not been ours'
    C. have not been our's
    D. are not ours
    E. are not ours'

21. <u>Each of your papers is filed</u> for future reference.
    A. No change
    B. Each of your papers are filed
    C. Each of your papers have been filed
    D. Each of your papers are to be filed
    E. Each of your paper is filed

22. I wish that <u>he would take his work more serious</u>.
    A. No change
    B. he took his work more serious
    C. he will take his work more serious
    D. he shall take his work more seriously
    E. he would take his work more seriously

23. <u>After the treasurer report had been read</u>, the chairman called for the reports of the committees.
    A. No change
    B. After the treasure's report had been read
    C. After the treasurers' report had been read
    D. After the treasurerer's report had been read
    E. After the treasurer's report had been read

24. Last night the stranger <u>lead us down the mountain</u>.
    A. No change
    B. leaded us down the mountain
    C. let us down the mountain
    D. led us down the mountain
    E. had led us down the mountain

25. It would not be safe <u>for either you or I</u> to travel in Viet Nam.
    A. No change
    B. for either you or me
    C. for either I or you
    D. for either of you or I
    E. for either of I or you

KEY (CORRECT ANSWERS)

1.	A		11.	D
2.	D		12.	E
3.	E		13.	A
4.	C		14.	A
5.	D		15.	D
6.	E		16.	A
7.	E		17.	E
8.	A		18.	E
9.	D		19.	E
10.	E		20.	D

21. A
22. E
23. E
24. D
25. B

TEST 2

DIRECTIONS: See DIRECTIONS for Sample Questions on Page 1. *PRINT THE LETTER OF THE CORRECT ANSWER IN THE SPACE AT THE RIGHT.*

1. Both the body and the mind <u>needs exercise</u>.
   A. No change
   B. have needs of exercise
   C. is needful of exercise
   D. needed exercise
   E. need exercise

   1._____

2. <u>It's paw injured</u>, the animal limped down the road.
   A. No change
   B. It's paw injured
   C. Its paw injured
   D. Its' paw injured
   E. Its paw injure

   2._____

3. The butter <u>tastes rancidly</u>.
   A. No change
   B. tastes rancid
   C. tasted rancidly
   D. taste rancidly
   E. taste rancid

   3._____

4. <u>Who do you think</u> has sent me a letter?
   A. No change
   B. Whom do you think
   C. Whome do you think
   D. Who did you think
   E. Whom can you think

   4._____

5. If more nations <u>would have fought</u> against tyranny, the course of history would have been different.
   A. No change
   B. would fight
   C. could have fought
   D. fought
   E. had fought

   5._____

6. Radio and television programs, along with other media of communication, <u>helps us to appreciate the arts and to keep informed</u>.
   A. No change
   B. helps us to appreciate the arts and to be informed
   C. helps us to be appreciative of the arts and to keep informed
   D. helps us to be appreciative of the arts and to be informed
   E. help us to appreciate the arts and to keep informed

   6._____

7. Music, <u>for example most always</u> has listening and viewing audiences numbering in the hundreds of thousands.
   A. No change
   B. for example, most always
   C. for example, almost always
   D. for example nearly always
   E. for example, near always

   7._____

8. When operas are performed on radio or television, <u>they effect the listener</u>.
   A. No change
   B. they inflict the listener
   C. these effect the listeners
   D. they affects the listeners
   E. they affect the listener

   8._____

87

9. After hearing then the listener wants to buy recordings of the music.   9.____
   A. No change
   B. After hearing them, the listener wants
   C. After hearing them, the listener want
   D. By hearing them the listener wants
   E. By hearing them, the listener wants

10. To we Americans the daily news program has become important.   10.____
    A. No change   B. To we the Americans
    C. To us Americans   D. To us the Americans
    E. To we and us Americans

11. This has resulted from it's coverage of a days' events.   11.____
    A. No change
    B. from its coverage of a days' events
    C. from it's coverage of a day's events
    D. from its' coverage of a day's events
    E. from its coverage of a day's events

12. In schools, teachers advice their students to listen to or to view certain programs.   12.____
    A. No change
    B. teachers advise there students
    C. teachers advise their students
    D. the teacher advises their students
    E. teachers advise his students

13. In these ways we are preceding toward the goal of an educated and an   13.____
    informed public.
    A. No change
    B. we are preeceding toward the goal
    C. we are proceeding toward the goal
    D. we are preceding toward the goal
    E. we are proceeding toward the goal

14. The cost of living is raising again.   14.____
    A. No change   B. are raising again
    C. is rising again   D. are rising again
    E. is risen again

15. We did not realize that the boys' father had forbidden them to keep there   15.____
    puppy.
    A. No change
    B. had forbade them to keep there puppy
    C. had forbade them to keep their puppy
    D. has forbidden them to keep their puppy
    E. had forbidden them to keep their puppy

16. Her willingness to help others' was her outstanding characteristic.
    A. No change
    B. Her willingness to help other's,
    C. Her willingness to help others's
    D. Her willingness to help others
    E. Her willingness to help each other

17. Because he did not have an invitation, the girls objected to him going.
    A. No change
    B. the girls object to him going
    C. the girls objected to him's going
    D. the girls objected to his going
    E. the girls object to his going

18. Weekly dances have become a popular accepted feature of the summer schedule.
    A. No change
    B. have become a popular accepted feature
    C. have become a popular excepted feature
    D. have become a popularly excepted feature
    E. have become a popularly accepted feature

19. I couldn't hardly believe that he would desert our party.
    A. No change
    B. would hardly believe
    C. didn't hardly believe
    D. should hardly believe
    E. could hardly believe

20. I found the place in the book more readily than she.
    A. No change
    B. more readily than her
    C. more ready than she
    D. more quickly than her
    E. more ready than her

21. A good example of American outdoor activities are sports.
    A. No change
    B. is sports
    C. are sport
    D. are sports events
    E. are to be found in sports

22. My point of view is much different from your's.
    A. No change
    B. much different from your's
    C. much different than yours
    D. much different from yours
    E. much different than yours'

23. The cook was suppose to use two spoonfuls of dressing for each serving.
    A. No change
    B. was supposed to use two spoonful
    C. was suppose to use two spoonful
    D. was supposed to use two spoonsfuls
    E. was supposed to use two spoonfuls

4 (#2)

24. If anyone has any doubt about the values of the tour, <u>refer him to me</u>. 24._____
    A. No change
    B. refer him to I
    C. refer me to he
    D. refer them to me
    E. refer he to I

25. We expect that the affects of <u>the trip will be neneficial</u>. 25._____
    A. No change
    B. the effects of the trip will be beneficial
    C. the effects of the trip should be beneficial
    D. the affects of the trip would be beneficial
    E. the effects of the trip will be benificial

KEY (CORRECT ANSWERS)

1.	E		11.	E
2.	C		12.	C
3.	B		13.	E
4.	A		14.	C
5.	E		15.	E
6.	E		16.	D
7.	C		17.	D
8.	E		18.	E
9.	B		19.	E
10.	C		20.	A

21.	B
22.	D
23.	E
24.	A
25.	B

TEST 3

DIRECTIONS: See DIRECTIONS for Sample Questions on Page 1. *PRINT THE LETTER OF THE CORRECT ANSWER IN THE SPACE AT THE RIGHT.*

1. <u>That, my friend</u> is not the proper attitude. 1.____
   A. No change
   B. That my friend
   C. That my fried,
   D. That—my friend
   E. That, my friend,

2. The girl refused to admit <u>that the note was her's</u>. 2.____
   A. No change
   B. that the note were her's
   C. that the note was hers'
   D. that the note was hers
   E. that the note might be hers

3. There <u>were fewer candidates that we had been lead</u> to expect 3.____
   A. No change
   B. was fewer candidates than we had been lead
   C. were fewer candidates than we had been lead
   D. was fewer candidates than we had been led
   E. were fewer candidates than we had been led

4. When I first saw the car, <u>its steering wheel was broke</u>. 4.____
   A. No change
   B. its' steering wheel was broken
   C. it's steering wheel had been broken
   D. its steering wheel were broken
   E. its steering wheel was broken

5. I find that the essential spirit for <u>we beginners is missing</u>. 5.____
   A. No change
   B. we who begin are missing
   C. us beginners are missing
   D. us beginners is missing
   E. we beginners are missing

6. I believe that <u>you had ought</u> to study harder. 6.____
   A. No change
   B. you should have ought
   C. you had better
   D. you ought to have
   E. you ought

7. This is <u>Tom, whom I am sure,</u> will be glad to help you. 7.____
   A. No change
   B. Tom whom, I am sure,
   C. Tom, whom I am sure
   D. Tom who I am sure,
   E. Tom, who, I am sure,

8. His father or his mother <u>has read to him</u> every night since he was very small. 8.____
   A. No change
   B. did read to him
   C. have been reading to him
   D. had read to him
   E. have read to him

9. He become an authority
   A. No change
   B. becomed an authority
   C. become the authority
   D. became an authority
   E. becamed an authority

10. I know of no other reason in the club who is more kind-hearted than her.
    A. No change
    B. who are more kind-hearted than they
    C. who are more kind-hearted than them
    D. whom are more kind-hearted than she
    E. who is more kind-hearted than she

11. After Bill had ran the mile, he was breathless.
    A. No change
    B. had runned the mile
    C. has ran the mile
    D. had ranned the mile
    E. had run the mile

12. Wilson has scarcely no equal as a pitcher.
    A. No change
    B. has scarcely an equal
    C. has hardly no equal
    D. had scarcely no equal
    E. has scarcely any equals

13. It was the worse storm that the inhabitants of the island could remember.
    A. No change
    B. were the worse storm
    C. was the worst storm
    D. was the worsest storm
    E. was the most worse storm

14. If only we had began before it was too late.
    A. No change
    B. we had began
    C. we would have begun
    D. we had begun
    E. we had beginned

15. Lets evaluate our year's work.
    A. No change
    B. Let us' evaluate
    C. Lets' evaluate
    D. Lets' us evaluate
    E. Let's evaluate

16. This is an organization with which I wouldn't want to be associated with.
    A. No change
    B. with whom I wouldn't want to be associated with
    C. that I wouldn't want to be associated
    D. with which I would want not to be associated with
    E. with which I wouldn't want to be associated

17. The enemy fled in many directions, leaving there weapons on the field.
    A. No change
    B. leaving its weapons
    C. letting their weapons
    D. leaving alone there weapons
    E. leaving their weapons

18. I hoped that John could effect a compromise between the approved forces.   18.____
    A. No change
    B. could accept a compromise between
    C. could except a compromise between
    D. would have effected a compromise among
    E. could effect a compromise among

19. I was surprised to learn that he has not always spoke English fluently.   19.____
    A. No change
    B. that he had not always spoke English
    C. that he did not always speak English
    D. that he has not always spoken English
    E. that he could not always speak English

20. The lawyer promised to notify my father and I of his plans for a new trial.   20.____
    A. No change   B. to notify I and my father
    C. to notify me and our father   D. to notify my father and me
    E. to notify mine father and me

21. The most important feature of the series of tennis lessons were the large amount of strokes taught.   21.____
    A. No change   B. were the large number
    C. was the large amount   D. was the largeness of the amount
    E. was the large number

22. That the prize proved to be beyond her reach did not surprise him.   22.____
    A. No change
    B. has not surprised him
    C. had not ought to have surprised him
    D. should not surprise him
    E. would not have surprised him

23. I am not all together in agreement with the author's point of view.   23.____
    A. No change   B. all together of agreement
    C. all together for agreement   D. altogether with agreement
    E. altogether in agreement

24. Windstorms have recently established a record which meteorologists hope will not be equal for many years to come.   24.____
    A. No change   B. will be equal
    C. will not be equalized   D. will be equaled
    E. will not be equaled

25. A large number of Shakespeare's soliloquies must be considered <u>as representing thought</u>, not speech.
    A. No change
    B. as representative of speech, not thought
    C. as represented by thought, not speech
    D. as indicating thought, not speech
    E. as representative of thought, more than speech

25.____

KEY (CORRECT ANSWERS)

1.	E	11.	E
2.	D	12.	B
3.	E	13.	C
4.	E	14.	D
5.	D	15.	E
6.	E	16.	E
7.	E	17.	E
8.	A	18.	A
9.	D	19.	D
10.	E	20.	D

21.	E
22.	A
23.	E
24.	E
25.	A

TEST 4

DIRECTIONS: See DIRECTIONS for Sample Questions on Page 1. *PRINT THE LETTER OF THE CORRECT ANSWER IN THE SPACE AT THE RIGHT.*

1. A sight to inspire fear <u>are wild animals on the lose</u>.
   A. No change
   B. are wild animals on the loose
   C. is wild animals on the loose
   D. is wild animals on the lose
   E. are wild animals loose

   1.____

2. For many years, the settlers <u>had been seeking to workship as they please</u>.
   A. No change
   B. had seeked to workship as they pleased
   C. sought to workship as they please
   D. sought to have worshiped as they pleased
   E. had been seeking to worship as they pleased

   2.____

3. The girls stated that the dresses were <u>their's</u>.
   A. No change
   B. there's
   C. theirs
   D. theirs'
   E. there own

   3.____

4. <u>Please fellows</u> don't drop the ball.
   A. No change
   B. Please, fellows
   C. Please fellows;
   D. Please, fellows,
   E. Please! fellows

   4.____

5. Your sweater <u>has laid</u> on the floor for a week.
   A. No change
   B. has been laying
   C. has been lying
   D. laid
   E. has been lain

   5.____

6. I wonder whether <u>you're sure that scheme of yours'</u> will work.
   A. No change
   B. your sure that scheme of your's
   C. you're sure that scheme of yours
   D. your sure that scheme of yours
   E. you're sure that your scheme's

   6.____

7. Please let <u>her and me</u> do it.
   A. No change
   B. she and I
   C. she and me
   D. her and I
   E. her and him

   7.____

8. I expected him to be angry <u>and to scold</u> her.
   A. No change
   B. and that he would scold
   C. and that he might scold
   D. and that he should scold
   E. , scolding

   8.____

9. Knowing little about algebra, <u>it was difficult to solve the equation</u>.   9.____
   A. No change
   B. the equation was difficult to solve
   C. the solution to the equation was difficult to find
   D. I found it difficult to solve the equation
   E. it being difficult to solve the equation

10. He <u>worked more diligent</u> now that he had become vice president of the company.   10.____
    A. No change
    B. works more diligent
    C. works more diligently
    D. began to work more diligent
    E. worked more diligently

11. <u>Flinging himself at the barricade he</u> pounded on it furiously.   11.____
    A. No change
    B. Flinging himself at the barricade: he
    C. Flinging himself at the barricade—he
    D. Flinging himself at the barricade; he
    E. Flinging himself at the barricade, he

12. When he <u>begun to give us advise</u>, we stopped listening.   12.____
    A. No change
    B. began to give us advise
    C. begun to give us advice
    D. began to give us advice
    E. begin to give us advice

13. John was only one of the boys <u>whom as you know was</u> not eligible.   13.____
    A. No change
    B. who as you know were
    C. whom as you know were
    D. who as you know was
    E. who as you know is

14. Why <u>was Jane and he</u> permitted to go?   14.____
    A. No change
    B. was Jane and him
    C. were Jane and he
    D. were Jane and him
    E. weren't Jane and he

15. <u>Take courage Tom: we</u> all make mistakes.   15.____
    A. No change
    B. Take courage Tom—we
    C. Take courage, Tom; we
    D. Take courage, Tom we
    E. Take courage! Tom: we

16. Henderson, the president of the class and <u>who is also captain of the team</u>, will lead the rally.   16.____
    A. No change
    B. since he is captain of the team
    C. captain of the team
    D. also being captain of the team
    E. who be also captain of the team

17. Our car has always <u>run good</u> on that kind of gasoline.   17.____
    A. No change
    B. run well
    C. ran good
    D. ran well
    E. done good

18. There was a serious difference of opinion among her and I.
    A. No change
    B. among she and I
    C. between her and I
    D. between her and me
    E. among her and me

19. "This is most unusual," said Helen, "the mailman has never been this late before."
    A. No change
    B. Helen, "The
    C. Helen—"The
    D. Helen; "The
    E. Helen." The

20. The three main characters in the story are Johnny Hobart a teenager, his mother a widow, and the local druggist.
    A. No change
    B. teenager; his mother, a widow; and
    C. teenager; his mother a widow; and
    D. teenager, his mother, a widow and
    E. teenager, his mother, a widow; and

21. How much has food costs raised during the past year?
    A. No change
    B. have food costs rose
    C. have food costs risen
    D. has food costs risen
    E. have food costs been raised

22. "Will you come too" she pleaded?
    A. No change
    B. too?"she pleaded
    C. too?" she pleaded
    D. too," she pleaded?
    E. too, she pleaded?"

23. If he would have drank more milk, his health would have been better.
    A. No change
    B. would drink
    C. had drank
    D. had he drunk
    E. had drunk

24. Jack had no sooner laid down and fallen asleep when the alarm sounded.
    A. No change
    B. no sooner lain down and fallen asleep than
    C. no sooner lay down and fell asleep when
    D. no sooner laid down and fell asleep than
    E. no sooner lain down than he fell asleep when

25. Jackson is one of the few Sophomores, who has ever made the varsity team.
    A. No change
    B. one of the few Sophomores, who have
    C. one of the few sophomores, who has
    D. one of the few sophomores who have
    E. one of the few sophomores who has

KEY (CORRECT ANSWERS)

1.	C		11.	E
2.	E		12.	D
3.	C		13.	B
4.	D		14.	C
5.	C		15.	C
6.	C		16.	C
7.	A		17.	B
8.	A		18.	D
9.	D		19.	E
10.	E		20.	B

21. C
22. C
23. E
24. B
25. D

TEST 5

DIRECTIONS: See DIRECTIONS for Sample Questions on Page 1. *PRINT THE LETTER OF THE CORRECT ANSWER IN THE SPACE AT THE RIGHT.*

1. The lieutenant had ridden almost a kilometer when the scattering shells <u>begin landing</u> uncomfortably close.
    A. No change
    B. beginning to land
    C. began to land
    D. having begun to land
    E. begin to land

    1._____

2. <u>Having studied eight weeks</u>, he now feels sufficiently prepared for the examination.
    A. No change
    B. For eight weeks he studies so
    C. Due to eight weeks of study
    D. After eight weeks of studying
    E. Since he's been spending the last eight weeks in study

    2._____

3. <u>Coming from the Greek, and the word "democracy" means government by the people.</u>
    A. No change
    B. "Democracy," the word which comes from the Greek, means government by the people.
    C. Meaning government by the people, the word "democracy" comes from the Greek.
    D. Its meaning being government by the people in Greek, the word is "democracy."
    E. The word "democracy" comes from the Greek and means government by the people.

    3._____

4. Moslem universities were one of the chief agencies <u>in the development</u> and spreading Arabic civilization.
    A. No change
    B. in the development of
    C. to develop
    D. in developing
    E. for the developing of

    4._____

5. The water of Bering Strait <u>were closing</u> to navigation by ice early in the fall.
    A. No change
    B. has closed
    C. have closed
    D. had been closed
    E. closed

    5._____

6. The man, <u>since he grew up</u> on the block, felt sentimental when returning to it.
    A. No change
    B. having grown up
    C. growing up
    D. since he had grown up
    E. whose growth had been

    6._____

99

7. <u>Jack and Jill watched the canoe to take their parents out of sight round the bend of the creek</u>.
   A. No change
   B. The canoe, taking their parents out of sight, rounds the bend as Jack and Jill watch.
   C. Jack and Jill watched the canoe round the bend of the creek, taking their parents out of sight,
   D. The canoe rounded the bend of the creek as it took their parents out of sight, Jack and Jill watching.
   E. Jack and Jill watching, the canoe is rounding the bend of the creek to take their parents out of sight.

8. Chaucer's best-known work is THE CANTERBURY TALES, a collection of stories <u>which he tells</u> with a group of pilgrims as they travel to the town of Canterbury.
   A. No change
   B. which he tells through
   C. who tell
   D. told by
   E. told through

9. The Estates-General, the old feudal assembly of France, <u>had not met</u> for one hundred and seventy-five years when it convened in 1789.
   A. No change
   B. has not met
   C. has not been meeting
   D. had no meeting
   E. has no meeting

10. Just forty years ago, <u>there had been</u> fewer than one hundred symphony orchestras in the United States.
    A. No change
    B. there had
    C. there were
    D. there was
    E. there existed

11. Mrs. Smith complained that her son's temper tantrums <u>aggravated her</u> and caused her to have a headache.
    A. No change
    B. gave her aggravation
    C. were aggravating to her
    D. aggravated her condition
    E. instigated

12. A girl <u>like I</u> would never be seen in a place like that.
    A. No change
    B. as I
    C. as me
    D. like I am
    E. like me

13. <u>Between you and me,</u> my opinion is that this room is certainly nicer than the first one we saw.
    A. No change
    B. between you and I
    C. among you and me
    D. betwixt you and I
    E. between we

14. It is important to know for <u>what kind of a person you are working</u>.   14.____
    A. No change
    B. what kind of a person for whom you are working
    C. what kind of person you are working
    D. what kind of person you are working for
    E. what kind of a person you are working for

15. I had <u>all ready</u> finished the book before you came in.   15.____
    A. No change   B. already   C. previously
    D. allready   E. all

16. <u>Ask not for who the bell tolls, it tolls for thee</u>.   16.____
    A. No change
    B. Ask not for whom the bell tolls, it tolls for thee.
    C. Ask not whom the bell tolls for; it tolls for thee.
    D. Ask not for whom the bell tolls; it tolls for thee.
    E. As not who the bell tolls for: It tolls for thee.

17. It is a far better thing I do, than <u>ever I did</u> before.   17.____
    A. No change   B. never I did
    C. I have ever did   D. I have ever been done
    E. ever have I done

18. <u>Ending a sentence with a preposition is something up with which I will not put</u>.   18.____
    A. No change
    B. Ending a sentence with a preposition is something with which I will not put up.
    C. To end a sentence with a preposition is that which I will not put up with.
    D. Ending a sentence with a preposition is something of which I will not put up.
    E. Something I will not put up with is ending a sentence with a preposition.

19. Everyone <u>took off their hats and stand up</u> to sing the national anthem.   19.____
    A. No change
    B. took off their hats and stood up
    C. take off their hats and stand up
    D. took off his hat and stood up
    E. have taken off their hats and standing up

20. <u>She promised me that if she had the opportunity she would have came irregardless of the weather</u>.   20.____
    A. No change
    B. She promised me that if she had the opportunity she would have come regardless of the weather.
    C. She assured me that had she had the opportunity he would have come regardless of the weather.
    D. She assured me that if she would have had the opportunity she would have come regardless of the weather.

E. She promised me that if she had had the opportunity she would have came irregardless of the weather.

21. The man decided it would be advisable to marry a girl <u>somewhat younger than him</u>.
    A. No change
    B. somehow younger than him
    C. some younger than him
    D. somewhat younger from him
    E. somewhat younger than he

22. Sitting near the campfire, the old man told <u>John and I about many exciting adventures he had had</u>.
    A. No change
    B. John and me about many exciting adventures he had,
    C. John and I about much exciting adventure which he'd had
    D. John and me about many exciting adventures he had had
    E. John and me about many exciting adventures he has had.

23. <u>If you had stood at home and done your homework</u>, you would not have failed the course.
    A. No change
    B. If you had stood at home and done you're homework,
    C. If you had staid at home and done your homework,
    D. Had you stayed at home and done your homework,
    E. Had you stood at home and done your homework,

24. The children didn't, as a rule, <u>do anything beyond</u> what they were told to do.
    A. No change
    B. do hardly anything beyond
    C. do anything except
    D. do hardly anything except for
    E. do nothing beyond

25. <u>Either the girls or him is</u> right.
    A. No change
    B. Either the girls or he is
    C. Either the girls or him are
    D. Either the girls or he are
    E. Either the girls nor he is

KEY (CORRECT ANSWERS)

1.	C	11.	D
2.	A	12.	E
3.	E	13.	A
4.	D	14.	C
5.	D	15.	B
6.	B	16.	D
7.	C	17.	E
8.	D	18.	E
9.	A	19.	D
10.	C	20.	C

21. E
22. D
23. D
24. A
25. B

WRITTEN ENGLISH EXPRESSION
EXAMINATION SECTION
TEST 1

DIRECTIONS: In each of the sentences below, four portions are underlined and lettered. Read each sentence and decide whether any of the UNDERLINED parts contains an error in spelling, punctuation, or capitalization, or employs grammatical usage which would be inappropriate for carefully written English. If so, note the letter printed under the unacceptable form and indicate this choice in the space at the right. If all four of the underlined portions are acceptable as they stand, select the answer E. (No sentence contains more than ONE unacceptable form.)

1. The revised <u>procedure</u> was <u>quite</u> different <u>than</u> the one which <u>was</u> employed up   1.____
           A   B   C   D
to that time. <u>No error</u>
            E

2. <u>Blinded</u> by the storm that <u>surrounded</u> him, his plane <u>kept going</u> in <u>circles</u>.   2.____
   A   B   C   D
<u>No error</u>
E

3. They <u>should</u> give the book to <u>whoever</u> <u>they</u> think deserves <u>it</u>. <u>No error</u>   3.____
         A   B   C   D E

4. The <u>government</u> will not consent to your <u>firm</u> <u>sending</u> that package as   4.____
      A   B   C
<u>second class</u> matter. <u>No error</u>
     D   E

5. She <u>would have</u> avoided all the trouble <u>that</u> followed if she <u>would have</u> waited   5.____
        A   B   C
ten minutes <u>longer</u>. <u>No error</u>
          D   E

6. <u>His</u> poetry, <u>when</u> it was carefully examined, showed <u>characteristics</u> not unlike   6.____
   A   B   C
<u>Wordsworth</u>. <u>No error</u>
    D   E

7. <u>In my opinion</u>, based upon long years of research, <u>I think</u> the plan offered by   7.____
       A   B
my opponent is <u>unsound</u>, because it is not <u>founded</u> on true facts. <u>No error</u>
                C   D   E

2 (#1)

8. The soldiers of <u>Washington's</u> army at Valley Forge <u>were</u> men ragged in
                            A   B
<u>appearance</u> but <u>who were</u> noble in character. <u>No error</u>
   C   D   E

9. Rabbits <u>have a distrust</u> of man <u>due to</u> the fact <u>that</u> they are <u>so often</u> shot.
                A   B   C   D
<u>No error</u>
  E

10. <u>This</u> is the man <u>who</u> I believe <u>is</u> best <u>qualified</u> for the position. <u>No error</u>
    A   B   C   D   E

11. Her voice was <u>not only</u> <u>good</u>, but <u>she</u> also very clearly <u>enunciated</u>.
                    A   B   C   D
<u>No error</u>
  E

12. <u>Today he</u> is wearing a <u>different</u> suit <u>than</u> the <u>one</u> he wore yesterday. <u>No error</u>
      A   B   C   D   E

13. Our work <u>is</u> to improve the club; if anybody <u>must</u> resign, let it <u>not</u> be you or <u>I</u>.
            A   B   C   D
<u>No error</u>
  E

14. There was so much talking <u>in back of</u> me <u>as</u> I <u>could</u> not <u>enjoy</u> the music.
                                     A   B   C   D
<u>No error</u>
  E

15. <u>Being that</u> he is that <u>kind of</u> <u>boy</u>, he cannot be blamed <u>for</u> the mistake.
    A   B   C   D
<u>No error</u>
  E

16. <u>The king, having read</u> the speech, <u>he</u> and the <u>queen</u> <u>departed</u>. <u>No error</u>
                A   B   C   D   E

17. I <u>am</u> <u>so tired</u> I <u>can't</u> <u>scarcely</u> stand. <u>No error</u>
   A   B   C   D   E

18. We are <u>mailing bills</u> to our customers <u>in Canada</u>, and, <u>being</u> eager to
                A   B   C
clear our books before the new season opens, it is <u>to be hoped</u> they will
                                                                           D
send their remittances promptly. <u>No error</u>
                                       E

19. I reluctantly acquiesced to the proposal. No error   19.____
    A   B   C   D   E

20. It had lain out in the rain all night. No error   20.____
    A   B   C   D   E

21. If he would have gone there, he would have seen a marvelous sight.   21.____
           A   B   C   D
    No error
    E

22. The climate of Asia Minor is somewhat like Utah. No error   22.____
                 A   B   C   D   E

23. If everybody did unto others as they would wish others to do unto them, this   23.____
       A   B   C   D
    world would be a paradise. No error
                                E

24. This was the jockey whom I saw was most likely to win the race. No error   24.____
    A   B   C   D   E

25. The only food the general demanded was potatoes. No error   25.____
        A   B   C   D   E

KEY (CORRECT ANSWERS)

1.	C	11.	C
2.	A	12.	C
3.	B	13.	D
4.	B	14.	B
5.	C	15.	A
6.	D	16.	A
7.	B	17.	C
8.	D	18.	C
9.	B	19.	E
10.	E	20.	E

21.	A
22.	D
23.	D
24.	B
25.	E

TEST 2

DIRECTIONS: In each of the sentences below, four portions are underlined and lettered. Read each sentence and decide whether any of the UNDERLINED parts contains an error in spelling, punctuation, or capitalization, or employs grammatical usage which would be inappropriate for carefully written English. If so, note the letter printed under the unacceptable form and indicate this choice in the space at the right. If all four of the underlined portions are acceptable as they stand, select the answer E. (No sentence contains more than ONE unacceptable form.)

1. A party <u>like</u> <u>that</u> <u>only</u> <u>comes</u> once a year. <u>No error</u>
         A   B   C   D   E

1.____

2. <u>Our's</u> <u>is</u> <u>a</u> <u>swift moving</u> age. <u>No error</u>
   A   B C   D   E

2.____

3. The <u>healthy</u> climate soon <u>restored</u> him <u>to</u> his <u>accustomed</u> vigor. <u>No error</u>
        A   B   C   D   E

3.____

4. <u>They</u> needed six typists and hoped that <u>only</u> that <u>many</u> <u>would</u> apply for the position. <u>No error</u>
    A   B   C   D
                 E

4.____

5. He <u>interviewed</u> people <u>whom</u> he thought had <u>something</u> <u>to impart</u>. <u>No error</u>
         A   B   C   D   E

5.____

6. <u>Neither</u> of his three sisters <u>is</u> older <u>than</u> <u>he</u>. <u>No error</u>
    A   B   C D   E

6.____

7. <u>Since</u> he is <u>that</u> <u>kind</u> <u>of</u> <u>a</u> boy, he cannot be expected to cooperate with us. <u>No error</u>
    A   B   C   D   E

7.____

8. When <u>passing</u> <u>through</u> the tunnel, the air pressure <u>affected</u> <u>our</u> years. <u>No error</u>
         A   B   C   D   E

8.____

9. <u>The story having</u> a sad ending, <u>it</u> never <u>achieved</u> popularity <u>among</u> the students. <u>No error</u>
        A   B   C   D
          E

9.____

10. <u>Since</u> we are both hungry, <u>shall</u> we go <u>somewhere</u> for lunch? <u>No error</u>
     A   B   C   D E

10.____

2 (#2)

11. <u>Will</u> you please <u>bring</u> this book <u>down to</u> the library and give it to my friend<u>,</u>
    A   B   C   D
    who is waiting for it? <u>No error</u>
                              E

12. You <u>may</u> <u>have</u> the book; I <u>am</u> finished <u>with</u> it. <u>No error</u>
         A   B   C   D   E

13. I <u>don't</u> know <u>if</u> I <u>should</u> mention <u>it</u> to her or not. <u>No error</u>
       A   B   C   D   E

14. Philosophy is not <u>a subject</u> <u>which</u> <u>has to do</u> with philosophers and
                       A   B   C
    mathematics <u>only</u>. <u>No error</u>
                 D   E

15. The thoughts of the scholar <u>in his library</u> are little different <u>than</u> the old woman
                                 A   B
    who first said, <u>"It's</u> no use crying over spilt milk.<u>"</u> <u>No error</u>
                     C   D   E

16. A complete <u>system</u> of philosophical ideas <u>are</u> <u>implied</u> in many simple
                A   B   C
    <u>utterances</u>. <u>No error</u>
     D   E

17. Even <u>if</u> one has never put <u>them</u> into words, <u>his</u> ideas <u>compose</u> a kind of a
          A   B   C   D
    philosophy. <u>No error</u>
                 E

18. Perhaps it <u>is</u> <u>well enough</u> that most <u>people</u> do not attempt this <u>formulation</u>.
                A   B   C   D
    <u>No error</u>
     E

19. <u>Leading their</u> ordered lives, this <u>confused</u> <u>body</u> of ideas and feelings <u>is</u>
     A   B   C   D
    sufficient. <u>No error</u>
                 E

20. Why <u>should</u> we <u>insist upon</u> <u>them</u> <u>formulating</u> it? <u>No error</u>
         A   B   C   D   E

21. <u>Since</u> it includes <u>something</u> of the wisdom of the ages, it is <u>adequate</u> for the
     A   B   C
    <u>purposes</u> of ordinary life. <u>No error</u>
     D   E

22. Therefore, I <u>have sought</u> to make a pattern <u>of mine</u>, <u>and so</u> there were, early   22.____
         A   B   C
moments of <u>my trying</u> to find out what were the elements with which I had to
              D
deal. <u>No error</u>
           E

23. I <u>wanted</u> <u>to get</u> <u>what</u> knowledge I <u>could</u> about the general structure of the   23.____
       A   B   C   D
universe. <u>No error</u>
              E

24. I wanted to <u>know</u> <u>if</u> life <u>per se</u> had any meaning or <u>whether</u> I must strive to give   24.____
                  A   B   C   D
it one. <u>No error</u>
              E

25. <u>So,</u> in a <u>desultory</u> way, I <u>began</u> <u>to read</u>. <u>No error</u>   25.____
      A   B   C   D   E

KEY (CORRECT ANSWERS)

1. C
2. A
3. A
4. C
5. B

6. A
7. D
8. A
9. A
10. E

11. B
12. C
13. B
14. D
15. B

16. B
17. A
18. C
19. A
20. D

21. E
22. C
23. C
24. B
25. E

WRITTEN ENGLISH EXPRESSION
EXAMINATION SECTION
TEST 1

DIRECTIONS: In each of the sentences below, four portions are underlined and lettered. Read each sentence and decide whether any of the underlined parts contains an error in spelling, punctuation, or capitalization, or employs grammatical usage which would be inappropriate for carefully written English. If so, note the letter printed under the unacceptable form and print it in the space at the right. If all four of the underlined portions are acceptable as they stand, print the letter E. No sentences contains more than one unacceptable form.

1. A low ceiling <u>is</u> <u>when</u> the atmospheric conditions <u>make</u> <u>flying</u> inadvisable. 1._____
               A B   C   D

2. <u>They</u> couldn't <u>tell</u> <u>who</u> the card was <u>from</u>. 2._____
   A   B C   D

3. No one <u>but</u> you and <u>I</u> <u>are</u> <u>to help</u> them. 3._____
          A   B C D

4. To <u>him</u> <u>fall</u> the <u>duties</u> of <u>foster parent</u>. 4._____
      A. B.   C   D

5. If the word <u>should</u> somehow find peace <u>within itself</u>, so that all <u>her</u> people 5._____
             A   B   C
<u>would</u> stop fighting everlastingly…that would be the day!
D

6. <u>Everyone</u> of the <u>teachers</u> prepared <u>his</u> lesson in a <u>consummate</u> manner. 6._____
   A   B   C   D

7. <u>Didn't</u> <u>they</u> <u>used</u> to <u>pay</u> promptly? 7._____
   A   B   C   D

8. The services <u>rendered</u> by these people and <u>their</u> share <u>in making</u> the work a 8._____
               A   B   C
success <u>is</u> to be commended.
D

9. <u>They</u> <u>couldn't</u> tell <u>whom</u> the cable was <u>recieved</u> from… 9._____
   A   B   C   D

10. We like <u>these</u> <u>better</u> than <u>those</u> <u>kind</u>. 10._____
          A   B   C   D

11. It is a test of you more than I.
    A   B   C   D

12. The person in charge being him there can be no change in policy.
        A   B   C   D

13. A large amount of information and news are to be found there.
      A   B   C   D

14. I should have liked to have seen it again.
        A   B   C D

15. The desire to travel made him restless.
               A   B   C   D

16. Should that effect their decision?
    A   B   C   D

17. Do as we do for the celebration of the childrens' event.
    A B   C   D

18. Do either of you care to join us?
    A B   C   D

19. A child's food requirements differ from the adult.
      A   B   C   D

20. A large family, including two uncles and four grandparents live at the hotel.
            A   B   C   D

21. If they would have done that, they might have succeeded.
              A   B   C   D

22. Neither the hot days or the humid nights annoy our Southern visitor.
       A   B   C   D

23. Some people do not gain favor because they are kind of tactless.
      A   B   C   D

24. No sooner had the turning point come than a new embarassing issue arose.
        A   B   C   D

25. An usher seldom rises above a theatre manager.
             A   B   C   D

KEY (CORRECT ANSWERS)

1. B
2. C
3. B
4. E
5. C

6. D
7. C
8. D
9. D
10. C

11. D
12. C
13. C
14. B
15. E

16. B
17. D
18. A
19. D
20. C

21. A
22. B
23. D
24. D
25. C

TEST 2

DIRECTIONS: In each of the sentences below, four portions are underlined and lettered. Read each sentence and decide whether any of the underlined parts contains an error in spelling, punctuation, or capitalization, or employs grammatical usage which would be inappropriate for carefully written English. If so, note the letter printed under the unacceptable form and print it in the space at the right. If all four of the underlined portions are acceptable as they stand, print the letter E. No sentences contains more than one unacceptable form.

1. The <u>epic,</u> "Gone With the Wind<u>,"</u> deals with events that <u>ocurred</u> during the Civil War <u>era</u>.
      A   B   C   D

   1.____

2. <u>Shall</u> you <u>be at home,</u> <u>let us say</u>, on Sunday at two o'clock?
     A   B   C   D

   2.____

3. We <u>see</u> Mr. <u>Lewis'</u> <u>take</u> his car <u>out of the garage</u> daily.
       A   B   C   D

   3.____

4. We <u>have</u> <u>no</u> place <u>to keep</u> our rubbers, <u>only</u> in the hall closet.
       A B   C   D

   4.____

5. <u>Isn't it</u> true <u>what</u> <u>you</u> <u>told</u> me about the best way to prepare for an examination?
      A   B   C D

   5.____

6. "<u>Who</u> <u>shall</u> I say called," the butler <u>asked</u> <u>?</u>
     A   B   C D

   6.____

7. The museum <u>is</u> often visited by students who <u>are</u> fond of <u>Primitive</u> paintings, and by <u>patent</u> attorneys.
               A   B   C

   7.____

8. I <u>rose</u> <u>to nominate</u> the <u>superintendant,</u> the man <u>who</u> most of us felt was the best.
     A   B   C   D

   8.____

9. The child <u>was</u> sent to the store to <u>purchase</u> a bottle of milk and <u>brought</u> home fresh rolls, <u>too</u>.
           A   B   C

   9.____

10. The garden tool <u>was sent</u> <u>to be sharpened</u> and a new handle <u>to be</u> <u>put on</u>.
                    A   B   C D

    10.____

11. At the end of her vacation, Joan came home with little money, nevertheless, 11.____
                                                          A   B   C
    it was a joyous occasion.
                   D

12. We people have opportunities to show the rest of the world how real 12.____
        A   B
    democracy functions and leads to the perfectability of man.
                              C   D

13. The guide paddled along and then fell into a reverie where he related the 13.____
                                       A   B   C   D
    history of the region.

14. We should have investigated the cause of the noise in the Hotel by bringing 14.____
           A   B   C   D
    the car to a halt.

15. The first few strokes of the brush were enough to convince me that Tom 15.____
                                   A   B
    could paint much better than me.
               C   D

16. We inquired whether we could see the owner of the store, after we waited 16.____
                A   B   C
    for one hour.
       D

17. The irratation of the high-strung parent was aggravated by the slightest 17.____
          A   B   C
    noise that the baby made.
                        D

18. There is a large demand for men interested in the field of Information Retrieval. 18.____
          A B   C   D

19. Snow after the rains delay the coming crops. 19.____
     A   B   C   D

20. They intend to partially do away with ceremonies. 20.____
      A   B C   D

21. If that be done and turns out badly we shall see horror. 21.____
     A   B   C   D

22. The new plant is to be electrically lighted; increasing brightness by 50%. 22.____
            A   B   C D

23. The reason the speaker was offended was that the audience was inattentive.　　23._____
　　　　　A　　　　　　　　　　　　　B　　C　　　　　　　D

24. There appear to be conditions that govern the behavioral Sciences.　　24._____
　　　　　　A　　B　　　　　　　　C　　　　　　　　　　D

25. Either of the men are influential enough to control the situation.　　25._____
　　　A　　　　　　　B　　　　　　　C　　　D

KEY (CORRECT ANSWERS)

1.	C		11.	A
2.	E		12.	D
3.	B		13.	C
4.	D		14.	C
5.	B		15.	D
6.	D		16.	C
7.	C		17.	A
8.	C		18.	D
9.	C		19.	C
10.	C		20.	E

21.	C
22.	C
23.	E
24.	D
25.	B

TEST 3

DIRECTIONS: In each of the sentences below, four portions are underlined and lettered. Read each sentence and decide whether any of the underlined parts contains an error in spelling, punctuation, or capitalization, or employs grammatical usage which would be inappropriate for carefully written English. If so, note the letter printed under the unacceptable form and print it in the space at the right. If all four of the underlined portions are acceptable as they stand, print the letter E. No sentences contains more than one unacceptable form.

1. <u>Who</u> <u>did</u> you predict <u>would win</u> the election <u>this</u> year?   1._____
   A   B   C   D

2. <u>It</u> takes a <u>lot</u> <u>more</u> effort <u>to sell</u> houses this year than last year.   2._____
   A   B C   D

3. <u>Having pranced</u> into the arena <u>with little grace and unsteady hoof</u>   3._____
        A   B
<u>for the jumps ahead,</u> <u>the driver reined his horse</u>.
       C   D

4. Once the dog wagged <u>it's</u> tail, <u>you</u> knew <u>it</u> <u>was</u> a friendly animal.   4._____
                              A   B   C D

5. The record of the winning team was <u>among</u> the <u>most</u> <u>noteworthy</u>   5._____
                                          A   B   C
<u>of the season</u>.
    D

6. <u>When</u> <u>asked</u> to choose corn, cabbage, <u>or</u> potatoes, the diner selected the   6._____
   A   B   C
<u>latter</u>.
  D

7. The maid <u>wasn't</u> <u>so</u> small <u>that</u> she <u>couldn't</u> reach the top window for cleaning.   7._____
                A   B   C   D

8. Many people <u>feel</u> that powdered coffee <u>produces</u> a <u>really</u> <u>abhorent</u> flavor.   8._____
               A   B   C   D

9. <u>Would you mind</u> <u>me</u> <u>trying</u> that coat on for <u>size</u>?   9._____
      A   B C   D

10. This chair <u>looks</u> <u>much</u> <u>different</u> <u>than</u> the chair we selected in the store.   10._____
            A   B   C   D

11. After <u>trying</u> unsuccessfully <u>to land</u> a <u>job</u> in the city, Will <u>settled</u> in the   11._____
       A   B   C   D
country on a farm.

12. On the last attempt, the pole-vaulter <u>came</u> <u>nearly</u> <u>to getting</u> <u>hurt.</u>   12.____
                                                        A   B   C   D

13. The <u>observance</u> of <u>armistice day</u> <u>throughout the world</u> offers an opportunity   13.____
            A   B   C
<u>to reflect</u> on the horrors of war.
D

14. <u>Outside of</u> the mistakes in spelling, the child's letter <u>was</u> a <u>very</u> good <u>one.</u>   14.____
    A   B   C   D

15. <u>Scisors</u> <u>are</u> always dangerous <u>for</u> a child to <u>handle.</u>   15.____
    A   B   C   D

16. I assure <u>you</u> <u>that</u> I <u>will not yield</u> to pressure <u>to sell</u> my interest.   16.____
             A B   C   D

17. Ask <u>him</u> <u>if</u> he <u>recalls</u> the incident which <u>took place</u> at our first meeting.   17.____
       A B   C   D

18. The manager <u>felt</u> <u>like as not to order</u> his <u>usher-captain</u> <u>to surrender</u> his   18.____
                          A   B   C   D
uniform.

19. The mother of the bride <u>climaxed</u> the <u>occasion</u> <u>by exclaiming,</u> "I want my   19.____
                                   A   B   C
children <u>should</u> be happy forever."
         D

20. We <u>read</u> <u>in the papers</u> <u>where</u> the prospects for peace <u>are</u> improving.   20.____
      A   B   C   D

21. "<u>Can I share</u> the <u>cab</u> with you?" <u>was</u> frequently heard during the period of   21.____
    A   B   C   D
gas rationing.

22. <u>Had</u> the police <u>suspected</u> the ruse, they <u>would have taken</u> <u>relevant</u>   22.____
    A   B   C   D
precautions.

23. The teacher admonished the <u>other</u> students <u>neither</u> to speak to John, <u>nor</u>   23.____
                             A   B   C
<u>should they</u> annoy him.
   D

24. Fortunately, <u>we had been told</u> <u>that</u> there was <u>but</u> one <u>availible</u> service   24.____
                  A   B   C   D
station in that area.

25. We haven't hardly enough time to make it.   25. ____
        A   B   C   D

KEY (CORRECT ANSWERS)

1.	E	11.	B
2.	B	12.	B
3.	D	13.	B
4.	A	14.	A
5.	E	15.	A
6.	D	16.	E
7.	B	17.	B
8.	D	18.	B
9.	B	19.	D
10.	A	20.	C

21. A
22. D
23. D
24. D
25. A

TEST 4

DIRECTIONS: In each of the sentences below, four portions are underlined and lettered. Read each sentence and decide whether any of the underlined parts contains an error in spelling, punctuation, or capitalization, or employs grammatical usage which would be inappropriate for carefully written English. If so, note the letter printed under the unacceptable form and print it in the space at the right. If all four of the underlined portions are acceptable as they stand, print the letter E. No sentences contains more than one unacceptable form.

1. He <u>either</u> <u>will fail</u> in his attempt <u>or</u> will seek other <u>Government</u> employment.
       A   B   C   D   1.____

2. <u>After</u> each side <u>gave</u> <u>their</u> version, the case <u>was</u> closed.   2.____
    A   B C   D

3. <u>Every</u> <u>one</u> of the cars <u>were</u> <u>tagged</u> by the police.   3.____
    A   B   C   D

4. They <u>can't</u> <u>seem</u> <u>to see</u> <u>it</u> when I explain the theory.   4.____
        A   B   C D

5. <u>It</u> is difficult <u>to find</u> the genuine signature <u>between</u> all <u>those</u> submitted.   5.____
   A   B   C   D

6. She can't understand why <u>they</u> <u>don't remember</u> <u>who</u> to give the letter <u>to</u>.   6.____
                                 A   B   C   D

7. <u>Every</u> <u>man and woman</u> in America <u>is</u> interested in <u>his</u> tax bill.   7.____
    A   B   C   D

8. A guard <u>was called</u> <u>to prevent</u> <u>them</u> <u>carrying away</u> souvenirs.   8.____
            A   B   C   D

9. <u>Neither</u> you <u>nor</u> <u>I</u> <u>am</u> to blame for the sudden slump in business.   9.____
    A   B C D

10. To <u>you</u> and <u>him</u> <u>belong</u> the <u>credit</u>.   10.____
        A   B   C   D

11. The auctioneer had <u>less</u> items to <u>sell</u> this year <u>than</u> last <u>year</u>.   11.____
                         A   B   C   D

12. <u>Theirs</u> <u>instead of</u> <u>his</u> instructions <u>will be followed</u>.   12.____
      A   B   C   D

13. <u>It</u> is the <u>same</u> at his local <u>broker's</u> Frank <u>Smith</u>.   13.____
     A   B   C   D

14. The teacher politely requested each pupil to step in the room. 14._____
               A   B   C   D

15. Too many parents leave their children do as they please. 15._____
      A   B   C   D

16. He arrived safe, his papers untouched, his composure unruffled. 16._____
     A   B   C   D

17. I do not have any faith in John running for office. 17._____
       A   B   C   D

18. The musicians began to play tunefully ; keeping the proper tempo indicated 18._____
                                         A   B   C   D
    for the selection.

19. Mary's maid of honor bought the kind of an outfit suitable for an afternoon 19._____
      A   B C D
    wedding.

20. After the debate, every one of the Speakers realized that, given another 20._____
                       A   B   C
    chance, he could have done better.
                  D

21. The reason given by the physician for the patient's trouble was because of 21._____
             A   B   C
    his poor eating habits.
                   D

22. The fog was so thick that the driver couldn't hardly see more than ten feet 22._____
               A   B   C
    ahead.
      D

23. I suggest that you present the medal to who you deem best. 23._____
                   A   B   C   D

24. A decision made by a man without much deliberation is sometimes no 24._____
                              A   B
    different than a slow one.
         C   D

25. By the time Jones graduates from Dental School, he will be twenty-six years 25._____
      A   B   C   D
    of age.

KEY (CORRECT ANSWERS)

1.	D		11.	A
2.	C		12.	A
3.	C		13.	D
4.	C		14.	D
5.	C		15.	B
6.	C		16.	D
7.	E		17.	C
8.	C		18.	B
9.	E		19.	C
10.	C		20.	B

21. C
22. B
23. B
24. D
25. C

TEST 5

Questions 1-18.

DIRECTIONS: Each of the sentences numbered 1 through 18 may be classified most appropriately under one of the following three categories:
    A. faulty because of incorrect grammar
    B. faulty because of incorrect punctuation
    C. correct
Examine each sentence carefully. Then, in the space at the right, print the letter preceding the option which is BEST of those suggested above. All incorrect sentences contain but one type of error. Consider a sentence correct if it contains none of the types of errors mentioned, even though there may be other correct ways of expressing the same thought.

1. He sent the notice to the clerk who you hired yesterday.   1._____

2. It must be admitted, however that you were not informed of this change.   2._____

3. Only the employees who have served in this grade for at least two years are eligible for promotion.   3._____

4. The work was divided equally between she and Mary.   4._____

5. He thought that you were not available at that time.   5._____

6. When the messenger returns; please give him this package.   6._____

7. The new secretary prepared, typed, addressed, and delivered, the notices.   7._____

8. Walking into the room, his desk can be seen at the rear.   8._____

9. Although John has worked here longer than she, he produces a smaller amount of work.   9._____

10. She said she could of typed this report yesterday.   10._____

11. Neither one of these procedures are adequate for the efficient performance of this task.   11._____

12. The typewriter is the tool of the typist; the cash register, the tool of the cashier.   12._____

13. "The assignment must be completed as soon as possible" said the supervisor.   13._____

14. As you know, office handbooks are issued to all new employees.   14._____

15. Writing a speech is sometimes easier than to deliver it before an audience.   15._____

123

16. Mr. Brown our accountant, will audit the accounts next week.   16._____

17. Give the assignment to whomever is able to do it most efficiently.   17._____

18. The supervisor expected either your or I to file these reports.   18._____

Questions 19-28.

DIRECTIONS: Each of the following sentences may be classified most appropriately under one of the following four categories:
- A. faulty because of incorrect grammar
- B. faulty because of incorrect punctuation
- C. faulty because of incorrect spelling
- D. correct

Examine each sentence carefully. Then, in the space at the right, print the letter preceding the option which is BEST of those suggested above. All incorrect sentences contain but one type of error. Consider a sentence correct if it contains none of the types of errors mentioned, even though there may be other correct ways of expressing the same thought.

19. The fire apparently started in the storeroom, which is usually locked.   19._____

20. On approaching the victim two bruises were noticed by the officer.   20._____

21. The officer, who was there examined the report with great care.   21._____

22. Each employee in the office had a separate desk.   22._____

23. All employees including members of the clerical staff, were invited to the lecture.   23._____

24. The suggested procedure is similar to the one now in use.   24._____

25. No one was more pleased with the new procedure than the chauffeur.   25._____

26. He tried to pursuade her to change the procedure.   26._____

27. The total of the expenses charged to petty cash were high.   27._____

28. An understanding between him and I was finally reached.   28._____

KEY (CORRECT ANSWERS)

1.	A	11.	A	21.	B
2.	B	12.	C	22.	C
3.	C	13.	B	23.	B
4.	A	14.	C	24.	D
5.	C	15.	A	25.	D
6.	B	16.	B	26.	C
7.	B	17.	A	27.	A
8.	A	18.	A	28.	A
9.	C	19.	D		
10.	A	20.	A		

WRITTEN ENGLISH EXPRESSION
EXAMINATION SECTION
TEST 1

DIRECTIONS: In each of the following groups of sentences, one of the four sentences is faulty in grammar, punctuation, or capitalization. Select the INCORRECT sentence in each case. *PRINT THE LETTER OF THE CORRECT ANSWER IN THE SPACE AT THE RIGHT.*

1.
   A. If you had stood at home and done your homework, you would not have failed in arithmetic.
   B. Her affected manner annoyed every member of the audience.
   C. How will the new law affect our income taxes?
   D. The plants were not affected by the long, cold winter, but they succumbed to the drought of summer.

   1.____

2.
   A. He is one of the most able men who have been in the Senate.
   B. It is he who is to blame for the lamentable mistake.
   C. Haven't you a helpful suggestion to make at this time?
   D. The money was robbed from the blind man's cup.

   2.____

3.
   A. The amount of children in this school is steadily increasing.
   B. After taking an apple from the table, she went out to play.
   C. He borrowed a dollar from me.
   D. I had hoped my brother would arrive before me.

   3.____

4.
   A. Whom do you think I hear from every week?
   B. Who do you think is the right man for the job?
   C. Who do you think I found in the room?
   D. He is the man whom we considered a good candidate for the presidency.

   4.____

5.
   A. Quietly the puppy laid down before the fireplace.
   B. You have made your bed; now lie in it.
   C. I was badly sunburned because I had lain too long in the sun.
   D. I laid the doll on the bed and left the room.

   5.____

6.
   A. Sailing down the bay was a thrilling experience for me.
   B. He was not consulted about your joining the club.
   C. This story is different than the one I told you yesterday.
   D. There is no doubt about his being the best player.

   6.____

7. A. He maintains there is but one road to world peace.
    B. It is common knowledge that a child sees much he is not supposed to see.
    C. Much of the bitterness might have been avoided if arbitration had been restored to earlier in the meeting.
    D. The man decided it would be advisable to marry a girl somewhat younger than him.

8. A. In this book, the incident I liked least is where the hero tries to put out the forest fire.
    B. Learning a foreign language will undoubtedly give a person a better understanding of his mother tongue.
    C. His actions made us wonder what he planned to do next.
    D. Because of the war, we were unable to travel during the summer vacation.

9. A. The class had no sooner become interested in the lesson than the dismissal bell rang.
    B. There is little agreement about the kind of world to be planned at the peace conference.
    C. "Today," said the teacher, "we shall read 'The Wind in the Willows.' I am sure you'll like it."
    D. The terms of the legal settlement of the family quarrel handicapped both sides for many years.

10. A. I was so surprised that I was not able to say a word.
    B. She is taller than any other member of the class.
    C. It would be much more preferable if you were never seen in his company.
    D. We had no choice but to excuse her for being late.

KEY (CORRECT ANSWERS)

1. A   6. C
2. D   7. D
3. A   8. A
4. C   9. C
5. A   10. C

TEST 2

DIRECTIONS: In each of the following groups of sentences, one of the four sentences is faulty in grammar, punctuation, or capitalization. Select the INCORRECT sentence in each case. *PRINT THE LETTER OF THE CORRECT ANSWER IN THE SPACE AT THE RIGHT.*

1. A. Please send me these data at the earliest opportunity.
   B. The loss of their material proved to be a severe handicap.
   C. My principal objection to this plan is that it is impracticable.
   D. The doll had laid in the rain for an hour and was ruined.

   1.____

2. A. The garden scissors, left out all night in the rain, were in a badly rusted condition.
   B. The girls felt bad about the misunderstanding which had arisen.
   C. Sitting near the campfire, the old man told John and I about many exciting adventures he had had.
   D. Neither of us is in a position to undertake a task of that magnitude.

   2.____

3. A. The general concluded that one of the three roads would lead to the besieged city.
   B. The children didn't, as a rule, do hardly anything beyond what they were told to do.
   C. The reason the girl gave for her negligence was that she had acted on the spur of the moment.
   D. The daffodils and tulips look beautiful in that blue vase.

   3.____

4. A. If I was ten years older, I should be interested in this work.
   B. Give the prize to whoever has drawn the best picture.
   C. When you have finished reading the book, take it back to the library.
   D. My drawing is as good as or better than yours.

   4.____

5. A. He asked me whether the substance was animal or vegetable.
   B. An apple which is unripe should not be eaten by a child.
   C. That was an insult to me who am your friend.
   D. Some spy must of reported the matter to the enemy.

   5.____

6. A. Limited time makes quoting the entire message impossible.
   B. Who did she say was going?
   C. The girls in your class have dressed more dolls this year than we.
   D. There was such a large amount of books on the floor that I couldn't find a place for my rocking chair.

   6.____

7. A. What with his sleeplessness and his ill health, he was unable to assume any responsibility for the success of the meeting.
   B. If I had been born in February, I should be celebrating my birthday soon.
   C. In order to prevent breakage, she placed a sheet of paper between each of the plates when she packed them.
   D. After the spring shower, the violets smelled very sweet.

   7.____

8. A. He had laid the book down very reluctantly before the end of the lesson.
   B. The dog, I am sorry to say, had lain on the bed all night.
   C. The cloth was first lain on a flat surface; then it was pressed with a hot iron.
   D. While we were in Florida, we lay in the sun until we were noticeably tanned.

9. A. If John was in New York during the recent holiday season, I have no doubt he spent most of time with his parents.
   B. How could he enjoy the television program; the dog was barking and the baby was crying.
   C. When the problem was explained to the class, he must have been asleep.
   D. She wished that her new dress were finished so that she could go to the party.

10. A. The engine not only furnishes power but light and heat as well.
    B. You're aware that we've forgotten whose guilt was established, aren't you?
    C. Everybody knows that the woman made many sacrifices for her children.
    D. A man with his dog and gun is a familiar sight in this neighborhood.

KEY (CORRECT ANSWERS)

1. D   6. D
2. C   7. B
3. B   8. C
4. A   9. B
5. D   10. A

TEST 3

DIRECTIONS: Each of sentences 1 through 18 may be classified most appropriately under one of the following three categories:
A. faulty because of incorrect grammar
B. faulty because of incorrect punctuation
C. correct

Examine each sentence carefully. Then, in the space at the right, print the capital letter preceding the option which is BEST of the three suggested above. All incorrect sentences contain but one type of error. Consider a sentence correct if it contains none of the types of errors mentioned, even though there may be other correct ways of expressing the same thought.

1. He sent the notice to the clerk who you hired yesterday. 1.____
2. It must be admitted, however that you were not informed of this change. 2.____
3. Only the employees who have served in this grade for at least two years are eligible for promotion. 3.____
4. The work was divided equally between she and Mary. 4.____
5. He thought that you were not available at that time. 5.____
6. When the messenger returns; please give him this package. 6.____
7. The new secretary prepared, typed, addressed, and delivered, the notices. 7.____
8. Walking into the room, his desk can be seen at the rear. 8.____
9. Although John has worked here longer than she, he produces a smaller amount of work. 9.____
10. She said she could of typed this report yesterday. 10.____
11. Neither one of these procedures are adequate for the efficient performance of this task. 11.____
12. The typewriter is the tool of the typist; the cash register, the tool of the cashier. 12.____
13. "The assignment must be completed as soon as possible" said the supervisor. 13.____
14. As you know, office handbooks are issued to all new employees. 14.____
15. Writing a speech is sometimes easier than to deliver it before an audience. 15.____

16. Mr. Brown, our accountant, will audit the accounts next week.   16._____

17. Give the assignment to whomever is able to do it most efficiently.   17._____

18. The supervisor expected either your or I to file these reports.   18._____

KEY (CORRECT ANSWERS)

1.	A	11.	A
2.	B	12.	C
3.	C	13.	B
4.	A	14.	C
5.	C	15.	A
6.	B	16.	B
7.	B	17.	A
8.	A	18.	A
9.	C		
10.	A		

TEST 4

DIRECTIONS: Each sentence may be classified most appropriately under one of the following four categories:
    A. faulty because of incorrect grammar
    B. faulty because of incorrect punctuation
    C. faulty because of incorrect spelling
    D. correct

Examine each sentence carefully. Then, in the space at the right, print the capital letter preceding the BEST of the four suggested above. All incorrect sentences contain but one type of error. Consider a sentence correct if it contains none of the types of errors mentioned, even though there may be other correct ways of expressing the same thought.

1. The fire apparently started in the storeroom, which is usually locked.   1.____
2. On approaching the victim two bruises were noticed by this officer.   2.____
3. The officer, who was there examined the report with great care.   3.____
4. Each employee in the office had a seperate desk.   4.____
5. All employees including members of the clerical staff, were invited to the lecture.   5.____
6. The suggested procedure is similar to the one now in use.   6.____
7. No one was more pleased with the new procedure than the chauffeur.   7.____
8. He tried to pursuade her to change the procedure.   8.____
9. The total of the expenses charged to petty cash were high.   9.____
10. An understanding between him and I was finally reached.   10.____

KEY (CORRECT ANSWERS)

1.	D		6.	D
2.	A		7.	D
3.	B		8.	C
4.	C		9.	A
5.	B		10.	A

TEST 5

Questions 1-5.

DIRECTIONS: Each of sentences 1 to 5 may be classified under one of the following four categories:
    A. faulty because of incorrect grammar
    B. faulty because of incorrect punctuation
    C. faulty because of incorrect capitalization or incorrect spelling
    D. correct
Examine each sentence carefully to determine under which of the above four options it is best classified. Then, in the space at the right, print the capital letter preceding the option which is the BEST of the four suggested above. Each faulty sentence contains but one type of error. Consider a sentence to be correct if it contains none of the types of errors mentioned, even though there may be other correct ways of expressing the same thought.

1. They told both he and I that the prisoner had escaped.   1.____

2. Any superior officer, who, disregards the just complaints of his subordinates, is remiss in the performance of his duty.   2.____

3. Only those members of the National organization who resided in the Middle West attended the conference in Chicago.   3.____

4. We told him to give the investigation assignment to whoever was available.   4.____

5. Please do not disappoint and embarass us by not appearing in court.   5.____

Questions 6-10.

DIRECTIONS: Each of questions 6 through 10 consists of a sentence. Read each sentence carefully and then write your answer to each question according to the following scheme:
    A. Sentence contains an error in spelling only
    B. Sentence contains an error in grammar or word usage only
    C. Sentence contains one error in spelling and one error in grammar or word usage
    D. Sentence is correct; contains no errors

6. Although the officer's speech proved to be entertaining, the topic was not relevant to the main theme of the conference.   6.____

7. In February all new officers attended a training course in which they were learned their principal duties and the fundamental operating procedures of the department.   7.____

8. I personally seen inmate Jones threaten inmates Smith and Green with bodily harm if they refused to participate in the plot.   8.____

9. To the layman, who on a chance visit to the prison observes everything functioning smoothly, the maintenance of prison discipline may seem to be a relatively easily realizable objective.   9.____

10. The prisoners in cell block fourty were forbidden to lay on the cell cots during the recreation hour.   10.____

KEY (CORRECT ANSWERS)

1.	A	6.	D
2.	B	7.	C
3.	C	8.	B
4.	D	9.	D
5.	C	10.	C

TEST 6

DIRECTIONS: Each of the following sentences may be classified under one of the following four categories:
    A. faulty because of incorrect grammar
    B. faulty because of incorrect punctuation
    C. faulty because of incorrect capitalization or incorrect spelling
    D. correct

Examine each sentence carefully to determine under which of the above four options it is best classified. Then, in the space at the right, print the capital letter preceding the option which is the BEST of the four suggested above. Each faulty sentence contains but one type of error. Consider a sentence to be correct if it contains none of the types of errors mentioned, even though there may be other correct ways of expressing the same thought.

1. I cannot encourage you any.
2. You always look well in those sort of clothes.
3. Shall we go to the park?
4. The man whome he introduced was Mr. Carey.
5. She saw the letter laying here this morning.
6. It should rain before the Afternoon is over.
7. They have already went home.
8. That Jackson will be elected is evident.
9. He does not hardly approve of us.
10. It was he, who won the prize.

KEY (CORRECT ANSWERS)

1. A   6. C
2. A   7. A
3. D   8. D
4. C   9. A
5. A   10. B

TEST 7

DIRECTIONS: Each of the following sentences may be classified under one of the following four categories:
    A. faulty because of incorrect grammar
    B. faulty because of incorrect punctuation
    C. faulty because of incorrect capitalization or incorrect spelling
    D. correct

Examine each sentence carefully to determine under which of the above four options it is best classified. Then, in the space at the right, print the capital letter preceding the option which is the BEST of the four suggested above. Each faulty sentence contains but one type of error. Consider a sentence to be correct if it contains none of the types of errors mentioned, even though there may be other correct ways of expressing the same thought.

1. Shall we go to the park.   1._____
2. They are, alike, in this particular.   2._____
3. They gave the poor man sume food when he knocked on the door.   3._____
4. I regret the loss caused by the error.   4._____
5. The students' will have a new teacher.   5._____
6. They sweared to bring out all the facts.   6._____
7. He decided to open a branch store on 33rd street.   7._____
8. His speed is equal and more than that of a racehorse.   8._____
9. He felt very warm on that Summer day.   9._____
10. He was assisted by his friend, who lives in the next house.   10._____

KEY (CORRECT ANSWERS)

1.	B	6.	A
2.	B	7.	C
3.	C	8.	A
4.	D	9.	C
5.	B	10.	D

TEST 8

DIRECTIONS: Each of the following sentences may be classified under one of the following four categories:
- A. faulty because of incorrect grammar
- B. faulty because of incorrect punctuation
- C. faulty because of incorrect capitalization or incorrect spelling
- D. correct

Examine each sentence carefully to determine under which of the above four options it is best classified. Then, in the space at the right, print the capital letter preceding the option which is the BEST of the four suggested above. Each faulty sentence contains but one type of error. Consider a sentence to be correct if it contains none of the types of errors mentioned, even though there may be other correct ways of expressing the same thought.

1. The climate of New York is colder than California. 1.____
2. I shall wait for you on the corner. 2.____
3. Did we see the boy who, we think, is the leader. 3.____
4. Being a modest person, John seldom talks about his invention. 4.____
5. The gang is called the smith street boys. 5.____
6. He seen the man break into the store. 6.____
7. We expected to lay still there for quite a while. 7.____
8. He is considered to be the Leader of his organization. 8.____
9. Although I recieved an invitation, I won't go. 9.____
10. The letter must be here some place. 10.____

KEY (CORRECT ANSWERS)

1. A   6. A
2. D   7. A
3. B   8. C
4. D   9. C
5. C   10. A

TEST 9

DIRECTIONS: Each of the following sentences may be classified under one of the following four categories:
- A. faulty because of incorrect grammar
- B. faulty because of incorrect punctuation
- C. faulty because of incorrect capitalization or incorrect spelling
- D. correct

Examine each sentence carefully to determine under which of the above four options it is best classified. Then, in the space at the right, print the capital letter preceding the option which is the BEST of the four suggested above. Each faulty sentence contains but one type of error. Consider a sentence to be correct if it contains none of the types of errors mentioned, even though there may be other correct ways of expressing the same thought.

1. I thought it to be he.   1.____
2. We expect to remain here for a long time.   2.____
3. The committee was agreed.   3.____
4. Two-thirds of the building are finished.   4.____
5. The water was froze.   5.____
6. Everyone of the salesmen must supply their own car.   6.____
7. Who is the author of Gone With The Wind?   7.____
8. He marched on and declaring that he would never surrender.   8.____
9. Who shall I say called?   9.____
10. Everyone has left but they.   10.____

KEY (CORRECT ANSWERS)

1.	A	6.	A
2.	D	7.	B
3.	A	8.	A
4.	A	9.	D
5.	A	10.	D

TEST 10

DIRECTIONS: Each of the following sentences may be classified under one of the following four categories:
- A. faulty because of incorrect grammar
- B. faulty because of incorrect punctuation
- C. faulty because of incorrect capitalization or incorrect spelling
- D. correct

Examine each sentence carefully to determine under which of the above four options it is best classified. Then, in the space at the right, print the capital letter preceding the option which is the BEST of the four suggested above. Each faulty sentence contains but one type of error. Consider a sentence to be correct if it contains none of the types of errors mentioned, even though there may be other correct ways of expressing the same thought.

1. Who did we give the order to?
2. Send your order in immediately.
3. I believe I paid the Bill.
4. I have not met but one person.
5. Why aren't Tom, and Fred, going to the dance?
6. What reason is there for him not going?
7. The seige of Malta was a tremendous event.
8. I was there yesterday I assure you.
9. Your ukulele is better than mine.
10. No one was there only Mary.

KEY (CORRECT ANSWERS)

1. A
2. D
3. C
4. A
5. B
6. A
7. C
8. B
9. C
10. A

WRITTEN ENGLISH EXPRESSION
EXAMINATION SECTION
TEST 1

DIRECTIONS: The following questions are designed to test your knowledge of grammar, sentence structure, correct usage, and punctuation. In each group, there is one sentence that contains an error. Select the letter of the INCORRECT sentence. *PRINT THE LETTER OF THE CORRECT ANSWER IN THE SPACE AT THE RIGHT.*

1.
   A. All things considered, he did unusually well.
   B. The poor boy takes everything too seriously.
   C. Our club sent two delegates, Ruth and I, to Oswego.
   D. I like him better than her.
   E. His eccentricities continually made good newspaper copy.

   1.____

2.
   A. If we except Benton, no one in the club foresaw the changes.
   B. The two-year-old rosebushes are loaded with buds—and beetles!
   C. Though the pitcher had been broken by the cat, Teena was furious.
   D. Virginia got the cake recipe off of her grandmother.
   E. Neither one of the twins was able to get a summer vacation.

   2.____

3.
   A. "What do you wish?" he asked, "may I help you?"
   B. Whose gloves are these?
   C. Has he drink all the orange juice?
   D. It was he who spoke to the manager of the store.
   E. Mary prefers this kind of evening dress.

   3.____

4.
   A. Charles himself said it before the assembled peers of the realm.
   B. The wind stirred the rose petals laying on the floor.
   C. The storm beat hard on the frozen windowpanes.
   D. Worn out by the days of exposure and storm, the sailor clung pitifully to the puny raft.
   E. The day afterward he thought more kindly of the matter.

   4.____

5.
   A. Between you and me, I think Henry is wrong.
   B. This is the more interesting of the two books.
   C. This is the most carefully written letter of all.
   D. During the opening course I read not only four plays but also three historical novels.
   E. This assortment of candies, nuts, and fruits are excellent.

   5.____

6.
   A. According to your report card, you are not so clever as he.
   B. If he had kept his eyes open, he would not have fallen into that trap.
   C. We were certain that the horse had broken it's leg.
   D. The troop of scouts and the leader are headed for the North Woods.
   E. I knew it to be him by the knock at the door.

   6.____

7. A. Being one of the earliest spring flowers, we welcome the crocus.
    B. The cold running water became colder as time sped on.
    C. Those boys need not have stood in line for lunch.
    D. Can you, my friend, donate ten dollars to the cause?
    E. Because it's a borrowed umbrella, return it in the morning.

8. A. If Walter would have planted earlier in the spring, the rosebushes would have survived.
    B. The flowers smell overpoweringly sweet.
    C. There are three *e*'s in dependent.
    D. May I be excused at the end of the test?
    E. Carl has three brothers-in-law.

9. A. We have bought neither the lumber nor the tools for the job.
    B. Jefferson was re-elected despite certain powerful opposition.
    C. The Misses Jackson were invited to the dance.
    D. The letter is neither theirs nor yours.
    E. The retail price for those items are far beyond the wholesale quotations.

10. A. To find peace of mind is to gain treasure beyond price.
    B. Fred is cheerful, carefree; his brother is morose.
    C. Whoever fails to understand the strategic importance of the Arctic fails to understand modern geography.
    D. They came promptly at 8 o'clock on August 7, 2020, without prior notification.
    E. Every one tried their best to guess the answer, but no one succeeded.

11. A. Is this hers or theirs?
    B. Having been recognized, Frank took the floor.
    C. Alex invited Sue; Paul, Marion; and Dan, Helen.
    D. If I were able to do the task, you can be sure that I'd do it.
    E. Stamp collecting, or philately as it is otherwise called is truly an international hobby.

12. A. He has proved himself to be reliable.
    B. The fisherman had arisen before the sun.
    C. By the time the truck arrived, I had put out the blaze.
    D. The doctor with his colleagues were engaged in consultation.
    E. I chose to try out a new method, but in spite of my efforts it failed.

13. A. He has drunk too much iced tea.
    B. I appreciated him doing that job for me.
    C. The royal family fled, but they were retaken.
    D. The secretary and the treasurer were both present on Friday,
    E. Iago protested his honesty, yet he continued to plot against Desdemona.

14. A. The family were all together at Easter.
    B. It is altogether too fine a day for us to stay indoors.
    C. However much you dislike him, you should treat him fairly.
    D. The judges were already there when the contestants arrived.
    E. The boy's mother reported that he was alright again after the accident.

    14._____

15. A. Ham and eggs is a substantial breakfast.
    B. By the end of the week the pond had frozen.
    C. I should appreciate any assistance you could offer me.
    D. Being that tomorrow is Sunday, we expect to close early.
    E. If he were to win the medal, I for one would be disturbed.

    15._____

16. A. Give the letter to whoever comes for it.
    B. He feels bad, but his sister is the one who looks sicker.
    C. He had an unbelievable large capacity for hard physical work.
    D. Earth has nothing more beautiful to offer than the autumn colors of this section of the country.
    E. Happily we all have hopes that the future will soon bring forth fruits of a lasting peace.

    16._____

17. A. This kind of apples is my favorite.
    B. Either of the players is capable of performing ably.
    C. Though trying my best to be calm, the choice was not an easy one for me.
    D. The nearest star is not several light years away; it is only 93,000,000 miles away.
    E. There were two things I still wished to do—to see the Lincoln Memorial and to climb up the Washington Monument.

    17._____

18. A. It is I who is to blame.
    B. That dress looks very good on Jane.
    C. People often take my brother to be me.
    D. I could but think she had deceived me.
    E. He himself told us that the story was true.

    18._____

19. A. They all went but Mabel and me.
    B. Has he ever swum across the river?
    C. We have a dozen other suggestions besides these.
    D. The Jones's are going to visit their friends in Chicago.
    E. The ideal that Arthur and his knights were in quest of was a better world order.

    19._____

20. A. Would I were able to be there with you!
    B. Whomever he desires to see should be admitted.
    C. It is not for such as we to follow fashion blindly.
    D. His causing the confusion seemed to affect him not at all.
    E. Please notify all those whom you think should have this information.

    20._____

21. A. She was not only competent but also friendly in nature.   21._____
    B. Not only must we visualize the play we are reading; we must actually hear it.
    C. The firm was not only acquiring a bad reputation but also indulging in illegal practices.
    D. The bank was not only uncooperative but also was indifferent to new business offered them.
    E. I know that a conscious effort was made not only to guard the material but also to keep it from being used.

22. A. How old shall you be on your next birthday?   22._____
    B. I am sure that he has been here and did what was expected of him.
    C. Near to the bank of the river, stood, secluded and still, the house of the hermit.
    D. Because of its efficacy in treating many ailments, penicillin has become an important addition to the druggist's stock.
    E. ROBINSON CRUSOE, which is a fairy tale to the child, is a work of social philosophy to the mature thinker.

23. A. We had no sooner started than it rained.   23._____
    B. The fact that the prisoner is a minor will be taken into consideration.
    C. Many parents think more of their older children than of their younger ones.
    D. The boy laid a book, a knife and a fishing line on the table.
    E. John is the tallest of any boy in his class.

24. A. Although we have been friend for many years, I must admit that May is most inconsiderate.   24._____
    B. He is not able to run, not even to walk.
    C. You will bear this pain as you have so many greater ones.
    D. The harder the work, the more studious she became.
    E. Too many "and's" in a sentence produce an immature style.

25. A. It would be preferable to have you submit questions after, not before, the lecture.   25._____
    B. Plan your work; then work your plan.
    C. At last John met his brother, who had been waiting two hours for him.
    D. Should one penalize ones self for not trying?
    E. There are other considerations besides this one.

KEY (CORRECT ANSWERS)

1.	C		11.	E
2.	D		12.	D
3.	A		13.	B
4.	B		14.	E
5.	E		15.	D
6.	C		16.	C
7.	A		17.	C
8.	A		18.	A
9.	E		19.	D
10.	E		20.	E

21. D
22. B
23. E
24. C
25. D

TEST 2

DIRECTIONS: The following questions are designed to test your knowledge of grammar, sentence structure, correct usage, and punctuation. In each group, there is one sentence that contains an error. Select the letter of the INCORRECT sentence. *PRINT THE LETTER OF THE CORRECT ANSWER IN THE SPACE AT THE RIGHT.*

1. A. "Halt!" cried the sentry, "Who goes there?"
    B. "It is in talk alone," said Robert Louis Stevenson, "that we can learn our period and ourselves."
    C. The world will long remember the "culture" of the Nazis.
    D. When duty says, "You must," the youth replies, "I can."
    E. Who said, "Give me liberty or give me death?"

    1.____

2. A. Why are you so quiet, Martha?
    B. Edward Jones, a banker who lives near us, expects to retire very soon.
    C. I picked up the solid-gold chain.
    D. Any boy, who refuses to tell the truth, will be punished.
    E. Yes, honey tastes sweet.

    2.____

3. A. I knew it to be him by the style of his clothes.
    B. No one saw him doing it.
    C. Her going away is a loss to the community.
    D. Mary objected to her being there.
    E. Illness prevented him graduating in June.

    3.____

4. A. Being tired, I stretched out on a grassy knoll.
    B. While we were rowing on the lake, a sudden squall almost capsized the boat.
    C. Entering the room, a strange mark on the floor attracted my attention.
    D. Mounting the curb, the empty car crossed the sidewalk and came to rest against a building.
    E. Sitting down, they watched him demonstrate his skill.

    4.____

5. A. The coming of peace effected a change in her way of life.
    B. Spain is as weak, if not weaker than, she was in 1900.
    C. In regard to that, I am not certain what my attitude will be.
    D. That unfortunate family faces the problem of adjusting itself to a new way of life.
    E. Fred Eastman states in his essay that one of the joys of reading lies in discovering courage.

    5.____

6. A. Not one in a thousand readers take the matter seriously.
    B. Let it lie there.
    C. You are not as tall as he.
    D. The people began to realize how much she had done.
    E. He was able partially to accomplish his purpose.

    6.____

2 (#2)

7.
  A. In the case of members who are absent, a special letter will be sent.
  B. The visitors were all ready to see it.
  C. I like Burns's poem "To a Mountain Daisy."
  D. John told William that he was sure he had seen it.
  E. Both men are Yale alumni.

  7._____

8.
  A. The audience took their seats promptly.
  B. Each boy and girl must finish his examination this morning.
  C. Every person turned their eyes toward the door.
  D. Everyone has his own opinion.
  E. The club nominated its officers by secret ballot.

  8._____

9.
  A. I can do that more easily than you.
  B. This kind of weather is more healthful.
  C. Pick out the really important points.
  D. Because of his aggressive nature, he only plays the hardest games.
  E. He pleaded with me to let him go.

  9._____

10.
  A. It is I who am mistaken.
  B. Is it John or Susie who stand at the head of the class?
  C. He is one of those who always do their lessons.
  D. He is a man on whom I can depend in time of trouble.
  E. Had he known who it was, he would have come.

  10._____

11.
  A. Somebody has forgotten his umbrella.
  B. Please let Joe and me use the car.
  C. We thought the author to be he.
  D. Whoever they send will be welcome.
  E. They thought the intruders were we.

  11._____

12.
  A. If I had known that you were coming, I should have met you.
  B. All the girls but her were at the game.
  C. I expected to have heard the concert before the present time.
  D. Walter would not have said it if he had thought it would make her unhappy.
  E. I have always believed that cork is the best material for insulation.

  12._____

13.
  A. Their contributions amounted to the no insignificant sum of ten thousand dollars.
  B. None of them was there.
  C. Ten dollars is the amount I agreed to pay.
  D. Fewer than one hundred persons assembled.
  E. Exactly what many others have done and are doing, Frank did.

  13._____

14.
  A. Neither Jane or her sister has arrived.
  B. Either Richard or his brother is going to drive.
  C. Refilling storage batteries is the work of the youngest employee.
  D. Helen has to lie still for two weeks.
  E. Mother lay down for an hour yesterday.

  14._____

15. A. He is not the man whom you saw entering the house.   15._____
    B. He asked why I wouldn't come.
    C. This is the cow whose horns are the longest.
    D. Helen, this is a man I met on the train one day last February.
    E. He greeted every foreign representative which came to the conference.

16. A. You, but not I, are invited.   16._____
    B. Guy's technique of service and return is masterly.
    C. Please pass me one of the books that are lying on the table.
    D. Mathematics is my most difficult subject.
    E. Unable to agree on a plan of organization, the class has departed in several directions.

17. A. He spoke to Gertrude and to me of the seriousness of the occasion.   17._____
    B. They seem to have decided to invite everyone except you and I.
    C. Your attitude is insulting to me who am your friend.
    D. He wished to know who our representative was.
    E. You may tell whomsoever you wish.

18. A. My favorite studies were Latin and science.   18._____
    B. The committee made its report.
    C. To get your work done promptly is better than leaving it until the last minute.
    D. That's what he would do if he were governor.
    E. He said that his chosen colors were red and blue.

19. A. Punish whoever disobeys orders.   19._____
    B. Come here, Henry; and sit with me.
    C. Has either of them his notebook?
    D. He talked as if he meant it.
    E. You did well; therefore you should be rewarded.

20. A. Many of us students were called to work.   20._____
    B. He shot the albatross with a crossbow.
    C. A house that is set on a hill is conspicuous.
    D. The wooden beams had raised slowly about a foot and then had settled back into place.
    E. Whom do you want to go with you?

21. A. He does not drive as he should.   21._____
    B. I can't hardly wait for the holidays.
    C. I like it less well than last week's.
    D. You were troubled by his coming.
    E. I don't know but that you are correct.

22. A. He was angry at both of us, her and me.   22._____
    B. When one enters the town, they see big crowds.
    C. They laid the tools on the ground every night.
    D. He is the only one of my friends who has written.
    E. He asked for a raise in wages.

23. A. None came with his excuse.
     B. Walking down the street, a house comes into view.
     C. "Never!" shouted the boy.
     D. Both are masters of their subject.
     E. His advice was to drive slowly.

24. A. There is both beef and lamb on the market.
     B. Either beans or beets are enough with potatoes.
     C. Where does your mother buy bananas?
     D. Dinners at the new restaurant are excellent.
     E. Each was rewarded according to his deeds.

25. A. Accordingly, we must prepare the food.
     B. The work, moreover, must be done today.
     C. Nevertheless, we must first have dinner.
     D. I always chose the most liveliest of the ponies.
     E. At six o'clock tomorrow the job will have been completed,

KEY (CORRECT ANSWERS)

1.	E		11.	C
2.	D		12.	C
3.	E		13.	A
4.	C		14.	A
5.	B		15.	E
6.	A		16.	E
7.	C		17.	B
8.	C		18.	C
9.	D		19.	B
10.	B		20.	D

21.	B
22.	B
23.	B
24.	A
25.	D

TEST 3

DIRECTIONS: In each group of five sentences below, one or more sentences contain an error in usage. Choose the lettered answer which indicates ALL the sentences containing errors in usage. *PRINT THE LETTER OF THE CORRECT ANSWER IN THE SPACE AT THE RIGHT.*

1. I. Shortly after the terms of the contract for the new road transpired, an aroused constituency showed its disapproval by voting the senator out of office.
    II. Neither father nor sons work for a living but spend their days in drinking and gambling at the pub.
    III. Like his Italian predecessor, Boccaccio, whose DECAMERON was used as a model, a company of people of various occupations and stations in life, brought together for a pilgrimage, are called upon to relate stories to help relieve the tedium of their journey,
    IV. Sarah hurried into the kitchen and after a half hour emerged with a nauseous brew which she called coffee.
    V. It was to the major that the people applied for redress and by his armed guards that they were driven away.
    The CORRECT answer is:
    A. I   B. III   C. I, II, III   D. IV, III   E. II, III

    1.____

2. I. As we approached the castle, which was illuminated suddenly by the full moon breaking through the clouds, we described a rider coming to meet us.
    II. The reason for his loss of interest in boxing, as far as I can see, was due to the pressure of his work and the distance of the local "Y" from his home.
    III. Accompanied by a handsome member of the British legation, Elsie was about to enter the luxuriously furnished salon to meet the countess.
    IV. In spite of all of John's gifts and attentions, little Rosalie, upon being asked to make a choice, said she liked me better than him.
    V. The scar of the clearing for the power line extended for a hundred miles over the mountains, and the great poles with fifty feet between each carried cable from Niagara to Albany.
    The CORRECT answer is:
    A. II, III   B. I, IV, III   C. I, II, IV, III
    D. II, V   E. III, V

    2.____

3. I. The high wind had blown the roofs of several houses; the water supply had been contaminated by the floods; transportation to the business center had ground to a half; but the mayor said there was no reason for alarm!
    II. Because there is a need to soften tragic or painful news, we resort to such euphuisms for the simple "to die" as "to pass away," "to go to a better world," or "to join the great majority."
    III. Hardly had the salient on the western shore of the river been obliterated than one on the eastern bank crossed on a pontoon bridge and in boats of all sorts.
    IV. The distinction between the man who gives in a spirit of charity and him who gives for social recognition is often to be seen in the nature of the gift.
    V. After a few months in office, the new superintendent effected many changes, not all of them for the good, in the administration of the plant.

    3.____

2 (#3)

The CORRECT answer is:
A. II, III   B. II, III, IV   C. III, IV   D. I, II, V   E. I, II, III

4. I. The defendants published an advertisement and notice giving information, directly and indirectly, stating where, how, and when, and by what means and what purports to be the said book can be purchased.
    II. In common with most Eskimos of her time, she had long spells of silence; and nature, while endowing her with immense sagacity, had thrust on her a compelling reticence.
    III. The entire report was read in less than half an hour to the full committee, giving no time for comment or question, and offered for vote.
    IV. Students going through this course almost always find themselves becoming critical of their own writing.
    V. In his report of 1968, Mr. Jones states that his chief problem is the rapid turnover of personnel which has prevailed to the moment of writing.
    The CORRECT answer is:
    A. I, IV   B. II, III   C. III, IV, V   D. I, IV, V   E. I, III

4._____

5. I. The material was destroyed after it had served our purposes, and after portions of it had been excluded and portions included in our report.
    II. We checked our results very carefully, too carefully perhaps, for we spent several hours on our task.
    III. We should keep constantly in mind the fact that writing has no purpose save to meet the needs of the reader.
    IV. Not even discussed in October, when Lathrop flew in from the Coast, the problem of expense was settled at the June meeting.
    V. Whether our facts were right or not, it was not necessary for you to rebuke him in such a discourteous manner.
    The CORRECT answer is:
    A. I only   B. I, IV   C. II, III   D. V only   E. I, V

5._____

6. I. At first the novel was interesting and liked by members of the class; but later the long reading assignments dampened the pupils' enthusiasm.
    II. Donnie had no love or confidence in his mother, who, when abandoned by her husband, put the boy in an orphanage and seldom went to visit him.
    III. Built during the Civil War, the house has a delicate air, supported as it is by iron columns and rimmed by an iron railing.
    IV. Recently a newspaper editor from the South returned from an eight-week trip through the Caribbean and made a number of recommendations on what we should do to counter the lack of accurate information about the United States.
    V. The need is to be candid about our problems, to be informed on what we are going about them, and to resolve them as expeditiously as possible.
    The CORRECT answer is:
    A. I, II   B. II, III   C. III, IV   D. I, V   E. I, III

6._____

7. I. "Man is flying too fast for a world that is round," he said. "Soon he will catch up with himself in a great rear-end collision."
    II. After the raid on the club, each of the men suspected of accepting racetrack bets, along with the owner of the club, were held for questioning at police headquarters.
    III. It seems to me that at the opening performance of the play the audience were of different opinions about its merit and about its chances for a long run.
    IV. Oak from the forests of Vermont and steel from the mills of Pittsburgh are the material of this magnificent modern structure.
    V. The machine is subjected to severe strains which it must withstand and at the same time work easily and rapidly.
    The CORRECT answer is:
    A. I, II B. II, III C. IV, V D. I, V E. II, V

8. I. We don't have to worry about cutting down on expenses; money is no object in this venture.
    II. And now, my dear, let you and I tell our guests of the plans we have for the future.
    III. For all his errors of the past, no one can or has said that he did not turn out on this occasion a perfectpiece of work.
    IV. Hercule Poirot, when looking for a suspect in the murder case never thought of its being me.
    V. During the interpellation the minister refused to answer any questions concerning his predecessor's conduct of the war.
    The CORRECT answer is:
    A. I, III B. I, IV, V C. II, III, IV D. III, IV E. II, III

9. I. John Steinbeck received the Nobel Prize only a few years ago for his work of the thirties, work, which now, according to some critics, has lost its timeliness and which never had timelessness.
    II. Respect is shown the flag by no matter when it is displayed, whether it be in the window of a private home or on the pole of a public building.
    III. When dinner was over we strolled through the garden and exclaimed at the beauty of the red gladioluses, the pride of the Jenkinses' gardener.
    IV. Mrs. Cosgrove's gift of $100,000 to the hospitals is only the latest of the many acts of generosity by which she has before now benefited her fellow men.
    V. Am I repeating your question exactly when I say, "How many of you are willing to join me in my attempt to rid America of the traitors who are threatening its freedom"?
    The CORRECT answer is:
    A. I, II, III, IV B. II, IV C. II, III, IV
    D. I, IV, V E. I, II, IV

10. I. Slashing the original 73 projects to 20 with little loss of subject matter in the consolidated schedule, a stalemate was avoided and the work of the Council speeded up.

II. I was particularly struck by the unselfishness of the American school children, many of whom willingly donating their allowances, because they felt that they should help the refugees.
III. As a result of Henry VIII's defiance of the Church of Rome, the ecclesiastical principle of government was substituted by the national.
IV. I wish you had invited me to the concert, for I should have liked particularly to hear Piatigorsky.
V. John will be in the best possible position for getting the most out of his vacation and of making business contacts in new markets.
The CORRECT answer is:
A. I, II, III, IV   B. I, II, III, V   C. I, II, III
D. III, IV, V   E. I, II, III, IV, V

11. I. They took him to be me despite ever so many differences in our appearance and despite his addiction to loquacity.
II. They may have more money, they may have more possessions, but they are not any happier than us, as we and they all know.
III. Either Betty or Bob must have thought the teacher's remarks were addressed to him.
IV. There was present at today's conference—and at next week's conference the same group is expected—representatives of many foreign countries, including Italy, France, England, and Germany.
V. The most important criteria in judging the performance of a pianist is not virtuosity but maturity of interpretation.
The CORRECT answer is:
A. I, IV   B. II, III, V   C. II, IV, V   D. I, III   E. I, IV, V

12. I. Thoroughly exhausted after we had swum for six hours, we lay breathless on the sand and oblivious of anything but our utter fatigue.
II. The jury seems in violent disagreement about the culpability of the defendant; such shouting as we hear from the jury room is most unusual among these halls.
III. The difference between the class' average grades for the first week and those for the eighth week, on alternate forms of the same test, were quite insignificant, indicating, we thought, that instruction had been ineffective.
IV. Each tree and each bush give forth a flaming hue such as we have not seen for many seasons in these climes.
V. We met a man whom we thought we had met many years since, when we lived in South Africa.
The CORRECT answer is:
A. III, IV, V   B. I, II, V   C. III, IV   D. I, II   E. I, III, IV

13. I. That old friend, whom I met again last night after a lapse of many a year, stands head and shoulders above any person I have ever known.
II. This is one of the finest pictures which have ever been put on canvas, bringing out rare qualities of tone-color, mature interpretation, and virtuosity in execution.
III. Which of them would you prefer to have working for you, considering the inordinate physical and mental demands of the work, him or his brother?

IV. Throughout Saturday and Sunday, the townsfolk took scarcely any notice of the absence of Jed Gorman, believing him to be off on a drunken spree; but on Monday a body was discovered in the river obviously that of the missing handyman.

V. Things being so pleasant as they were, we could not fathom the reason for John leaving so soon after he had started what we considered an excellent job with unlimited opportunities.

The CORRECT answer is:
  A. I, V   B. II, III, V   C. II, III   D. II, IV, V   E. I, IV, V

14.
I. He is unfailingly polite not only to his superiors and his colleagues but even to those who are in subordinate positions, and, in general, to whoever else he thinks is deserving of kindly consideration.

II. Without more ado, he took the books off the radiator, where they had lain quite neglected for several days and where their bindings were beginning to grow loose.

III. We can still include a discussion of the lunchroom situation among the topics, for the agenda have not yet been printed and will not be for another hour or two.

IV. We knew who would be at the party and who would take us home, but we didn't know who to expect to meet us at the station upon our arrival.

V. Despite his protestations, we know that the true reason why he was suffering such obvious anguish and failing to do his work was because of marital trouble.

The CORRECT answer is:
  A. I, III, IV   B. II, III, V   C. I, IV, V   D. I, II   E. IV, V

15.
I. A difficult stretch of bad road in addition to a long detour which caused a series of minor motor mishaps, have much delayed our visitor's arrival and have created an awkward situation for us all.

II. To make the campaign effective, there is posted in every building, in full view of all entrants, one notice of the location of the shelter, and a second notice intended to boost morale and win cooperation.

III. One day while leading sheep in the desert and musing upon his people's future, the angel of the Lord appeared to Moses.

IV. Though he plead with the tongue of an angel, he will not ever alter her cold eyes nor trouble her calm fount of speech.

V. Despite continuous and well-advised and well-directed efforts by each of us, neither he nor I am able to improve the situation.

The CORRECT answer is:
  A. I, V   B. III, IV, V   C. I, II, III   D. II, III, IV   E. I, III

16.
I. Though business has been brisk of late, this kind of appliances have not sold well at all, despite our continuous and concentrated efforts.

II. The return trip was a desperate one, with time of the essence; and partly blinded by the unexpected snowstorm, the trip was doubly hazardous.

III. I started on my journey by foot through forest and mountain, after a last warning to be careful about snake bites by my parents—a warning I knew I must heed on that dangerous terrain.

IV. That he was losing to a better man, a man who had worked diligently and a man of impeccable virtue, was a consideration of but small import to him.
V. The precarious state of affairs was aggravated by a new hazard, notwithstanding all our cautions to avoid any change in the situation.
The CORRECT answer is:
   A. I, III, V   B. II, IV   C. IV, V   D. I, II, III   E. II, III

17. I. Who's responsible for the feeding of his cat and its young, I'd like to know, we or they? If we, let's feed them.
    II. The books that had lain on the desk for many weeks were laid in the bookcase, where they lay until picked up by the messenger from the second-handbook shop.
    III. You say I merit the award for competence in my duties; but he deserves an award as well as I, for he is as good, without doubt, or even better than I.
    IV. The Joneses' car was more luxurious than, but not necessarily as expensive as, the Browns'.
    V. Slowly they tiptoed into the living room hoping not to be heard, but we were fully aware of it being they.
    The CORRECT answer is:
       A. II, IV   B. I, III, IV   C. I, V   D. I, II, V   E. III, V

18. I. I shall lay the rug in the sun, where it has laid many times before; and I shall lie in the sun, too, as always I have lain at leisure while the rug has been drying.
    II. Though he knew a great deal about printing machinery, he thought, mistakenly, that the new machine could be made to cast type as well as setting it up.
    III. Knowledge in several major fields with sympathy for varied points of view make him an excellent choice for student adviser.
    IV. You will find the girls' equipment in the teachers' lounge where the boy's father left it at Professor Wills's suggestion.
    V. I know that the Burnses have worked for the mill for generations, and that the Smiths have but recently removed from town, but does either of the Norton boys work here?
    The CORRECT answer is:
       A. I, II, III   B. II, III, IV   C. I, IV, V   D. III, V   E. I, II, IV

19. I. I can put two and two together as quick as most mean; but understanding how he, a slow-witted dolt, could achieve so notable a victory over his opponent is one of the things that puzzle and, forevermore, will puzzle me.
    II. Besides my two brothers, my sister, and I, there are a cousin and my father's nephew living at home with us,
    III. He has lived in the Reno for many years; previously he lived in Chicago for a short space, after he had come from Los Angeles.
    IV. Researchers have been baffled for a long time by this statistic, for it contradicts many of their most highly cherished hypotheses.
    V. So intense was the heat near the furnace that all the men at work could not carry on; consequently, production came to a halt,

The CORRECT answer is:
A. I, II, IV   B. III, V   C. I, III, IV   D. I, II, V   E. II, V

20. I. If we can escape from our desks for a brief interval, let's you, Henry, and I put in an appearance at the party.
   II. If you persevere in your ambitions, you are likely to achieve at least a modicum of success; if you malinger, you are liable to court failure.
   III. You may find conditions here congenial, but since I neither like he work nor the salary, it is to no avail for you to attempt to persuade me to stay.
   IV. He has never deigned to take a drink with us, his office colleagues, though we know him now for over fifteen years; and he takes an occasional drink, we know, at home and at his golf club,
   V. Though the results of your investigation are at variance with the hypothesis we advanced, I believe you have interpreted these data in the only ways that have scientific validity.
   The CORRECT answer is:
   A. I, II, IV   B. I, II   C. IV, V   D. II, III, V   E. I, III, IV

21. I. He can't hardly hear anything unless the room is completely quiet.
   II. His attitude seemed perfectly alright to me.
   III. One can't be too careful, can one?
   IV. He is one of those people who believe in the perfectability of man.
   V. His uneasiness is reflected in his unwillingness to compromise on even the smallest point.
   The CORRECT answer is:
   A. II, III, V   B. I, III   C. I, IV, V   D. I, II, IV   E. III, IV

22. I. "Have you found what you were looking for?" he asked.
   II. "I have never," she insisted, "Seen such careless disregard for the rights of others."
   III. "I found this ticket on the step," he said. "Did you lose it?"
   IV. "In one way I'd like to enter the contest," said Anne; "in another way I'm not too eager."
   V. "Did he say, 'I'm coming?'"
   The CORRECT answer is:
   A. I, III, IV   B. II, V   C. III, V   D. II, IV   E. I, II, IV

23. I. Were I the owner of the dog, I'd keep him muzzled.
   II. In the tennis match Don was paired with Bill; Ed, with Al.
   III. He was given an excellent trade-in allowance on his old car.
   IV. Why doesn't this window raise?
   V. The prow of the vessel had almost completely sank by the time the rescuers arrived on the scene.
   The CORRECT answer is:
   A. I, II, V   B. I, IV, V   C. I, II, III   D. II, V   E. IV, V

24. I. Turning the pages rapidly, his glance fell upon a peculiarly worded advertisement.
     II. Turning the pages rapidly, his eyes noticed a peculiarly worded advertisement.
     III. Turning the pages rapidly, he noticed a peculiarly worded advertisement.
     IV. Turning the pages rapidly made him more attentive to the unusual.
     V. Turning the pages rapidly does not guarantee rapid comprehension.
     The CORRECT answer is:
     A. III, IV, V   B. I, II, IV   C. III, V   D. I, II   E. I, II, III

25. I. They told us how they had suffered.
     II. It is interesting (a) to the student, (b) to the parent, and (c) to the teacher.
     III. There were blue, green and red banners.
     IV. "Will you help", he asked?
     V. In addition to reproducibility, an attitude scale must meet various other requirements characteristic of scale analysis procedures.
     The CORRECT answer is:
     A. I, II   B. II, III   C. I only   D. IV only   E. IV, V

KEY (CORRECT ANSWERS)

1.	C	11.	C
2.	D	12.	C
3.	A	13.	D
4.	E	14.	E
5.	A	15.	C
6.	A	16.	D
7.	E	17.	C
8.	A	18.	A
9.	B	19.	E
10.	B	20.	F

21.	D
22.	B
23.	E
24.	D
25.	D

WRITTEN ENGLISH EXPRESSION
EXAMINATION SECTION
TEST 1

DIRECTIONS: The questions that follow the paragraph below are designed to test your appreciation of correctness and effectiveness of expression in English. The paragraph is presented first in full so that you may read it through for sense. Disregard the errors you find, as you will be asked to correct them in the questions that follow. The paragraph is then presented sentence by sentence with portions underlined and numbered. At the end of this material, you will find numbers corresponding to those below the underlined portions, each followed by five alternatives lettered A to E. In every case, the usage in the alternative lettered A is the same as that in the original paragraph and is followed by four possible usages. Choose the usage you consider BEST in each case. *PRINT THE LETTER OF THE CORRECT ANSWER IN THE SPACE AT THE RIGHT.*

    When this war is over, no nation will either be isolated in war or peace. Each will be within trading distance of all the others and will be able to strike them. Every nation will be most as dependent on the rest for the maintainance of peace as is any of our own American states on all the others. The world that we have known was a world made up of individual nations, each of which has the priviledge of doing about as they pleased without being embarassed by outside interference. The world has dissolved before the impact of an invention, the airplane has done to our world what gunpowder did to the feudal world. Whether the coming century will be a period of further tragedy or one of peace and progress depend very largely on the wisdom and skill with which the present generation adjusts their thinking to the problems immediately at hand. Examining the principal movements sweeping through the world, it can be seen that they are being accelerated by the war. There is undoubtedly many of these whose courses will be affected for good or ill by the settlement that will follow the war. The United States will share the responsibility of these settlements with Russia, England and China. The influence of the United States, however, will be great. This country is likely to emerge from the war stronger than any other nation. Having benefitted by the absence of actual hostilities on our own soil, we shall probably be less exhausted than our allies and better able to help restore the devastated areas. However many mistakes have been made in our past, the tradition of America, not only the champion of freedom but also fair play, still lives among millions who can see light and hope scarcely nowhere else.

1. When this war is over, no nation will <u>either be isolated in war or peace</u>.   1.____
   - A. either be isolated in war or peace
   - B. be either isolated in war or peace
   - C. be isolated in neither war nor peace
   - D. be isolated either in war or in peace
   - E. be isolated neither in war or peace

2. <u>Each</u>   2.____
       A. Each   B. It   C. Some   D. They   E. A nation

3. within trading distance of all the others and will be able to strike them.
   A. within trading distance of all the others and will be able to strike them.
   B. near enough to trade with and strike all the others.
   C. trading and striking the others.
   D. within trading and striking distance of all the others.
   E. able to strike and trade with all the others,

4. Every nation will be most as dependent on
   A. most   B. wholly   C. much   D. mostly   E. almost

5. the rest for the maintainance of peace as is
   A. maintainance   B. maintainence   C. maintenence
   D. maintenance   E. maintanence

6. any of our own American states on all the others. The world that we have known was a world made up of individual nations, each
   A. nations, each   B. nations. Each   C. nations: each
   D. nations; each   E. nations each

7. of which had the priviledge of doing about as
   A. priviledge   B. priveledge   C. privelege
   D. privalege   E. privilege

8. they pleased without being
   A. they   B. it   C. they individually
   D. he   E. the nations

9. embarassed by outside interference. That
   A. embarassed   B. embarrassed   C. embaressed
   D. embarrased   E. embarressed

10. world has dissolved before the impact of an invention, the airplane has done to our world what gunpowder did to the feudal world. Whether the coming century will be a period of further tragedy or one of peace and
    A. invention, the   B. invention but the   C. invention: the
    D. invention. The   E. invention and the

11. progress depend very largely on the wisdom and skill with which the present generation
    A. depend   B. will have depended   C. depends
    D. depended   E. shall depend

12. adjusts their thinking to the problems immediately at hand.
    A. adjusts their   B. adjusts there   C. adjusts its
    D. adjust our   E. adjust it's

13. <u>Examining the principal movements sweeping through the world, it can be seen</u>
    A. Examining the principal movements sweeping through the world, it can be seen
    B. Having examined the principal movements sweeping through the world, it can be seen
    C. Examining the principal movements sweeping through the world can be seen
    D. Examining the principal movements sweeping through the world, we can see
    E. It can be seen examining the principal movements sweeping through the world

14. that they are being <u>accelerated</u> by the war.
    A. accelerated   B. acelerated   C. accelerated
    D. acellerated   E. acelerrated

15. There <u>is</u> undoubtedly many of these whose courses will be affected for good or ill by the settlements that will follow the war. The United States will share the responsibility of these settlements with Russia, England and China. The influence of the United
    A. is   B. were   C. was   D. are   E. might be

16. States, <u>however,</u> will be great. This country is likely to emerge from the war stronger than any other nation.
    A. , however,   B. however,   C. , however
    D. however   E. ; however

17. Having <u>benefitted</u> by the absence of actual hostilities on our own soil, we shall probably be less exhausted
    A. benefitted   B. benifitted   C. benefited
    D. benifited   E. benafitted

18. than our allies and better able than <u>them</u> to help restore the devastated areas. However many mistakes have been made in our past, the tradition of American,
    A. them   B. themselves   C. they
    D. the world   E. the nations

19. <u>not only the champion of freedom but also fair play</u>, still lives among millions who can
    A. not only the champion of freedom but also fair play,
    B. the champion of not only freedom but also of fair play,
    C. the champion not only of freedom but also of fair play,
    D. not only the champion but also freedom and fair play,
    E. not the champion of freedom only, but also fair play,

20. see light and hope <u>scarcely nowhere else.</u>   20.____
    A. scarcely nowhere else
    B. elsewhere
    C. nowhere
    D. scarcely anywhere else
    E. anywhere

KEY (CORRECT ANSWERS)

1. D   11. C
2. A   12. C
3. D   13. D
4. E   14. A
5. D   15. D

6. A   16. A
7. E   17. C
8. B   18. C
9. B   19. C
10. D   20. D

TEST 2

DIRECTIONS: The questions that follow the paragraph below are designed to test your appreciation of correctness and effectiveness of expression in English. The paragraph is presented first in full so that you may read it through for sense. Disregard the errors you find, as you will be asked to correct them in the questions that follow. The paragraph is then presented sentence by sentence with portions underlined and numbered. At the end of this material, you will find numbers corresponding to those below the underlined portions, each followed by five alternatives lettered A to E. In every case, the usage in the alternative lettered A is the same as that in the original paragraph and is followed by four possible usages. Choose the usage you consider BEST in each case. *PRINT THE LETTER OF THE CORRECT ANSWER IN THE SPACE AT THE RIGHT.*

    The use of the machine produced up to the present time outstanding changes in our modern world. One of the most significant of these changes have been the marked decreases in the length of the working day and the working week. The fourteen-hour day not only has been reduced to one of ten hours but also, in some lines of work, to one of eight or even six. The trend toward a decrease is further evidenced in the longer weekend already given to employees in many business establishments. There seems also to be a trend toward shorter working weeks and longer summer vacations. An important feature of this development is that leisure is no longer the privilege of the wealthy few,—it has become the common right of most people. Using it wisely, leisure promotes health, efficiency, and happiness, for there is time for each individual to live their own "more abundant life" and having opportunities for needed recreation.

    Recreation, like the name implies, is a process of revitalization. In giving expression to the play instincts of the human race, new vigor and effectiveness are afforded by recreation to the body and to the mind. Of course not all forms of amusement, by no means, constitute recreation. Furthermore, an activity that provides recreation for one person may prove exhausting for another. Today, however, play among adults, as well as children, is regarded as a vital necessity of modern life. Play being recognized as an important factor in improving mental and physical health and thereby reducing human misery and poverty,

    Among the most important forms of amusement available at the present time are the automobile, the moving picture, the radio, television, and organized sports. The automobile, especially, has been a boon to the American people, since it has been the chief means of them getting out into the open. The motion picture, the radio and television have tremendous opportunities to supply wholesome recreation and to promote cultural advancement. A criticism often leveled against organized sports as a means of recreation is because they make passive spectators of too many people. It has been said "that the American public is afflicted with "spectatoritis," but there is some recreational advantages to be gained even from being a spectator at organized games. Such sports afford a release from the monotony of daily toil, get people outdoors and also provide an exhilaration that is tonic in its effect.

    The chief concern, of course, should be to eliminate those forms of amusement that are socially undesirable. There are, however, far too many people who, we know, do not use their leisure to the best advantage. Sometimes leisure leads to idleness, and idleness may lead to demoralization. The value of leisure both to the individual and to society will depend on the uses made of it.

2 (#2)

1. The use of the machine produced up to the
   A. produced   B. produces   C. has produced
   D. had produced   E. will have produced

2. present time many outstanding changes in our modern world. One of the most significant of these changes have been the marked
   A. have been   B. was   C. were
   D. has been   E. will be

3. decreases in the length of the working day and the working week. The fourteen-hour day not only has been reduced to one of ten hour but also, in some line of work, to one of eight or even six.
   A. The fourteen-hour day not only has been reduced
   B. Not only the fourteen-hour day has been reduced
   C. Not the fourteen-hour day only has been reduced
   D. The fourteen-hour day has not only been reduced
   E. The fourteen-hour day has been reduced not only

4. The trend toward a decrease is further evidenced in the longer week end already given
   A. already   B. all ready   C. allready   D. ready   E. all in all

5. to employees in many business establishments. There seems also to be a trend toward shorter working weeks and longer summer vacations. An important feature of this development is that leisure is no longer the privilege of the wealthy few,—it has become the common right of people.
   A. , —it   B. : it   C. ; it
   D. ...it   E. omit punctuation

6. Using it wisely, leisure promotes health, efficiency, and happiness, for there is time for
   A. Using it wisely   B. If used wisely
   C. Having used it widely   D. Because of its wise use
   E. Because of usefulness

7. each individual to live their own "more abundant life"
   A. their   B. his   C. its   D. our   E. your

8. and having opportunities for needed recreation.
   A. having   B. having had   C. to have
   D. to have had   E. had

9. Recreation, like the name implies, is a
   A. like   B. since   C. through   D. for   E. as

164

3 (#2)

10. process of revitalization. In giving expression to the play instincts of the human race, <u>new vigor and effectiveness are afforded by recreation to the body and to the mind.</u>
    A. new vigor and effectiveness are afforded by recreation to the body and to the mind.
    B. recreation affords new vigor and effectiveness to the body and to the mind.
    C. there are afforded new vigor and effectiveness to the body and to the mind.
    D. by recreation the body and mind are afforded new vigor and effectiveness.
    E. the body and the mind afford new vigor and effectiveness to themselves by recreation.

10.____

11. Of course not all forms of amusement, <u>by no means,</u> constitute recreation. Furthermore, an activity that provides recreation for one person may prove exhausting for another. Today, however, play among adults, as well as children, is regarded as a vital necessity of modern life.
    A. by no means   B. by those means   C. by some means
    D. by every means   E. by any means

11.____

12. <u>Play being recognized</u> as an important factor in improving mental and physical health and thereby reducing human misery and poverty.
    A. . Play being recognized as   B. . by their recognizing play as
    C. . They recognizing play as   D. . Recognition of it being
    E. , for play is recognized as

12.____

13. Among the most important forms of amusement available at the present time are the automobile, the moving picture, the radio, television, and organized sports. The automobile, especially, has been a boon to the American people, since it has been the chief means of <u>them</u> getting out into the open. The motion picture, the radio, and television have tremendous opportunities to supply wholesome recreation and to promote cultural advancement. A criticism often leveled against organized
    A. them   B. their   C. his   D. our   E. the people

13.____

14. sports as a means of recreation is <u>because</u> they make passive spectators of too many people
    A. because   B. since   C. as   D. that   E. why

14.____

15. It has been said "<u>that</u> the American public is afflicted with "spectatoritis,"
    A. "that   B. "that"   C. that"   D. 'that   E. that

15.____

16. but there <u>is</u> some recreational advantages to be gained even from being a spectator at organized games
    A. is   B. was   C. are   D. were   E. will be

16.____

165

17. Such sports afford a release from the monotony of daily toil, get people outdoors and also provide an exhilaration that is tonic in its effect. The chief concern, of course, should be to eliminate those forms of amusement that are socially undesirable. There are, however, far too many people who, we know, do not use their leisure to the best advantage. Sometimes leisure leads to idleness, and idleness may lead to demoralization. The value of leisure both to the individual and to society will depend on the uses made of it.
A. who   B. whom   C. which   D. such as   E. that which

17.____

KEY (CORRECT ANSWERS)

1. C
2. D
3. E
4. A
5. C

6. B
7. B
8. C
9. E
10. B

11. E
12. E
13. B
14. D
15. E

16. C
17. A

TEST 3

DIRECTIONS: The questions that follow the paragraph below are designed to test your appreciation of correctness and effectiveness of expression in English. The paragraph is presented first in full so that you may read it through for sense. Disregard the errors you find, as you will be asked to correct them in the questions that follow. The paragraph is then presented sentence by sentence with portions underlined and numbered. At the end of this material, you will find numbers corresponding to those below the underlined portions, each followed by five alternatives lettered A to E. In every case, the usage in the alternative lettered A is the same as that in the original paragraph and is followed by four possible usages. Choose the usage you consider BEST in each case. *PRINT THE LETTER OF THE CORRECT ANSWER IN THE SPACE AT THE RIGHT.*

    The process by which the community influence the actions of its members is known as social control. Imitation which takes place when the action of one individual awakens the impulse in each other to attempt the same thing, is one of the means by which society gains this control. When the child acts as other members of his group acts, he receives their approval. There is also adults who seem almost equally imitative. Advertisers of luxuries are careful to convey the idea that important persons use and indorse the merchandise concerned, for most folk will do their utmost to follow the example of those whom they think are the best people.
    Akin to imitation as a means of social control is suggestion. The child is taught to think and feel as do the adults of his community. He is neither encouraged to be critical or to examine all the evidence for his opinion. To be sure, there would be scarcely no time left for other things if school children would have been expected to have considered all sides of every matter on which they hold opinions. It is possible, however and probably very desirable, for pupils of high school age to learn that the point of view accepted in their community is not the only one, and that many widely held opinions may be mistaken. The way in which suggestion operates is illustrated by advertising methods. Depending on skillful suggestion, argument is seldom used in advertising. The words accompanying the picture do not seek to convince the reason but only to intensify the suggestion.
    Some persons are more susceptible to suggestion than others. The ignorant person is more easily moved to action by suggestion than he who is well educated, education developing the habit of criticizing what is read and heard. Whoever would think clearly, freeing himself from emotion and prejudice, must beware of the influence of the crowd or mob. A crowd is a group of people in a highly suggestible condition, each stimulating the feelings of the others until an intense uniform emotion has control of the group. Such a crowd may become irresponsible and anonymous, and whose activity may lead in any direction. The educated person ought to be beyond reach of this kind of appeal, no one may be said to have a real individuality who, at the mercy of the suggestions of others, allow themselves to succumb to "crowd-mindedness."

1. The process by which the community <u>influence the action of its members</u> is known as social control.
    A. influence the actions of its members
    B. influences the actions of its members
    C. had influenced the actions of its members
    D. influences the actions of their members
    E. will influence the actions of its members

1.____

2. Imitation which takes place when the action
   A. which   B. , which   C. —which   D. that   E. what

3. of one individual awakens the impulse in each other to attempt the same thing, is one of the means by which society gains this control.
   A. each other   B. some other   C. one other
   D. another   E. one another

4. When the child acts as other members of his group acts, he receives their approval
   A. acts   B. act   C. has acted
   D. will act   E. will have acted

5. There is also adults who seem almost equally imitative.
   A. is   B. are   C. was   D. were   E. will be

6. Advertisers of luxuries are careful to convey the idea that important persons use and indorse the merchandise concerned, for most folk will do their utmost to follow the example of those whom they think are the best people.
   A. whom   B. what   C. which
   D. who   E. that which

7. Akin to imitation as a means of social control is suggestion. The child is taught to think and feel as do the adults of his community.
   A. do   B. does   C. had   D. may   E. might

8. He is neither encouraged to be critical or to examine all the evidence for his opinions.
   A. neither encouraged to be critical or to examine
   B. neither encouraged to be critical nor to examine
   C. either encouraged to be critical or to examine
   D. encouraged either to be critical nor to examine
   E. not encouraged either to be critical or to examine

9. To be sure, there would be scarcely no time left for other things.
   A. scarcely no   B. hardly no   C. scarcely any
   D. enough   E. but only

10. if school children would have been expected
    A. would have been   B. should have been   C. would have
    D. were   E. will be

11. to have considered all sides of every matter on which they hold opinions
    A. to have considered   B. to be considered
    C. to consider   D. to have been considered
    E. and have considered

3 (#3)

12. It is possible, <u>however</u> and probably very desirable, for pupils of high school age to learn that the point of view accepted in their community is not the only one, and that many widely held opinions may be mistaken. The way in which suggestion operates is illustrated by advertising methods.
    A. , however
    B. however,
    C. ; however,
    D. however
    E. , however,

12.____

13. <u>Depending on skillful suggestion, argument is seldom used in advertising.</u> The words accompanying the picture do not seek to convince the reason but only to intensify the suggestion.
    A. Depending on skillful suggestion, argument is seldom used in advertising.
    B. Argument is seldom used by advertisers, who depend instead on skillful suggestion.
    C. Skillful suggestion is depended on by advertisers instead of argument.
    D. Suggestion, which is more skillful, is used in place of argument by advertisers.
    E. Instead of suggestion, depending on argument is used by skillful advertisers.

13.____

14. Some persons are more susceptible to suggestion than others. The ignorant person is more easily moved to action by suggestion than he who is well educated, <u>education developing</u> the habit of criticizing what is read and heard. Whoever would think clearly, freeing himself from emotion and prejudice, must beware of the influence of the crowd or mob.
    A. , education developing
    B. , education developed by
    C. , for education develops
    D. . Education will develop
    E. . Education developing

14.____

15. A crowd is a group of people in a highly suggestible condition, each stimulating the feelings of the others until an intense uniform emotion has control of the group. Such a crowd may become irresponsible and anonymous, <u>and whose</u> activity may lead in any direction. The educated person ought to be beyond reach of this kind of appeal,
    A. and whose
    B. whose
    C. and its
    D. and the
    E. and the crowd's

15.____

16. <u>no</u> one may be said to have a real individuality who,
    A. , no
    B. : no
    C. —no
    D. . No
    E. omit punctuation

16.____

17. at the mercy of the suggestions of others, <u>allow themselves</u> to succumb to "crowd-mindedness."
    A. allow themselves
    B. allows themselves
    C. allow himself
    D. allows himself
    E. allow ourselves

17.____

KEY (CORRECT ANSWERS)

1.	B	11.	C
2.	B	12.	E
3.	D	13.	B
4.	B	14.	C
5.	B	15.	C
6.	D	16.	D
7.	A	17.	D
8.	E		
9.	C		
10.	D		

TEST 4

DIRECTIONS: The questions that follow are designed to test your appreciation of correctness and effectiveness of expression in English. In each statement, you will find underlined portions. In some cases, the usage in the underlined portion is correct. In other cases, it requires correction. Five (5) alternatives lettered A to E are presented. In every case, the usage in the alternative lettered A (No Change) is the same as that in the original statement and is followed by four (4) other possible usages. Choose the usage you consider BEST in each case. *PRINT THE LETTER OF THE CORRECT ANSWER IN THE SPACE AT THE RIGHT.*

Sample Questions and Answers

Questions
1. John <u>ran</u> home.
   A. No change B. run C. runned
   D. runed E. None right

2. John <u>aint</u> here.
   A. No change B. ain't C. am not
   D. arre'nt E. None right

Answers
1. A
   (The sentence is obviously correctly written. Therefore, the correct answer is A. No change.)

2. E
   (word <u>aint</u> is unacceptable in usage today. The correct answer should be <u>is not</u> or <u>isn't</u>. Since the alternatives offered in A, B, C, and D are all incorrect, the correct answer is, therefore, E. None right.)

1. It takes study <u>to become</u> a lawyer. 1.____
   A. No change B. before you can become
   C. in becoming D. for becoming
   E. None right

2. His novels never <u>concern old people who wished</u> to be young. 2.____
   A. No change
   B. concerned old people who wish
   C. concerned old people who had wished
   D. concern old people who wish
   E. None right

3. You people like <u>we boys as much as we.</u> boys like you. 3.____
   A. No change B. we boys as much as us
   C. us boys as much as us D. us boys as much as we
   E. None right

171

4. Jane and Mary are <u>more poised than he, but Bill is the brighter</u> of all three.   4.____
   A. No change
   B. more poised than he, but Bill is the brightest
   C. more poised than him, but Bill is the brightest
   D. more poised than him, but Bill is the brighter
   E. None right

5. It is a thing of joy, beauty, <u>and containing</u> terror.   5.____
   A. No change   B. and abounding in   C. and of
   D. and contains   E. None right

6. If he <u>was able, he would demand that she return</u> home.   6.____
   A. No change
   B. were able, he would demand that she return
   C. was able, he would demand that she returns
   D. were able, he would demand that she returns
   E. None right

7. He <u>use to visit when he was supposed to.</u>   7.____
   A. No change
   B. use to visit when he was suppose to.
   C. used to visit when he was suppose to.
   D. used to visit when he was supposed to.
   E. None right

8. I saw the <u>seamstress and asked her for a needle, hook and eye,</u> and thimble.   8.____
   A. No change
   B. seamstress, and asked her for a needle, hook and eye
   C. seamstress and asked her for a needle, hook and eye
   D. seamstress, and asked her for a needle, hook and eye
   E. None right

9. A tall, young<u>, man threw the heavy, soggy,</u> ball.   9.____
   A. No change
   B. , young man threw the heavy, soggy
   C. young man threw the heavy, soggy
   D. , young man threw the heavy soggy
   E. None right

10. The week <u>before my sister, thinking of other matters,</u> thrust her hand into the fire.   10.____
    A. No change
    B. before, my sister thinking of other matters
    C. before my sister thinking of other matters
    D. before my sister, thinking of other matters
    E. None right

11. We seldom eat a roast at our house. <u>My</u> wife being a vegetarian.   11.____
    A. No change   B. my   C. , my
    D. ; my   E. None right

3 (#4)

12. I have only one request. That you leave at once.
    A. No change B. that C. ; that
    D. : that E. None right

13. I admire stimulating conversation and appreciative listening, therefore I talk to myself.
    A. No change B. , therefore, C. therefore
    D. therefore, E. None right

14. The battle-scarred veteran was as bald as a newlaid egg.
    A. No change
    B. battlescarred veteran was as bald as a new-laid egg.
    C. battle-scarred veteran was as bald as a new-laid egg.
    D. battle scarred veteran was as bald as a new laid egg.
    E. None right

15. The President's proclamation opened with the following statement: "The intention of the government is, to make the people aware of one of the greatest dangers to the safety of the country."
    A. No change
    B. , "The intention of the government is
    C. : "The intention of the government is:
    D. : "The intention of the government is
    E. None right

16. I get only a week vacation after two years work.
    A. No change
    B. week's vacation after two years work.
    C. week's vacation after two years' work.
    D. weeks vacation after two years work.
    E. None right

17. You first wash your brush in turpentine. Then hang it up to dry.
    A. No change B. First you C. First you should
    D. First E. None right

18. The teacher insisted that you and he were responsible for the mistakes of Joe and me.
    A. No change
    B. him were responsible for the mistakes of Joe and me.
    C. he were responsible for the mistakes of Joe and I.
    D. him were responsible for the mistakes of Joe and I.
    E. None right

19. He sometimes in a generous mood gave the flowers to others that he had grown in his garden.
    A. No change
    B. He in a generous mood sometimes gave to others the flowers
    C. In a generous mood he sometimes gave the flowers to others

4 (#4)

    D. Sometimes in a generous mood he gave to others the flowers
    E. None right

20. He is attending college since September.
    A. No change
    B. has attended
    C. was attending
    D. attended
    E. None right

21. He enjoys me hearing him singing.
    A. No change
    B. my hearing him sing
    C. me hearing him sing
    D. me hearing his singing
    E. None right

22. Even patients of anxious temperament occasionally feel an element of primitive pleasure.
    A. No change
    B. temperament occassionally feel an element of primitive
    C. temperment occasionally feel an element of primitive
    D. temperament occasionally feel an element of primitive
    E. None right

23. Undoubtedly even the loneliest patient feels tranquill.
    A. No change
    B. Undoubtably even the loneliest patient feels tranquill.
    C. Undoubtedly even the loneliest patient feels tranquil.
    D. Undouvtably even the loneliest patient feels tranquil.
    E. None right

24. Sophmores taking behavioral psychology must pay a labratory fee.
    A. No change
    B. Sophmores taking behavioral psychology must pay a laboratory
    C. Sophmores taking behavioral psychology must pay a laboratory
    D. Sophomores taking behavioral psychology must pay a labratory
    E. None right

25. Atheletic heroes often find their studies an unnecessary hinderance.
    A. No change
    B. Athletic heroes often find their studies an unnecessary hinderance.
    C. Athletic heros often find their studies an unnecessary hindrance.
    D. Athletic heroes often find their studies an unnecessary hindrance.
    E. None right

KEY (CORRECT ANSWERS)

1.	A		11.	C
2.	D		12.	D
3.	D		13.	E
4.	B		14.	C
5.	E		15.	D
6.	B		16.	C
7.	D		17.	D
8.	D		18.	A
9.	C		19.	D
10.	E		20.	B

21. B
22. A
23. E
24. C
25. D

TEST 5

DIRECTIONS: The questions that follow are designed to test your appreciation of correctness and effectiveness of expression in English. In each statement, you will find underlined portions. In some cases, the usage in the underlined portion is correct. In other cases, it requires correction. Five (5) alternatives lettered A to E are presented. In every case, the usage in the alternative lettered A (No Change) is the same as that in the original statement and is followed by four (4) other possible usages. Choose the usage you consider BEST in each case. *PRINT THE LETTER OF THE CORRECT ANSWER IN THE SPACE AT THE RIGHT.*

1. Many of the <u>childrens' games were supervised by students who's</u> interests lay in teaching.
   A. No change
   B. children's games were supervised by students who's
   C. childrens' games were supervised by students whose
   D. children's games were supervised by students whose
   E. None right

   1.____

2. I told <u>father that a college president</u> was invited to speak.
   A. No change
   B. Father that a college president
   C. father that a College President
   D. Father that a College president
   E. None right

   2.____

3. One should either <u>be able to read</u> German or French.
   A. No change
   B. be able either to read
   C. be able to either read
   D. be able to read either
   E. None right

   3.____

4. <u>Twirling around on my piano stool, my head begins to swim.</u>
   A. No change
   B. My head begins to swim, twirling around on my piano stool.
   C. Twirling around on my piano stool, a dizzy spell ensues.
   D. Twirling around on my piano stool, I begin to feel dizzy.
   E. None right

   4.____

5. As the reverberations of my deep bass voice <u>increase, one of my dogs starts</u> to howl.
   A. No change
   B. increase, one of my dogs start
   C. increases, one of my dogs start
   D. increases, one of my dogs starts
   E. None right

   5.____

6. Roy bellows at Eve that it is <u>her, not he</u> who shouts.
   A. No change
   B. her, not him
   C. she, not him
   D. she, not he
   E. None right

   6.____

7. The only man who I think will knock out whoever he fights is Roy. 7.____
   A. No change
   B. who I think will knock out whomever
   C. whom I think will knock out whomever
   D. whom I think will knock out whoever
   E. None right

8. The more prettier of my eyes is the glass one. 8.____
   A. No change B. most pretty C. prettier
   D. prettiest E. None right

9. When a good actress cries, she feels real sad. 9.____
   A. No change B. feels real sadly
   C. feels really sadly D. really feels sad
   E. None right

10. I asked the instructor what I should do with this examina-paper. Can you 10.____
    imagine what he said?
    A. No change B. ? Can you imagine what he said.
    C. ? Can you imagine what he said? D. . Can you imagine what he said.
    E. None right

11. Not wishing to hurt my friend's feeling, I tell him that I am leaving, because 11.____
    I have a previous engagement.
    A. No change B. I tell him that I am leaving
    C. , I tell him that I am leaving D. I tell him that I am leaving,
    E. None right

12. I remember Utopia College where I studied, while I lived abroad, when the 12.____
    world was at peace.
    A. No change
    B. College where I studied, while I lived abroad
    C. College, where I studied while I lived abroad
    D. College, where I studied, while I lived abroad
    E. None right

13. Would Robinson Crusoe have survived if he was less unimaginative? 13.____
    A. No change B. were C. had been
    D. would have been E. None right

14. Neither time nor tide delay either the traveler or the stay-at-home from his 14.____
    pastime.
    A. No change
    B. delays either the traveler or the stay-at-home from his
    C. delay either the traveler or the stay-at-home from their
    D. delays either the traveler or the stay-at-home from their
    E. None right

15. When the committee reports its findings somebody will lose their composure.   15.____
    A. No change
    B. their findings somebody will lose their
    C. their findings somebody will lose his
    D. its findings somebody will lose his
    E. None right

16. The worst one of the problems which is confronting me concern money.   16.____
    A. No change   B. are confronting me concern
    C. is confronting me concerns   D. are confronting me concerns
    E. None right

17. Far in the distance rumble the motors of the convoy, but there's no signs of   17.____
    it yet.
    A. No change
    B. rumbles the motors of the convoy, but there is
    C. rumbles the motors of the convoy, but there are
    D. rumble the motors of the convoy, but there are
    E. None right

18. Neither of the patients believe that Hansel or Gretel are alive.   18.____
    A. No change   B. believes that Hansel or Gretel are
    C. believe that Hansel or Gretel is   D. believes that Hansel or Gretel is
    E. None right

19. Its in untried emergencies that a man's native metal receives its ultimate test.   19.____
    A. No change
    B. It's in untried emergencies that a man's native metal receives its
    C. It's in untried emergencies that a man's native metal receives its
    D. It's in untried emergencies that a man's native metal receives its'
    E. None right

20. Expecting my friends to be on time, their tardiness seemed almost an insult.   20.____
    A. No change
    B. it seemed that their tardiness was almost an insult.
    C. resentment at their tardiness grew in my mind.
    D. only an accident on the way could account for their tardiness.
    E. None right

21. On first reading "The Wasteland" seems obscure.   21.____
    A. No change
    B. On first reading it, "The Wasteland" seems obscure.
    C. "The Wasteland" seems an obscure poem on first reading it.
    D. On first reading "The Wasteland," it seems an obscure poem.
    E. None right

4 (#5)

22. A special light will be required to inspect the engine. 22._____
    A. No change
    B. To inspect the engine, a special light will be required.
    C. To inspect the engine, you will require a special light.
    D. To inspect the engine, your light must be special.
    E. None right

23. When mixing it, the cake batter must be thoroughly beaten. 23._____
    A. No change   B. mixing   C. being mixed
    D. being mix   E. None right

24. What you say may be different from me. 24._____
    A. No change   B. from what I say   C. than me
    D. than mine   E. None right

25. Trumping is playing a trump when another suit has been led. 25._____
    A. No change   B. to play   C. if you play
    D. where one plays   E. None right

KEY (CORRECT ANSWERS)

1.	D		11.	C
2.	A		12.	C
3.	D		13.	C
4.	D		14.	B
5.	A		15.	D
6.	D		16.	D
7.	B		17.	D
8.	C		18.	D
9.	D		19.	B
10.	A		20.	E

21. B
22. B
23. C
24. B
25. A

ENGLISH EXPRESSION
EXAMINATION SECTION
TEST 1

DIRECTIONS: Each question or incomplete statement is followed by several suggested answers or completions. Select the one that BEST answers the question or completes the statement. *PRINT THE LETTER OF THE CORRECT ANSWER IN THE SPACE AT THE RIGHT.*

Questions 1-9.

DIRECTIONS: The following sentences contain problems in grammar, usage diction (choice of words), and idiom. Some sentences are correct. No sentence contains more than one error. You will find that the error, if there is one, is underlined and lettered. Assume that all other elements of the sentence are correct and cannot be changed. In choosing answers, follow the requirements of standard written English. If there is an error, select the *one underlined* part that must be changed in order to make the sentence correct. If there is no error, mark E.

1. <u>In planning</u> your future, <u>one must be</u> as honest with yourself as possible, make careful   1.____
       A   B
   decisions about the best course <u>to follow to achieve</u> a particular purpose, and, above all,
                                              C
   have the courage <u>to stand by those</u> decisions. <u>No error</u>
                      D   E

2. <u>Even though</u> history does not actually repeat itself, knowledge <u>of</u> history <u>can give</u>   2.____
       A   B   C
   current problems a familiar, <u>less</u> formidable look. <u>No error</u>
                              D   E

3. The Curies <u>had almost exhausted</u> their resources, and <u>for a time it seemed</u>   3.____
                    A   B
   <u>unlikely that they ever</u> would find the <u>solvent to their financial problems</u>. <u>No error</u>
           C   D   E

4. <u>If the rumors are</u> correct, Deane <u>will not be convicted</u>, for each of the officers   4.____
            A   B
   on the court realizes that Colson and Holdman may be <u>the real culprit and</u> that
                                                                     C
   <u>their</u> testimony is not completely trustworthy. <u>No error</u>
    D   E

5. The citizens of Washington, <u>like Los Angeles</u>, prefer to commute by automobile,   5._____
                                      A

    even though motor vehicles contribute <u>nearly as many</u> contaminants to the air
                                                           B

    <u>as do all other</u> sources <u>combined</u>. <u>No error</u>
             C   D   E

6. <u>By the time Robert Vasco completes</u> his testimony, every major executive of our   6._____
                      A

    company but Ray Ashurst <u>and I</u> <u>will have been</u> <u>accused of</u> complicity in the stock
                                      B   C   D

    swindle. <u>No error</u>
                E

7. <u>Within six months</u> the store was operating <u>profitably and efficient</u>; shelves   7._____
       A   B

    <u>were well stocked</u>, goods were selling rapidly, and the cash register
             C

    <u>was ringing constantly</u>. <u>No error</u>
             D   E

8. Shakespeare's comedies have an advantage <u>over Shaw</u> <u>in that Shakespeare's</u> were   8._____
                                                     A   B

    <u>written primarily</u> to entertain and <u>not to</u> argue for a cause. <u>No error</u>
         C   D   E

9. Any true insomniac <u>is well aware of</u> the futility of <u>such measures as</u> drinking   9._____
                           A   B

    hot milk, <u>regular hours, deep breathing</u>, counting sheep, and <u>concentrating on</u>
                           C   D

    black velvet. <u>No error</u>
                      E

Questions 10-15.

DIRECTIONS: In each of the following sentences, some part of the sentence or the entire sentence is underlined. Beneath each sentence you will find five ways of phrasing the underlined part. The first of these repeats the original; the other four are different. If you think the original is better than any of the alternatives, choose answer A; otherwise choose one of the others. In choosing answers, follow the requirements of standard written English; that is, pay attention to grammar, choice of words, sentence construction, and punctuation. Choose the answer that produces the most effective sentence—clear and exact, without awkwardness or ambiguity. Do not make a choice that changes the meaning of the original sentence.

10. The tribe of warriors believed that boys and girls should be <u>reared separate, and,</u>   10._____
<u>as soon as he was weaned, the boys were taken from their mothers.</u>
    A. reared separate, and, as soon as he was weaned, the boys were taken
       from their mothers

B. reared separate, and, as soon as he was weaned, a boy was taken from his mother
C. reared separate, and, as soon as he was weaned, the boys were taken from their mothers
D. reared separately, and, as soon as a boy was weaned, they were taken from their mothers
E. reared separately, and, as soon as a boy was weaned, he was taken from his mother

11. Despite Vesta being only the third largest, it is by far the brightest of the known asteroids.
    A. Despite Vesta being only the third largest, it is by far the brightest of the known asteroids.
    B. Vesta, though only the third largest asteroid, is by far the brightest of the known ones.
    C. Being only the third largest, yet Vesta is by far the brightest of the known asteroids.
    D. Vesta, though only the third largest of the known asteroids, is by far the brightest.
    E. Vesta is only the third largest of the asteroids, it being, however, the brightest one.

12. As a result of the discovery of the Dead Sea Scrolls, our understanding of the roots of Christianity has had to be revised considerably.
    A. has had to be revised considerably
    B. have had to be revised considerably
    C. has had to undergo revision to a considerable degree
    D. have had to be subjected to considerable revision
    E. has had to be revised in a considerable way

13. Because it is imminently suitable to dry climates, adobe has been a traditional building material throughout the southwestern states.
    A. it is imminently suitable to
    B. it is eminently suitable for
    C. It is eminently suitable when in
    D. of its eminent suitability with
    E. of being imminently suitable in

14. Martell is more concerned with demonstrating that racial prejudice exists than preventing it from doing harm, which explains why his work is not always highly regarded.
    A. Martell is more concerned with demonstrating that racial prejudice exists than preventing it from doing harm, which explains
    B. Martell is more concerned with demonstrating that racial prejudice exists than with preventing it from doing harm, and this explains
    C. Martell is more concerned with demonstrating that racial prejudice exists than with preventing it from doing harm, an explanation of
    D. Martell's greater concern for demonstrating that racial prejudice exists than preventing it from doing harm—this explains
    E. Martell's greater concern for demonstrating that racial prejudice exists than for preventing it from doing harm explains

15. Throughout this history of the American West there runs a steady commentary on the deception and mistreatment of the Indians.   15.____
    A. Throughout this history of the American West there runs a steady commentary on the deception and mistreatment of the Indians.
    B. There is a steady commentary provided on the deception and mistreatment of the Indians and it runs throughout this history of the American West.
    C. The deception and mistreatment of the Indians provide a steady comment that runs throughout this history of the American West.
    D. Comment on the deception and mistreatment of the Indians is steadily provided and runs throughout this history of the American West.
    E. Running throughout this history of the American West is a steady commentary that is provided on the deception and mistreatment of the Indians.

Questions 16-20.

DIRECTIONS: In each of the following questions you are given a complete sentence to be rephrased according to the directions which follow it. You should rephrase the sentence mentally to save time, although you may make notes in your test book if you wish. Below each sentence and its directions are listed words or phrases that may occur in your revised sentence. When you have thought out a good sentence, look in the choices A through E for the word or entire phrase that is included in your revised sentence, and print the letter of the correct answer in the space at the right. The word or phrase you choose should be the most accurate and most nearly complete of all the choices given, and should be part of a sentence that meets the requirements of standard written English. Of course, a number of different sentences can be obtained if the sentence is revised according to directions, and not all of these possibilities can be included in only five choices. If you should find that you have thought of a sentence that contains none of the words or phrases listed in the choices, you should attempt to rephrase the sentence again so that it includes a word or phrase that is listed. Although the directions may at times require you to change the relationship between parts of the sentence or to make slight changes in meaning in other ways, make only those changes that the directions require; that is, keep the meaning the same, or as nearly the same as the directions permit. If you think that more than one good sentence can be made according to the directions, select the sentence that is most exact, effective, and natural in phrasing and construction.

EXAMPLES

I. Sentence: Coming to the city as a young man, he found a job as a newspaper reporter.
    Directions: Substitute He came for Coming.
    A. and so he found   B. and found
    C. and there he had found   D. and then finding
    E. and had found

5 (#1)

Your rephrased sentence will probably read: "He came to the city as a young man and found a job as a newspaper reporter." This sentence contains the correct answer: <u>B. and found</u>. A sentence which used one of the alternate phrases would <u>change the</u> meaning or <u>intention</u> of the original sentence, would be a <u>poorly written sentence</u>, or would be <u>less effective</u> than another possible revision.

II. <u>Sentence</u>: Owing to her wealth, Sarah had many suitors.
<u>Directions</u>: Begin with <u>Many men courted</u>.
A. so   B. while   C. although   D. because   E. and

Your rephrased sentence will probably read: "Many men courted Sarah because she was wealthy." This new sentence contains only choice D, which is the correct answer. None of the other choices will fit into an effective, correct sentence that retains the original meaning.

16. The archaeologists could only mark out the burial site, for then winter came.
Begin with <u>Winter came before</u>.
  A. could do nothing more   B. could not do anything
  C. could only do   D. could do something
  E. could do anything more

17. The white reader often receives some insight into the reasons why black men are angry from descriptions by a black writer of the injustice they encounter in a white society.
Begin with <u>A black writer often gives</u>.
  A. when describing   B. by describing
  C. he has described   D. in the descriptions
  E. because of describing

18. The agreement between the university officials and the dissident students provides for student representation on every university committee and on the board of trustees.
Substitute <u>provides that</u> for <u>provides for</u>.
  A. be   B. are   C. would have
  D. would be   E. is to be

19. English Romanticism had its roots in German idealist philosophy, first described in England by Samuel Coleridge.
Begin with <u>Samuel Coleridge was the first in</u>.
  A. in which English   B. and from it English
  C. where English   D. the source of English
  E. the birth of English

20. Four months have passed since his dismissal, during which time Alan has looked for work daily.
Begin with <u>Each day</u>.
  A. will have passed   B. that have passed   C. that passed
  D. were to pass   E. had passed

KEY (CORRECT ANSWERS)

1.	B	11.	D
2.	E	12.	A
3.	D	13.	B
4.	C	14.	E
5.	A	15.	A
6.	B	16.	E
7.	B	17.	B
8.	A	18.	A
9.	C	19.	D
10.	E	20.	B

EXAMINATION SECTION
TEST 1

DIRECTIONS: Each question or incomplete statement is followed by several suggested answers or completions. Select the one that BEST answers the question or completes the statement. *PRINT THE LETTER OF THE CORRECT ANSWER IN THE SPACE AT THE RIGHT.*

1. 2/3 × 12 equals
   A. 4
   B. 6
   C. 8
   D. 18
   E. None of the above

2. 83.97
   1.78
   14.36
   9.03
   The sum of the above column is
   A. 99.13   B. 99.24   C. 109.14   D. 109.23   E. 109.24

3. The value of x in the equation 5x = 75 is
   A. 13
   B. 15
   C. 70
   D. 80
   E. None of the above

4. 65 ÷ .13 equals
   A. .501
   B. 5.01
   C. 50.1
   D. 501
   E. None of the above

5. The sum of 6 feet 8 inches and 3 feet 4 inches is
   A. 2 ft. 2 in.
   B. 9 ft.
   C. 10 ft.
   D. 10 ft. 12 in.
   E. None of the above

6. 3/4 – 1/2 + 1/8 equals
   A. 3/10
   B. 3/8
   C. 5/8
   D. 1 3/8
   E. None of the above

7. 4 5/16 – 2 3/8 equals
   A. 1 15/16
   B. 2 1/16
   C. 2 ¼
   D. 2 15/16
   E. None of the above

8. (-12)+(-3) equals
   A. -9
   B. +15
   C. +9
   D. -15
   E. None of the above

9. The ratio of the lengths of two lines is 5 to 3. The length of the shorter line is 30 inches. The length of the longer line is _____ inches.
   A. 18
   B. 48
   C. 50
   D. 140
   E. None of the above

2 (#1)

10. .025 written as a common fraction is
 A. 25/10
 B. 25/100
 C. 25/1000
 D. 25/10,000
 E. None of the above

 10._____

11. In the proportion 5/2 = 9/x the value of x is
 A. 1.8
 B. 3.6
 C. 22.5
 D. 36
 E. None of the above

 11._____

12. 33 1/3 percent of 3 equals
 A. 1
 B. 10
 C. 100/3
 D. 100
 E. None of the above

 12._____

13. $\sqrt{233}$ equals
 A. 15
 B. 20.5
 C. 25
 D. 112.5
 E. None of the above

 13._____

14. On the portion of the scale shown at the right, the reading to which the arrow points is _____ units.
 A. 6 3/16
 B. 6 3/5
 C. 6 3/4
 D. 7 5/8
 E. None of the above

 14._____

15. If 4x/5 − 6 = 10, then x equals
 A. 15 1/5
 B. 5
 C. 4
 D. 3 1/5
 E. None of the above

 15._____

16. The difference between 8 hours 0 minutes 6 seconds and 6 hours 4 minutes 15 seconds is _____ hr. _____ min. _____ seconds.
 A. 0; 54; 51
 B. 1; 54; 51
 C. 2; 4; 9
 D. 2; 54; 45
 E. None of the above

 16._____

17. The scores made by nine pupils on a science test are: 2, 4, 6, 6, 8, 10, 12, 14, 19.
 The MEAN score is
 A. 6
 B. 8
 C. 9
 D. 81
 E. None of the above

 17._____

18. A certain cost formula is represented graphically in the figure at the right. From the graph, when n = 7, the value of C is about
 A. 140
 B. 120
 C. 110
 D. 102
 E. None of the above

 18._____

188

19. A simplified form of the expression A = 1/2 bh + 1/2 ah is
    A. A = ½ h(b+a)   B. bh + ah   C. A = abh
    D. $\frac{A}{1/2 bh}$ = 1/2 ah   E. None of the above

    19.____

20. The ratio of 6 inches to 3 feet is
    A. 6/1   B. 2/1   C. 1/2
    D. 1/18   E. None of the above

    20.____

21. The value of s in the equation 3s = 12 – s is
    A. 6   B. 4   C. 3 2/3
    D. 3   E. None of the above

    21.____

22. 16 2/3 percent of what number is 30?
    A. 5   B. 18   C. 160
    D. 180   E. None of the above

    22.____

23. The line graph shown at the right represents the temperature readings in Albany, New York, at two-hour intervals from 4 A.M. to 10 P.M. on a certain day in February. The APPROXIMATE change in temperature between 7 A.M. and 9 A.M. is _____ degrees.
    A. 3.5
    B. 3.0
    C. 2.5
    D. 2.0
    E. None of the above

    23.____

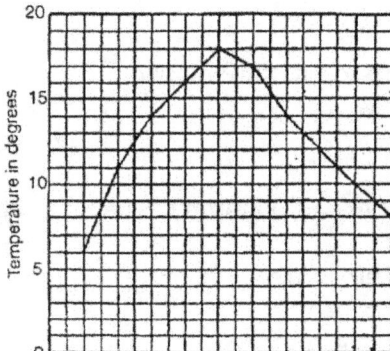

Questions 24-25.

DIRECTIONS: Questions 24 and 25 are to be answered on the basis of the following figure and information.

In the figure below, a square whose side is b is cut from a square whose side is a.

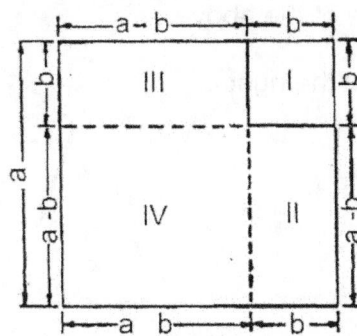

24. The sum of the perimeters of Section I and Section III can be represented by
    A. b^2
    B. $4a - 2b$
    C. $2a + 3b$
    D. $a(a-b)$
    E. None of the above

25. The sum of the areas of Section II and Section IV can be represented by
    A. b^2
    B. $4a - 2b$
    C. $2a + 3b$
    D. $a(a-b)$
    E. None of the above

26. The temperature reading (F) on the Fahrenheit scale equals 32 more than 9/5 of the Centigrade reading (C).
    This rule when translated into symbols is expressed by
    A. F = 9/5C + 32
    B. F = 9/5(C+32)
    C. F = 9/5 + 32C
    D. F + 32 = 9/5C
    E. None of the above

27. In the equation 6x − 114 = .3x, the value of x is
    A. 38
    B. 20
    C. 12 2/3
    D. 2
    E. None of the above

28. What percent of 42 is 84?
    A. 4%
    B. 2%
    C. 50%
    D. 200%
    E. None of the above

29. The CORRECT name of the solid figure at the right is
    A. semicircle
    B. circle
    C. sphere
    D. cone
    E. cylinder

30. Which of these fractions has the LARGEST value?
    A. 1/2
    B. 5/9
    C. 7/12
    D. 2/3
    E. 3/4

31. The formula for the area of a circle is A =
    A. π^2
    B. $2/3\, \pi^2$
    C. $2\pi r$
    D. bh
    E. None of the above

32. The CORRECT name of the figure at the right is
    A. pentagon
    B. hexagon
    C. rectangle
    D. trapezoid
    E. square

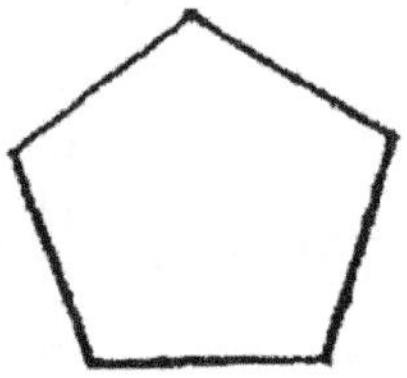

33. The figure at the right is a
    A. rectangle
    B. square
    C. pentagon
    D. trapezoid
    E. parallelogram

33._____

34. If x = -18, y = 3, and z = -2, then x – y + z equals
    A. 3   B. -3   C. -23   D. -52   E. -56

34._____

35. The number 335,560 rounded off to the nearest thousand is
    A. 335,000   B. 335,500   C. 336,000
    D. 340,000   E. None of the above

35._____

36. In the triangle ABC at the right, the sum of the angles is _____ degrees.
    A. 360
    B. 180
    C. 90
    D. 35
    E. None of the above

36._____

37. According to the map shown at the right, the APPROXIMATE distance between the southern point of New York City and Albany is _____ miles.
    A. 50
    B. 75
    C. 130
    D. 180
    E. 200

37._____

38. If 6 is added to a certain number n, the result is 1. An equation which expresses this relationship is
    A. n + 6 = 1   B. n – 1 = 6   C. 6 – n = 1
    D. n + 1 = 6   E. None of the above

38._____

39. In the expression $2n^3$, the 3 is called a(n)
    A. coefficient   B. factor   C. exponent
    D. multiplicand   E. None of the above

39._____

40. The number of inches in n feet is represented by
    A. 12n   B. 3n   C. n/3
    D. n/12   E. None of the above

40._____

41. The simple interest on $600 for 3 months at 4 percent per year is represented by 600 × .04x
    A. 1/4   B. 1/3   C. 3
    D. 4   E. None of the above

42. The circle graph shown at the right indicates how a family's annual budget of $3,000 was planned.
    Food   40 percent
    Shelter   25 percent
    Clothes   15 percent
    Operating Expenses   10 percent
    Insurance & Savings 10 percent
    The part of the circle representing Shelter is _____ degrees.
    A. 25   B. 45   C. 90
    D. 250   E. None of the above

43. In the parallelogram ABCD shown at the right, each small square represents 4 square inches. The area of the right triangle AED represents _____ square inches.
    A. 3
    B. 12
    C. 24
    D. 48
    E. None of the above

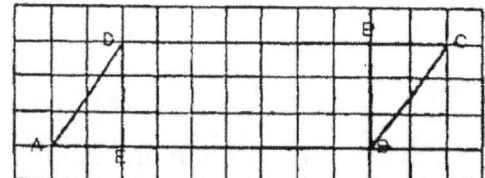

44. A surveyor measured angle x with a transit. (See figure at the right.) Angle x is called
    A. the angle of depression B from A
    B. an obtuse angle
    C. the supplement of angle
    D. the angle of elevation of B from A
    E. none of the above

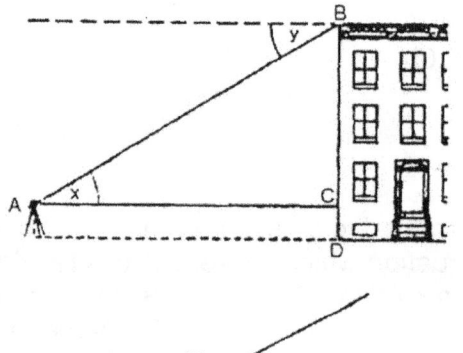

45. In the figure at the right, AOB is a straight line. An equation showing the relationship between u and v is
    A. u = 1/2v
    B. u = 180 − v
    C. u + v = 90
    D. v = 3u
    E. None of the above

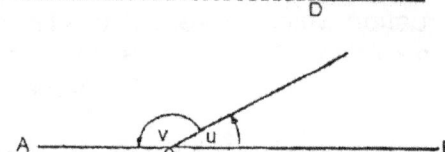

46. If x = 4 when y = 6 and x varies directly as y, then when y = 15, x equals
    A. 20   B. 10   C. 1 3/5
    D. 1 1/3   E. None of the above

47. A discount of 15 percent from a marked price produces a net price which is _____ of the marked price.
    A. .15%   B. .85%   C. 15%   D. 85%   E. 115%

48. When the formula A = P + Prt is solved for t, t equals
    A. A – P – Pr   B. $\frac{A-Pr}{P}$ C. $\frac{A-P}{1+r}$
    D. $\frac{A-P}{Pr}$ E. None of the above

49. The Greek letter π
    A. was assigned the value 3.1416 by the International Court of Law
    B. was given an arbitrary value of 22/7 by a famous mathematician
    C. was discovered to be exactly 3.142
    D. when multiplied by the radius of a circle equals the area
    E. is used as a symbol for the ratio of the circumference of a circle to its diameter

50. If the base and altitude of a triangle are doubled, the area
    A. remains constant   B. is multiplied by 4   C. is doubled
    D. is divided by 4   E. is none of the above

51. Each side of the equilateral triangle in the figure at the right is s inches long. The length of an altitude of the triangle is represented as
    A. s in.
    B. $s\sqrt{2}$
    C. $s\sqrt{3}$
    D. $\frac{s\sqrt{3}}{2}$ in.
    E. None of the above

52. The length of a meter is about _____ inches.
    A. 1   B. 6   C. 12   D. 40   E. 100

53. A point which lies on the straight-line graph of the equation 2x – 3y = 12 is
    A. (3,-2)   B. (2,-3)   C. (-4,0)
    D. (0,6)   E. None of the above

54. If the two parallel lines AB and CD in the figure at the right are cut by a third line, EF, then the FALSE statement is
    A. $\angle r + \angle s = \angle s + \angle y$
    B. $\angle y + \angle w = \angle t + \angle s$
    C. $\angle u + \angle w = \angle s + \angle x$
    D. $\angle r + \angle x = \angle t + \angle w$
    E. $\angle s + \angle u = \angle r + \angle t$

54._____

55. The product of n^4 and n^2 equals
    A. $2n^8$ B. $2n^6$ C. n^8
    D. n^2 E. None of the above

55._____

56. The volume of the rectangular solid shown at the right is
    A. 12 cu. in.
    B. 44 sq. in.
    C. 48 cu. in.
    D. 88 sq. in.
    E. None of the above

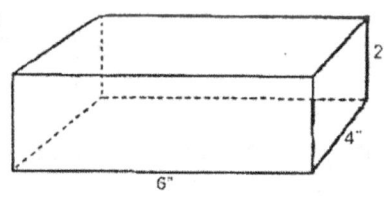

56._____

57. Baseball bats listed at twenty-one dollars per dozen are sold to schools at a discount of 20 percent.
    How much do they cost the schools per dozen?
    A. $4.20   B. $16.80   C. $20.80
    D. $25.20   E. None of the above

57._____

58. Last year a Chicago merchant's total business amounted to $30,000. For the goods sold, he paid $12,000, for rent he paid $2,500, for clerk services $4,742, and for other expenses $1,058.
    His average monthly net profit was
    A. $676.67   B. $891.67   C. $2,500.00
    D. $9,700.00   E. None of the above

58._____

59. If the marked price of an article is $100 and the first discount is 10 percent and the second discount 2 percent, the sale price is
    A. $78.20   B. $88.00   C. $88.20
    D. $88.80   E. None of the above

59._____

60. Mr. Smith agreed to pay an automobile agency a commission of 18 percent of the selling price of his car.
    If the selling price was $1,250, Mr. Smith would receive
    A. $225.00   B. $1,025.00   C. $1,227.50
    D. $1,475.00   E. None of the above

60._____

61. Mr. Browne receives $30.45 per year on an investment of $870.
    At this rate, if his total investment was $1,500, his annual interest would be
    A. $52.50   B. $62.50   C. $625.00
    D. $655.45   E. None of the above

61._____

9 (#1)

62. The Ephrata National Bank discounted a 60-day note for $3,500 at 3½ percent per year.
    The proceeds of the note were
    A. $3,377.50   B. $3,479.58   C. $3,520.42
    D. $3,622.50   E. None of the above

    62._____

63. The normal weight of an adult can be found by using the formula $w = 5.5(20+d)$, where w represents the weight in pounds and d the number of inches one's height exceeds 5 feet.
    By this formula, the normal weight of an adult who is 5'6" tall is _____ pounds.
    A. 134   B. 140.25   C. 140.8
    D. 143.0   E. None of the above

    63._____

64. In the figure at the right, triangles ACB and ADE are similar triangles. The length of side DE is _____ feet.
    A. 30
    B. 32
    C. 48
    D. 50
    E. None of the above

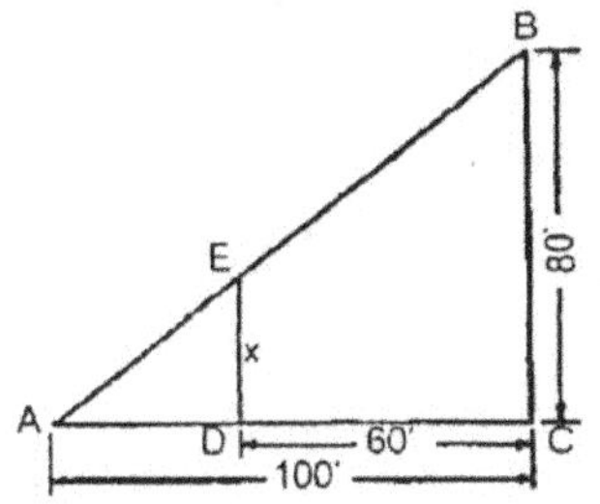

    64._____

65. A square piece of tin shown in the figure at the right is used to make an open box. One-inch squares are cut from each corner of the piece of tin and the sides then turned up, to form a box containing 49 cubic inches.
    The length of a side of the original square piece of tin required to make this box is _____ inches.
    A. 5
    B. 7
    C. 8
    D. 9
    E. None of the above

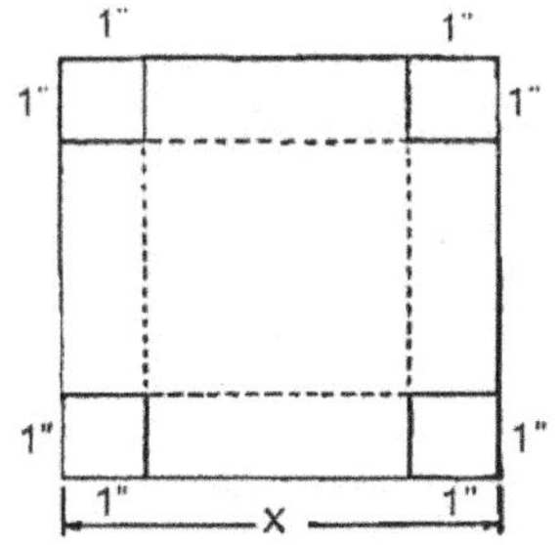

    65._____

KEY (CORRECT ANSWERS)

1.	C	11.	B	21.	D	31.	A	41.	A	51.	D	61.	A
2.	C	12.	A	22.	D	32.	A	42.	C	52.	D	62.	B
3.	B	13.	A	23.	C	33.	E	43.	B	53.	A	63.	D
4.	D	14.	E	24.	E	34.	C	44.	D	54.	E	64.	B
5.	C	15.	E	25.	D	35.	C	45.	B	55.	E	65.	D
6.	B	16.	E	26.	A	36.	B	46.	B	56.	C		
7.	A	17.	C	27.	B	37.	C	47.	D	57.	B		
8.	D	18.	A	28.	D	38.	A	48.	D	58.	E		
9.	C	19.	A	29.	E	39.	C	49.	E	59.	C		
10.	C	20.	E	30.	E	40.	A	50.	B	60.	B		

11 (#1)

SOLUTIONS TO PROBLEMS

1. $2/3 \times 12 = \frac{12}{1} = \frac{24}{3} = 8$

2. Adding, we get 109.14

3. If 5x = 75, x = 75/5 = 15

4. 65.13 ÷ 13 = 501

5. 6 ft. 8 in. + 3 ft. 4 in. = 9 ft. 12 in. = 10 ft.

6. 3/4 − 1/2 + 1/8 = 6/8 − 4/8 + 1/8 = 3/8

7. 4 15/16 − 2 3/8 = 3 21/16 − 2 6/16 = 1 15/16

8. (−12) + (−3) = −15

9. Let x = length of longer line. Then, 5:3 = x:30. Solving, x = 50

10. .025 = 25/1000 (Can also be reduced to 1/40)

11. Cross-multiplying, 5x = 18. Thus, 18/5 = 3.6

12. 33 1/3% of 3 = (1/3)(3) = 1

13. $\sqrt{225}$ = 15, since 15^2 = 225

14. The arrow points to 6 3/8

15. 4x/5 − 6 = 10. Adding 6, 4x/5 = 16. Then, x = 16 ÷ 4/5 = 20

16. 8 hrs. 0 min. 6 sec. − 6 hrs. 4 min. 15 sec. can be written as 7 hrs. 59 min. 66 sec. − 6 hrs. 4 min. 15 sec. to get 1 hr. 55 min. 51 sec.

17. Mean = (2+4+6+8+10+12+14+19) ÷ 9 = 9

18. When n = 0, c = 0. When n = 5, c = 100. Thus, c = 20n. Finally, for n = 7, c = (20)(7) = 140

19. A = 1/2 bh + 1/2 h(b+a)

20. 6 inches : 3 feet = 6 inches : 36 inches = 1/6

21. Add 5 to both sides to get 4s = 12, so s = 3

22. 16 2/3% of x is 30. Then, 1/6 x = 30. Then, 1/6 x = 180

12 (#1)

23. At 7:00 A.M. the temperature was 12.5, while at 9:00 A.M. the temperature was 15. The change was 2.5 degrees.

24. Perimeter of Section I is 4b and the perimeter of Section III is 2b + 2a − 2b = 2a. The sum of the perimeters is 4b + 2a,

25. Area of Section II is b(a-b) = ab − b^2 and the area of Section IV is $(a-b)^2 = a^2 − 2ab + b^2$. The sum of the areas is $a^2 − ab = a(a-b)$.

26. Direct translation of words to symbols yields F = 9/5C + 32

27. Subtract 6x to get -114 = 5.7x. Solving, x = 20

28. (84/42)(100)% = 200%

29. The figure is a cylinder.

30. Converting each choice to a decimal, we get .5, .$\bar{5}$, .58$\bar{3}$, .6, .75. The largest is .75 corresponding to 3/4.

31. For a circle, A = πr^2

32. A five-sided enclosed figure with straight sides is called a pentagon.

33. A quadrilateral with opposite sides parallel is called a parallelogram. Rectangles and squares are parallelograms with 90° angles.

34. x − y + z = 18 − 3 − 2 = 23

35. Since the digit in the hundreds place is 5 or greater, the answer is 336,000.

36. The sum of the angles of any triangle is 180°.

37. The scale difference is about 2 inches, and since 50 miles corresponds to 3/4 inch, the actual distance is about (50)(2÷3/4) = 133 1/3 mi. Closest answer given s 130 mi.

38. 6 added to n means 6 + n. Thus, 6 + n = 1 or n + 6 = 1.

39. 3 is an exponent for $2n^3$.

40. 12 inches in 1 foot means 12n inches in n feet.

41. 3 months = 1/4 year

42. 25% of 360 degrees = 90 degrees.

43. Area of △AED = (1/2)(2)(3) = 3 square units = 12 sq. inches.

44. Angle X is the angle of elevation to B from A.

13 (#1)

45. Since u + v = 180, we can also write u = 180 − v

46. 4/x = 6/15 Cross-multiplying, 6x = 60. Solving, x = 10

47. 100% - 15% = 85%

48. A = P + Prt becomes A − P = Prt. Dividing by Pr, we get: t = (A-P)/Pr

49. π = ratio of circumference to diameter of a circle.

50. Let B = base, H = altitude. Original area of triangle = 1/2BH. If new base and altitude are 2B and 2H, new area = ½(2B)(2H) = 2BH, which is 4 times the value of 1/2BH.

51. Let x = altitude. Then, $x^2 + (s/2)^2 = s^2$. This becomes $3/4s^2 = x^2$. Solving, x = s √3 /2

52. 1 meter ≈ 39.37 inches ≈ 40 inches.

53. Substituting (3,-2), 2(3) − 3(-2) = 12. The other points do not lie on 2x − 3y = 12.

54. The false statement is ∠2 + ∠u = ∠r + ∠t. It is only true that ∠x = ∠u and∠ r = ∠t).

55. $n^4 • n^2 = n^6$, since exponents are added in multiplication.

56. Volume = (6)(4)(2) = 48 cu. in.

57. ($21)(.80) = $16.80

58. $30,000 - $12,000 - $2,500 - $4,742 - $1,058 = $9,700. The monthly amount is $9,700 ÷ 12 = $808.33

59. ($100)(.90) = $90. Then, ($90)(.98) = $88.20

60. 1,250 − (1,250)(.18) = $1,025

61. $30.45/$870 = 3.5%. Then, 3.5% of $1,500 = $52.50

62. (.035)(60/360) = .00583̄ = discount for 60 days.
The value of the note = (1 - .00583̄)($3500) = $3,479.58.

63. W = 5.5(20+6) = (5.5)(26) = 143

64. x/80 = 40/100. Solving, x = 32. Note that AD:AC = DE:BC

65. When folded, each new side is √49 = 7

EXAMINATION SECTION
TEST 1

DIRECTIONS: Each question or incomplete statement is followed by several suggested answers or completions. Select the one that BEST answers the question or completes the statement. *PRINT THE LETTER OF THE CORRECT ANSWER IN THE SPACE AT THE RIGHT.*

1. Which ordered pair of numbers (x,y) is the solution of the following system of equations?
   $3x - 2y = 5$
   $2x + 2y = 10$
   A. (1,1)   B. (1,2)   C. (2,1)   D. (2,3)   E. (3,2)

   1._____

2. A certain microcomputer's memory contains 16K (K = 1,024) storage locations. If a program being run uses 12,517 storage locations, how many storage locations are still available?
   A. 3,767   B. 3,867   C. 4,867   D. 11,493   E. 16,384

   2._____

3. $(3.5 + 0.3) - 4(0.82 + 1.08) =$
   A. -3.800   B. -0.380   C. 0.304   D. 1.700   E. 4.840

   3._____

4.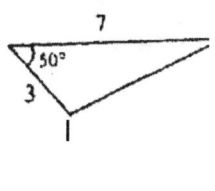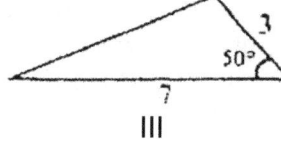

   4._____

   Which of the above triangles are congruent?
   A. I and II
   B. I and III
   C. II and III
   D. All of the above
   E. No triangle is congruent to any other triangle

5. A survey asked a sample of people to choose the better candidate in an upcoming election. Of the people surveyed, 20% said they would vote for Candidate A, 30% for Candidate B, and 50% said they were undecided.
   If 1,000 people said they would vote for Candidate A, how many people said they would vote for Candidate B?
   A. 300   B. 1,100   C. 1,500   D. 2,500   E. 5,000

   5._____

6. Sheila's salary is $110 per day. Due to financial problems in her company, her employer has asked Sheila too take a 10% cut in pay.
   How much will Sheila be earning per day if she takes the cut in pay?
   A. $11   B. $99   C. $100   D. $109   E. $121

7. The 6 M. temperature one day last winter was -13°F. From 6 M. until 1 P.M., the temperature rose an average of 3°F per hour.
   Which of the following expressions represents the temperature in °F at 1 P.M.?
   A. 7(-13+3)   B. -13-7(3)   C. 7+3(-13)   D. -13+5(3)   E. -13+7(3)

8.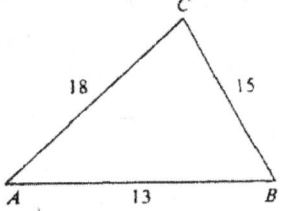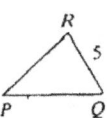

   In the figure above, △ABC is similar to △PQR, and the measure of ∠A is equal to the measure of ∠P. The length PR is
   A. 4 1/6   B. 4 1/3   C. 5 10/13   D. 6   E. 8

9. |-5|+|6|+(-5)+6 =
   A. -22   B. -1-   C. 2   D. 10   E. 12

10. A bread recipe calls for 1/2 cup of butter and 3 1/2 cups of flour. Using this recipe to make enough bread for a party, John will need 1 1/2 cups of butter. How many cups of flour will he need?
    A. 4 1/2   B. 5 1/2   C. 7 1/2   D. 9 1/2   E. 10 1/2

11.

Midland A/V Supply House			
Item	Price Each	Quantity Ordered	Total for Item(s)
8 GB Flash Drive	$4.50	6	
Bluetooth Earbuds	$36.00	1	
CD cases (plastic)	$0.10	25	
		Subtotal	$
		Add 4% Sales Tax	+
		Shipping	+150
		Total	$

   What would be the TOTAL cost of the order shown above?
   A. $42.10   B. $65.50   C. $67.00   D. $69.62   E. $69.68

12. The distance, in miles, from an observer to the horizon is 1.35 times the square root of the observer's elevation, in feet.
    If an observer's elevation is 16 feet, how many miles away is the horizon?
    A. 5.4   B. 7.0   C. 10.8   D. 11.9   E. 48.6

13. If 3x − 2y = 6, then y equals which of these expressions?
    A. $-\frac{3}{2}x-3$ B. $-\frac{3}{2}x+6$ C. $\frac{3}{2}x-3$ D. $\frac{3}{2}x+3$ E. 3x−3

13._____

14.

Age	Number of Students
14	50
15	180
16	180
17	340
18	210
19	40
Total	1,000

The ages of the students attending City High School this year are listed in the table above.
If a student is picked at random from this school, what is the probability that he or she will be 18 or older?
    A. 1/25   B. 1/4   C. 1/3   D. 1/2   E. 3/4

14._____

15.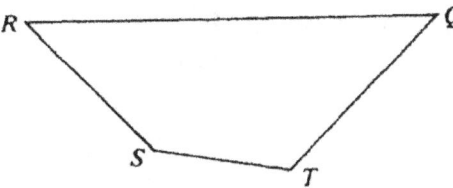

In quadrilateral QRST above, the measures of ∠Q, ∠R, and ∠S are 45°, 45°, and 140°, respectfully.
The measure of ∠T is _____ degrees.
    A. 120   B. 130   C. 135   D. 140   E. 220

15._____

16. If x = 3 and y = −2, then the GREATEST value is
    A. |x−y| B. |x|−|y| C. |x|−y   D. x−|y| E. x−y

16._____

17.

Name	Height in Inches
Adam	65
Barbara	64
Chris	69
Daniel	64
Ella	65

What is the average (arithmetic mean) height, in inches, of the five people whose heights are listed in the above table?
    A. 65.0   B. 65.2   C. 65.4   D. 66.0   E. 66.5

17._____

18. The Jones family wants to buy a refrigerator that costs $750. They agree to pay 15% of the cost initially and the balance in 5 equal monthly payments without interest.
    How much will each monthly payment be?
    A. $112.50   B. $127.50   C. $129.50   D. $147.00   E. $150.00

19. What is the SMALLEST positive integer that gives a remainder of 1 when divided by any of the integers 12, 18, and 27?
    A. 121   B. 109   C. 61   D. 55   E. 37

20. A serving of a certain cereal, with milk, provides 35% of the potassium required daily by the average adult. A serving of this cereal with milk contains 112 milligrams of potassium.
    How many milligrams of potassium does the average adult require each day?
    A. 35   B. 39   C. 147   D. 320   E. 392

21. Three people share $198 in the ratio 1:3:7.
    To the nearest dollar, how much is the LARGEST share?
    A. $18   B. $28   C. $54   D. $126   E. $134

22. Which of the following is a factorization of the polynomial $2x^2 + x - 10$?
    A. $2(x^2+x-5)$
    B. $(2x+2)(x-5)$
    C. $(2x+5)(x-2)$
    D. $(2x-5)(x+2)$
    E. $(2x+10)(x-1)$

23. In the figure at the right, B, E, and C are collinear; A, D, and C ae collinear; E is halfway between B and C; and $\overline{DE}$ and $\overline{AB}$ are each perpendicular to $\overline{BC}$.
    If $\overline{BE}$ is 40 units long and $\overline{AB}$ is 60 units long, how many units long is the perimeter of quadrilateral ABED?
    A. 100
    B. 140
    C. 180
    D. 200
    E. 220

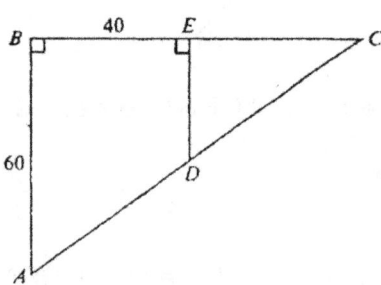

24. The circle graph at the right represents the relative sizes of the sources of a tax dollar. The degree measure of the central angle of the sector labeled *Income* is _____ degrees.
    A. 40
    B. 72
    C. 100
    D. 120
    E. 144

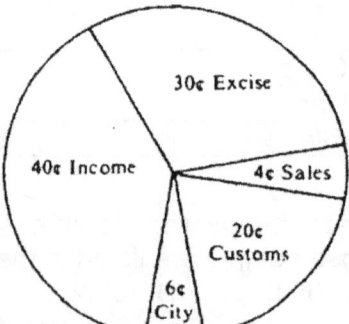

25. $\sqrt{8} + \sqrt{16} + 3\sqrt{2} - \sqrt{3} =$
    A. $4 + 5\sqrt{2} - \sqrt{3}$
    B. $11\sqrt{2} - \sqrt{3}$
    C. $3\sqrt{26} - \sqrt{3}$
    D. $15 - \sqrt{3}$
    E. $3\sqrt{23}$

26. Two lines have the equations 2x + y = 4 and x - 2y = 7, respectively. At what (x,y) point do they intersect?
    A. (3,2)   B. (6,-5)   C. (5,-6)   D. (-3,-2)   E. (-2,3)

27.

x	0	2	4	6	8	10
y	4	7	10	13	16	19

Which of these equations expresses the relationship shown in the above table?
A. y = 2x   B. y = x + 4   C. y = x + 9
D. 2y = 3x + 4 E. 2y = 3x + 8

28. A life insurance policy costs $0.75 per month for each $1,000 worth of insurance.
    At this rate, how much would someone have to pay in a year for $25,000 worth of this insurance?
    A. $225.00   B. $187.50   C. $156.25   D. $75.00   E. $18.75

29. In the circle at the right, which has O as its center, $\overline{OA}$ and $\overline{AB}$ are each 4 units long.
    If $\overline{OE}$ is perpendicular to $\overline{AB}$, how many units long is $\overline{OE}$?
    A. $\sqrt{3}$
    B. 2
    C. 3
    D. $2\sqrt{3}$
    E. 4

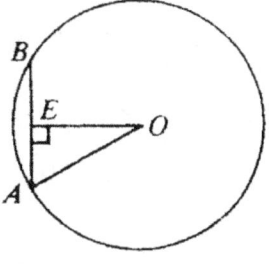

30. If the solutions of the equation $2x^2 - kx + 6 = 0$ are x = 1 and x = 3, then k =
    A. -4   B. 4   C. 7   D. 8   E. 10

31. If f(x) = x + 3 and g(x) = 3 − x, what is the value of f[g(3)]?
    A. 6   B. 3   C. 0   D. -3   E. -6

32. Let x equal the numerator of a certain fraction. The denominator of that fraction is 2 more than the numerator. When 5 is added to both the numerator and the denominator, the resulting fraction equals 5/6.
    Which of these equations determines the correct value of x, the numerator of the original fraction?

    A. $\dfrac{x+5}{x+3} = \dfrac{5}{6}$
    B. $\dfrac{x+3}{x+5} = \dfrac{5}{6}$
    C. $\dfrac{x+5}{x+7} = \dfrac{5}{6}$
    D. $\dfrac{x+5}{2x+5} = \dfrac{5}{6}$
    E. $\dfrac{2x+5}{x+5} = \dfrac{5}{6}$

33. A man throwing darts at a dartboard hit the board on 95% of the throws he made. He hit the board 114 times.
   Which equation determines the CORRECT value of x, the number of throws he made?
   A. $(0.95)114 = x$
   B. $0.95x = 114$
   C. $114x = 95$
   D. $\frac{x}{95} = 114$
   E. $x = \frac{0.95}{114}$

34. Which equation determines the line that is parallel to the line with the equation $y = 3x + 1$ and intersects the line with the equation $y = 6x$ at the y-axis?
   y =
   A. $3x - 1$ B. $2x - 1$ C. $1/3x - 1$ D. $1/3x + 1$ E. $1/2x - 1$

35.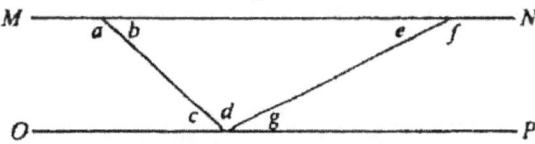

   In the figure above, 2 line segments intersect $\overline{MN}$ and $\overline{OP}$, $\overline{MN}$ is parallel to $\overline{OP}$, and a, b, c, d, e, f, and g are the measures, in degrees, of the indicated angles. Which of these statements is NOT necessarily true?
   A. $b = 180° - d - c$
   B. $e = 180° - d - c$
   C. $a = 180° - c$
   D. $f = 180° - g$
   E. $g = 180° - f$

36. If $x = 2$, $y = 3$, and $z = 5$, then the product xyz is how much GREATER than the sum $x + y + z$?
   A. -34   B. -26   C. 20   D. 26   E. 34

37. If $n! = (n)(n-1)(n-2)....(2)(1)$, then $5! =$
   A. 12   B. 15   C. 30   D. 120   E. 54,321

38. For all x, $(2x+3)^2 + 2(2x+4) - 2$ equals which of these expressions?
   A. $4x^2 + 4x + 11$
   B. $(4x+15)(x+1)$
   C. $(2x+5)(2x+3)$
   D. $(2x+5)(2x+2)$
   E. $(2x+5)(2x-3)$

39. What is TRUE about the solutions of the equation $x^2 - 3x = 2$?
   They are
   A. real and unequal
   B. real and equal
   C. real and negative
   D. irrational and negative
   E. imaginary

40. If the retail price of a dinette set is 1 1/3 times the wholesale price, and the retail price of a dinette set is $200.00, what is its wholesale price?
   A. $133/33   B. $150.00   C. $166.67   D. $266.67   E. $300.00

KEY (CORRECT ANSWERS)

1.	E	11.	D	21.	D	31.	B
2.	B	12.	A	22.	C	32.	C
3.	A	13.	C	23.	C	33.	B
4.	B	14.	B	24.	E	34.	A
5.	C	15.	B	25.	A	35.	A
6.	B	16.	C	26.	A	36.	E
7.	E	17.	C	27.	E	37.	D
8.	D	18.	B	28.	A	38.	C
9.	E	19.	B	29.	D	39.	A
10.	E	20.	D	30.	D	40.	B

8 (#1)

SOLUTIONS TO PROBLEMS

1. Adding the equations, 5x = 15, so x = 3. Substituting this value of x into the first equation, 9 – 2y = 5. Then, y = 2.

2. (16)(1024) = 16,384. Then, 16,384 – 12,517 = 3867.

3. Simplify to 3.8 – 4(1.9) = -3.8 or 3.800

4. Triangles I and III are congruent by SAS, which refers to two pairs of matching sides and an included equivalent angle.

5. The ratios of votes for Candidate A to votes for Candidate B is 2:3. Then, letting x = number of votes for Candidate B, 2:3 = 1000:x. Solving, x = 1500.

6. Her pay after a 10% cut is ($110)(.90) = $99

7. Since the temperature rose 3° per hour for 7 hours, the temperature at 1:00 P.M. was -13° + 7(3°)

8. 18:PR = 15:5. Solving, PR = 6

9. |-5|+|6| + (-5) + 6 = +6 – 5 + 6 = 12

10. Let x = cups of flour. Then, $\frac{1}{2} : 3\frac{1}{2} = 1\frac{1}{2} : x$. This becomes $\frac{1}{2}x = 5\frac{1}{4}$. Solving, $x = 10\frac{1}{2}$

11. Total for items before tax is 6($4.50) + 1($36.00) + 25($0.10) = $65.50. Then, $65.50 + (.04)($65.50) + $1.50 = $69.62.

12. $(1.35)(\sqrt{16}) = (1.35 \times 4) = 5.4$

13. Subtract 3x from both sides of the equation to get -2y = -3x + 6.3. Dividing by -2, $y = \frac{3}{2}x - 3$

14. There are 250 students 18 or older out of 1,000 students in the school. Probability of selecting a student 18 or older is 250/1000 = ¼

15. ∠T = 360° - 45° - 45° - 140° = 130°. Note that the sum of the angles in any quadrilateral is 360°

16. Choice C has a value of |-3|-|(-2) = 3 + 2 = 5, which exceeds the value of each of the other choices.

17. Total of heights = 327. Average height is 327/5 = 65'4"

9 (#1)

18. ($750)(.15) = $112.50. The balance is $637.50. If this is paid in 5 equal installments, each installment is $637.50/5 = $127.50.

19. The number 109 when divided by any of 12, 18, or 27 gives a remainder of 1.

20. The amount of potassium required is 112 ÷ .35 = 320 milligrams

21. Let x, 3x, 7x represent each person's share. Then, x + 3x + x = 198, so x = $18. Then, largest share is 7($18) = $126

22. $2x^2 + x - 10 = (2x+5)(x-2)$, which can be checked by multiplication.

23. Because △GED is similar to △CBA, ED = 1/2(BA) = 30
Now, AC = $\sqrt{80^2 + 60^2}$ = 100, so AD = 1/2(100) = 50. The perimeter of ABED is 40 + 60 + 50 + 30 = 180

24. Total of all sources is 100 cents. The central angle for income is, in degrees, (40/100)(360) = 144

25. $\sqrt{8} + \sqrt{16} + 3\sqrt{2} - \sqrt{3} = 2\sqrt{2} + 4 + 3\sqrt{2} - \sqrt{3} = 4 + 5\sqrt{2} - \sqrt{3}$

26. Double the 2nd equation to get 2x – 4y = 14. Subtract the 1st equation to get -5y = 10, so y = 2. Substitute into the 1st equation to get 2x – 2 = 4. Then, x = 3. The point of intersection is (3,-2).

27. Determine the slope to be (7-4)7(2-0) = 3/2. Then, $y = \frac{3}{2}x + k$, where k is a constant. Substituting the point (0,4), $4 = \frac{3}{2}x + 4$ or equivalently 2y = 3x + 8.

28. ($0.75)(25) = $18.75 per month = $225 per year.

29. BE = 1/2(4) = 2. Then, $(QE)^2 + 2^2 = 4^2$. Solving, OE = $\sqrt{12} = 2\sqrt{3}$

30. Substituting x = 1, $2(1^2) - k(1) + 6 = 0$. Simplifying, 8 – k = 0. So, k = 8. Note that if we used x = 3, $2(3^2) - k(3) + 6 = 0$. This would lead to 24 – 3k = 0, and still k = 8.

31. g(3) = 3 – 3 = 0. Then, f[g(3)] = f(0) = 0 + 3 = 3

32. Since x = numerator, x + 2 = denominator. Adding 5 to each makes the new numerator x + 5 and the new denominator X + 7. Thus, (x+5)/(x+7) = 5/6

33. Let x = number of throws. Then, .95x = 114, since his 114 hits represent 95% of his throws.

34. A line parallel to y = 3x + 1 must be of the form y = 3x + k, where k is a constant. The equation y = 6x – 1 crosses the y-axis at (0,-1) and this point must lie on y = 3x + k. By substitution, -1 = 3(0) + k, k = -1. The resulting equation.

10 (#1)

35. The statement which is NOT necessarily true is b = 180° - d – c. We know that c + d + g = 180°, but b and g are not necessarily equal.

36. xyz = 30, x + y + z = 4. Then, xyz – (x+y+z) = 34.

37. 5! = (5)(4)(3)(2)(1) – 120

38. $(2x+3)^2 + 2(2x+4) - 2 = 4x^2 + 12x + 9 + 4x + 8 - 2 = 4x^2 + 16x + 15$. This last expression factors as (2x+5)(2x+3).

39. Rewrite as $x^2 - 3x + 2 = 0$, which becomes (x-2)(x-1) = 0. The solutions are x = 1 and x = 2, which are real and unequal.

40. Let x = wholesale price. Then, $200 = $1\frac{1}{3}$x. Solving, x = $150

EXAMINATION SECTION
TEST 1

DIRECTIONS: Each question or incomplete statement is followed by several suggested answers or completions. Select the one that BEST answers the question or completes the statement. *PRINT THE LETTER OF THE CORRECT ANSWER IN THE SPACE AT THE RIGHT.*

1. At 7:00 A.M., a student leaves his home in his automobile to drive to school 28 miles away. He averages 50 mph until 7:30 A.M., when his car breaks down. The student has to walk and run the rest of the way.
   If he wants to arrive at school at 8:00 A.M., how fast, in mph, must he travel on foot?
   A. 3   B. 4   C. 5   D. 6   E. 7

   1.____

2. Express $1 + \dfrac{\frac{1}{2+1}}{1+\frac{1}{4}}$ in simplest terms.
   A. 27/28   B. 30/43   C. 1 1/9   D. 1 1/27   E. 1 13/30

   2.____

3. A theater charges $5.00 admission for adults and $2.50 for children. At one showing, 240 admissions brought in a total of $800.
   How many adults attended the showing?
   A. 40   B. 80   C. 120   D. 160   E. 266

   3.____

4. $\sqrt{25+?} = 5 + 8$
   A. 8   B. 12   C. 64   D. 144   E. 169

   4.____

5. The perimeter of a square is 20.
   Which of the following represents the area?
   A. 5   B. 10   C. 20   D. 25   E. 100

   5.____

6. Evaluate the expression $\dfrac{1}{4} + \dfrac{3}{8} - \dfrac{6}{16} - \dfrac{8}{32}$
   A. 7/16   B. 1/32   C. 1/8   D. 1/4   E. 0

   6.____

7. Bill spent 20% of the money he initially had in his wallet on groceries and 25% on gas. He had $66.00 left.
   How much money did he have before he shopped?
   A. $85   B. $100   C. $110   D. $111   E. $120

   7.____

8. Express the product $(2x+5y)^2$ in simplest form.
   A. $4x^2 + 25y^2$ B. $4x^2 + 20xy + 25y^2$ C. $4x^2 + 10y + 25y^2$
   D. $4x^2 - 20xy + 25y^2$ E. $4x + 25y$

   8.____

9. A student received test grades of 83, 90, and 88.
   What was her grade on a fourth test if the average for the four tests is 84?
   A. 85   B. 80   C. 75   D. 70   E. 65

   9.____

211

10. A rectangular room is 3 meters wide, 4 meters long, and 2 meters high. How far is it from the northeast corner at the floor to the southwest corner at the ceiling?
_____ meters.
   A. $\sqrt{29}$ B. $\sqrt{11}$ C. $\sqrt{9}$ D. 9   E. 5

11. If an electron has a mass of 9.109×10^{-31} kg and a proton has a mass of 1.672×10^{-27} kg, approximately how many electrons are required to have the same mass as one proton?
   A. 150,000   B. 1,800   C. 5.4×10^4
   D. 5.4×10^{-4} E. 15×10^{-58}

12. The introduction of a new manufacturing process will affect a saving of $1,450 per week over the initial 8-week production period. New equipment, however, will cost 1/4 of the total savings.
How much did the equipment cost?
   A. $11.600.00   B. $2,900.00   C. $725.00
   D. $362.50   E. $181.25

13. If P dollars is invested at r percent compounded annually, at the end of n years it will have grown to $A = P(1+r)^n$. An investment made at 16% compounded annually. It grows to $1,740 at the end of one year.
How much was originally invested?
   A. $150   B. $278.40   C. $1,461.60
   D. $1,500   E. $1,700

14. What is 1/4% of 200?
   A. 0.05   B. 0.5   C. 5   D. 12.5   E. 50

15. Which of the following is .5% of .95?
   A. .000475   B. .00475   C. .0475   D. .475   E. 4.75

16. What is the value of (5 lbs. 1 oz.)/(3 lbs. 6 oz.) in ounces?
   A. 22   B. 1.66   C. 1.5   D. 0.66   E. 0.28

17. If 1 inch = 2.56 centimeters, 3/8 centimeter equals which of the following in inches?
   A. 6.77   B. .95   C. .39   D. .38   E. .15

18. If $2x + y = 7$ and $x - 4y = 4$, then x equals which of the following?
   A. -15/9   B. -1/9   C. 7/15   D. 11/9   E. 32/9

19. What part of an hour is 6 seconds?
   A. 1/600   B. 1/10   C. 1/360   D. 1/60   E. 1/5

20. If $1/3 + 5(x-1) = 8$, then which of the following is the value of x?
   A. 8/13   B. 8/5   C. 38/25   D. 38/15   E. 38

21. Which line is perpendicular to the x-axis?
    A. x = 3   B. y = 3   C. x = y   D. x = y/3   E. y = x/3

22. If a dental hygienist at a certain office is paid H dollars a week, the dental assistant works 36 hours a week at A dollars per hour, and the receptionist works 40 hours a week and receives R dollars every other week, which of the following represents the weekly payroll for these three employees?
    A. H/3 + 36A + 40R/3
    B. H + 36A + R/2
    C. H/3 + 12A + R/6
    D. 5H + 36 + 20R
    E. H/3 + 12A + 40R

23. Company A ordered five units of anesthetic at $12.00 per unit. Company B ordered 10 units at $13.00 per unit, and Company C ordered 4 at $10.00 per unit. Since all these companies were at one address, the three orders were put on one bill.
    Approximately what percent of the total bill did Company A have to pay?
    A. 5   B. 18   C. 26   D. 36   E. 55

24. Which of the following is the value of A, if 50(A/100) = 2A^2?
    A. 25   B. 1   C. 5/2   D. 1/4   E. 1/2

25. Five-eighths of the employees in the company are single males. What percentage of the employees in the company are single males?
    A. 12.5   B. 20.0   C. 25.0   D. 32.0   E. 62.5

26. If x = 20% of y, and z = 35% of x, then z = _____ % of y.
    A. 70   B. 57   C. 7   D. 1.75   E. .07

27. Which of the following is the value of the expression $\frac{|14-3|-|7-16|}{3|(-2)+1|}$?
    A. -20/3   B. -2/3   C. 0   D. 23   E. 20/3

28. A tank can be filled by a pipe in 30 minutes and emptied by another pipe in 50 minutes.
    How many minutes will it take to fill the tank if both pipes are open?
    A. 45   B. 60   C. 75   D. 80   E. 100

29. If (4/5)x = (2/5)y, then which of the following is equal to y/x?
    A. 1/2   B. 2/5   C. 25/8   D. 2   E. 3

30. Which of the following would NOT result in a straight line? x =
    A. 1/y   B. 2y + 5   C. (y+6)/(2)   D. 5 − y   E. 4(x+3y)

31. $\frac{5}{4} + \frac{4}{5} + \frac{3}{2} -$ _____ = a positive integer.
    A. 10/20   B. 11/20   C. 71/20   D. 3/20   E. 4/20

32. If $\frac{2}{x} + \frac{3}{5} = \frac{4}{3}$, then which of the following is the value of x?
    A. 30/11   B. 30/29   C. 11/30   D. -11/6   E. -5/2

33. Optometry school applicants decreased by 25% during a 4-year period. During the same time, the number of first-year openings in optometry school increased by 12%.
    If the ratio of applicants to first-year student openings had been 3 to 1, then which of the following would be the APPROXIMATE ratio at the end of the 4-year period?
    A. 1.5 to 1   B. 2 to 1   C. 3 to 2   D. 4 to 3   E. 6 to 5

34. If then which of the following is the value of x?
    A. 4   B. 27   C. 29   D. 40   E. 729

35. Two cars start at the same point and travel north and west at the rate of 24 and 32 mph, respectively.
    How far apart are they at the end of 2 hours?
    A. 63   B. 80   C. 112   D. 116   E. 100

36. Right triangle ABC with right angle C and AB = 6, BC = 3, find AC.
    A. 3   B. 6   C. 27   D. 33   E. $3\sqrt{3}$

37. When each of the sides of a square is increased by 1 yard, the area of the new square is 53 square yards more than that of the original square. What is the length of the sides of the original square?
    A. 25   B. 26   C. 27   D. 52   E. 54

38. Evaluate: $3(2)^2 + \sqrt{25} - (-2)^3$.
    A. 9   B. 24   C. 25   D. 33   E. 76

39. Which of the following is the length of the line segment BC if AB = 14, AD = 5, and angle BAD = 30°?
    A. $\sqrt{221}$
    B. $\sqrt{171}$
    C. $7\sqrt{3}$
    D. 7
    E. 9

    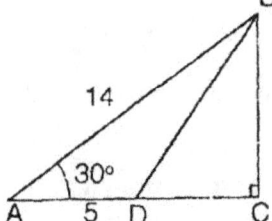

40. A bowl contains 7 green and 3 red marbles.
    What is the probability that two marbles selected at random from this bowl without replacement are both red?
    A. 1/15   B. 9/100   C. 21/100   D. 47/90   E. 6/10

41. If x pens cost 75 cents and y pencils cost 57 cents, then which equation below can be used to find the cost of 2 pens and 3 pencils?
    A. 2(75/x) + 3(57/y) B. 3x/75 + 2y/57 C. 75/2x + 57/3y
    D. 2(x/75) + 3(y/57) E. 3(75/x) + 2(57/y)

42. Maria has a number of dimes and quarters whose total value is less than $9.00. There are twice as many dimes as quarters.
    At most, how many quarters could she have?
    A. 14   B. 15   C. 19   D. 20   E. 35

43. The number (1, 2, 3, 6) have an average (arithmetic mean) of 3 and a variance of 3.5.
    What is the average (arithmetic mean) and variance of the set of numbers (3, 6, 9, 18)?
    A. 9, 31.5   B. 3, 10.5   C. 3, 31.5   D. 6, 7.5   E. 9, 27.5

44. A fence encloses a triangular-shaped region whose sides are 20 feet, 20 feet, and 10 feet in length.
    If the number of inches between fence posts (centers) is 30 inches, how many posts will be needed?
    A. 17   B. 20   C. 21   D. 22   E. 23

45. A ceiling 6 feet by 7 feet can be painted for $52.
    Find the cost of painting a ceiling 18 feet by 21 feet, all things equal except the dimensions.
    A. $104   B. $126   C. $156   D. $378   E. $468

46. Three consecutive odd numbers have a sum of 51.
    What is the LARGEST of these numbers?
    A. 15   B. 17   C. 18   D. 19   E. 21

47. It takes 5 hours for a qualified typist to complete a report. Coffee break begins at 10:15 A.M. It is now 9:55 A.M.
    How much of the task can the typist be expected to complete by coffee break?
    A. 1/8   B. 1/25   C. 1/3   D. 1/6   E. 1/15

48. A container in the form of a rectangular solid is 10 feet long, 9 feet wide, and 2 feet deep. The container is filled with a liquid weighing 100 pounds per cubic foot.
    A. 90   B. 180   C. 1,800   D. 9,000   E. 18,000

49. The value of cost ($\pi/3$) equals the value of
    A. $-\cos(2\pi/3)$ B. $\cos(2\pi/3)$ C. $\cos(6\pi/3)$
    D. $-\cos(5\pi/3)$ E. $\cos(4\pi/3)$

50. If $5 \leq x \leq 12$ and -2y9, then is as large as possible when x = _____ and y = _____.
    A. 12; 9   B. 12; 0   C. 12; -2   D. 0; 0   E. 0; 0

KEY (CORRECT ANSWERS)

1.	D	11.	B	21.	A	31.	B	41.	A
2.	E	12.	B	22.	B	32.	A	42.	C
3.	B	13.	D	23.	C	33.	B	43.	A
4.	D	14.	B	24.	D	34.	C	44.	B
5.	D	15.	B	25.	A	35.	B	45.	E
6.	E	16.	C	26.	C	36.	E	46.	D
7.	E	17.	E	27.	D	37.	B	47.	E
8.	B	18.	E	28.	C	38.	C	48.	E
9.	C	19.	A	29.	D	39.	D	49.	A
10.	A	20.	D	30.	A	40.	A	50.	B

SOLUTIONS TO PROBLEMS

1. Let x = rate of walking/running. Then, (50)(1/2) + (x)(1/2) = 28. Simplifying, 1/2x = 3. Solving, x = 6.

2. $3 + \frac{1}{4} = 3\frac{1}{4}$, $1/3\frac{1}{4} = \frac{4}{13}$, $2 + \frac{4}{13} = 2\frac{4}{13}$, $1/2\frac{4}{13} = \frac{13}{30}$
Finally, $1 + \frac{13}{30} = 1\frac{13}{30}$

3. Let x = number of adults, 240-x = number of children.
Then, 5x + 2.50(240-x) = 800. Simplifying, we get 5x + 600 – 2.50x = 800. This reduces to 2.50x = 200. Solving, x = 800

4. $\sqrt{25 + x} = 13$ squaring both sides, 25 + x = 169. So, x = 144.

5. If the perimeter of a square is 20, each side must be 5. The area is $5^2 = 25$.

6. Changing to a denominator of 32, we get 8/32 + 12/32 + 12/32 − 12/32 − 8/32 = 0/32 = 0

7. Let x = original amount. 100% - 20% - 25% = 55%. Then, $66 = .55x. Solving, x = $120

8. $(2x+5y)^2 = 4x^2 + 10xy + 25y^2 = 4x^2 + 20xy + 25y^2$

9. Let x = grade on her 4th test. Then, (83+90+88+x)/4 = 84. This becomes (261+x)/4 = 84. Further reduction leads to 261 + x = 336, so x – 75.

10. The required distance is $\sqrt{3^2 + 4^2 + 2^2} = \sqrt{9 + 16 + 4} = \sqrt{29}$

11. $(1.672 \times 10^{-27}) \div (9.1109 \times 10^{-31})$. $1836 \times 10^4 \approx 1800$

12. Total savings is $1450)(8) = $11,600. Equipment costs (1/4)($11,600) = $2900.

13. $1740 = P(l+.16)'. Then, P = $1740 ÷ 1.16 = $1500.

14. 1/4% of 200 is (.0025)(200) = .5

15. .5% of .95 is (.005)(.95) = .00475

16. 5 lbs. 1 oz. = 81 oz. and 3 lbs. 6 oz. = 54 oz. Then, 81 oz. ÷ 54 oz. = 1.5

17. 3/8 cm = 3/8 ÷ 2.54 = .375 ÷ 2.54 ≈ .1476 ≈ .15 inch.

18. From equation 1, y = 7 − 2x. Substituting into equation 2, x − 4(7-2x) = 4.
Simplifying, x − 28 + 8x = 4. This reduces to 9x = 32, so x = 32/9

19. Since there are 3600 seconds in 1 hour, 6 seconds would represent 6/3600 = 1/600 of an hour.

8 (#1)

20. 1/3 + 5(x-1) = 8. Simplify to 1/3 + 5x – 5 = 8. This will reduce to 5x = 12 2/3, so x = 38/15.

21. A line perpendicular to the x-axis must have an undefined slope. The equation must be x = constant. The only choice fitting this format is x = 3.

22. The receptionist works 40 hours at R/2 dollars per week. Thus, the weekly payroll for all three workers is H + 36A + R/2. (The 40 hours is not used in computing.)

23. The total bill was (5)($12) + (10)($13) + (4)($20) = $230. Company A's bill was $60. Thus, $60/$230 ≈ 26.1% ≈ 26%.

24. 50(A/100) = 2A² becomes A/2 = 2A². Simplifying further, we get A = 4A². Simplifying further, we get A = 4A² or A(4A-1) = 0. The two values of A are 0 and 1/4.

25. The number of single males is represented as (5/8)(1/5)(100)% = 12.5%

26. z = .35x and x = .20y. Thus, z = (.35)(.20)y = .07y.

27. The numerator is |11| - |-9| = 11 - 9 = 2. The denominator is 3|-1| = 3. Thus, the fraction = 2/3.

28. Let x = required number of minutes. Then, 1/30x – 1/50x = 1. Multiplying by 150, 5x – 3x = 150. Solving, x = 75.

29. $\frac{4}{5}x = \frac{2}{5}y$. Then, $\frac{y}{x} = \frac{4}{5} \div \frac{2}{5} = 2$

30. $x = \frac{1}{y}$ becomes xy = 1, which represents a hyperbola.

31. $\frac{5}{4} + \frac{4}{5} + \frac{3}{2}$ = (25+16+30)/20 = 71/20. If 71/20 – x = a positive integer, then the only correct values of x are 11/20, 31/20, 51/20.

32. Multiplying the equation by 15x, we get 30 + 9x = 20x. Then, 30 = 11x, so x = 30/11.

33. Let 3x = number of applicants, x = 1st year student openings. Over the 4-year period, the number of applicants dropped to .75(3x) = 2.25x and the number of openings rose to 1.12x. Now, 2.25x ÷ 1.12x ≈ 2 to 1.

34. $\sqrt{x - 25}$ = 2. Squaring both sides, x – 25 = 4, so x = 29.

35. At the end of 2 hours, their individual <u>distances</u> are 48 miles and 64 miles. Their distance apart is = 80 miles.

36. AC² + 3² = 6². This simplifies to AC² = 27. Thus, AC = $\sqrt{27}$ = 3$\sqrt{3}$

37. Let x = original length of each side, so that x + 1 = new length of each side of the square. Then, $(x+1)^2 - x^2 + 53$. This simplifies to $x^2 + 2x + 1 = x^2 + 53$. Then, $2x + 1 = 53$, so $x = 26$.

38. $3(2)^2 + \sqrt{25} - (-2)^3 = 12 + 5 + 8 = 25$.

39. Sine 30° = BC/14 1/2 = BC/14, so BC = 7.

40. Probability of 2 red marbles being drawn without replacement is (3/10)(2/9) = 1/15.

41. Each pen costs 75/x cents and each pencil costs 57/y cents. Then, 2 pens and 3 pencils cost 2(75/x) + 3(57/y).

42. Let x = number of quarters, 2x = number of dimes. Then, .25x + .10(2x) < 9.00. Solving, x < 20, so x = 19.

43. The new set of numbers is 3 times as large as the original set. Therefore, the mean is 3 times as big, which is 9, and the variance is 3^2 or 9 times as big, which is (9)(3.5)= 31.5.

44. Using the diagram shown at the right, for the fence $\overline{BC}$, we'll need 5 posts whose distance from each other is 12 1/2'. (This includes a post at B and a post at C.) Now along $\overline{AB}$, since AB = 20' and $20 \div 2\frac{1}{2} = 8$, we'll need 8 posts (including a post at A). Finally, starting at A and ending at C, we need to place only 20 ÷ 2 1/2 – 1 = 7 posts since a post already exists at A and at C. Thus, the total number of posts is 5 + 8 + 7 = 20.

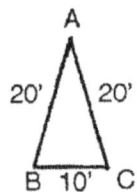

45. (6')(7') = 42 square feet costing $52, which means $52/$42 or $(26/21) per square foot. Now a ceiling 18 ft. by 21 ft. is 378 square feet and will cost (26/21)(378) = $468.

46. Let x, x+2, x+4 represent the three odd numbers. Then, x + x+2 + x+4 = 51. This reduces to 3x + 6 = 51, from which x = 15. The three numbers are 15, 17, 19 and so the largest is 19.

47. From 9:55 A.M. to 10:15 A.M. represents 20 minutes. Then, 20 minutes/5 hours = 20 minutes/300 minutes, which reduces to 1/15.

48. Volume is (10)(9)(2) = 180 cu. ft. The weight of the liquid is (100)(180) = 18,000 lbs.

49. Cosine $\frac{\pi}{3}$ = .5, which is also the value of -Cosine $\frac{2\pi}{3}$.

50. To make $(3x-4)(4+5y^2)$ as large as possible, we maximize the numerator and minimize the denominator. Given the restriction $5 \leq x \leq 12$, use x = 12. Given the restriction use y = 0. (Note carefully that y = 0 yields a smaller value of $4 + 5y^2$ than y = -2)

EXAMINATION SECTION
TEST 1

DIRECTIONS: Each question or incomplete statement is followed by several suggested answers or completions. Select the one that BEST answers the question or completes the statement. *PRINT THE LETTER OF THE CORRECT ANSWER IN THE SPACE AT THE RIGHT.*

1. Which of the following fractions is the SMALLEST?
   A. 2/3 B. 4/5 C. 5/7 D. 5/11

2. 40% is equivalent to which of the following?
   A. 4/5 B. 4/6 C. 2/5 D. 4/100

3. How many 100's are in 10,000?
   A. 10 B. 100 C. 10,000 D. 100,000

4. $\frac{6}{7} + \frac{11}{12}$ is approximately
   A. 1 B. 2 C. 17 D. 19

5. The time required to heat water to a certain temperature is directly proportional to the volume of water being heated.
   If it takes 12 minutes to heat 1 ½ gallons of water, how many minutes will it take to heat 2 gallons of water?
   A. 12 B. 16 C. 18 D. 24

6. The cost of an item increased by 25%.
   If the original cost was C dollars, identify the expression which gives the new cost of that item.
   A. C + 0.25 B. 1/4 C C. 25C D. 1.25C

7. Given the formula PV = nRT, all of the following are true EXCEPT
   A. T = PV/nR B. P = nRTN C. V = P/nRT D. n = PV/RT

8. If a Fahrenheit (F) temperature reading is 104, find its Celsius (C) equivalent, given that C = i(F-32).
   A. 36 B. 40 C. 72 D. 76

9. If 40% of a graduating class plans to go directly to work after graduation, which of the following must be TRUE?
   A. Less than half of the class plans to go directly to work.
   B. Forty members of the class plan to enter the job market.
   C. Most of the class plans to go directly to work.
   D. Six in ten members of the class are expected not to graduate.

10. Given a multiple-choice test item which has 5 choices, what is the probability of guessing the correct answer if you know nothing about the item content?
    A. 5%   B. 10%   C. 20%   D. 25%

11.

S	T
0	80
5	75
10	65
15	50
20	30
25	5

Which graph BEST represents the data shown in the above table?

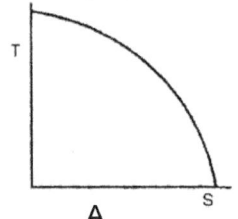
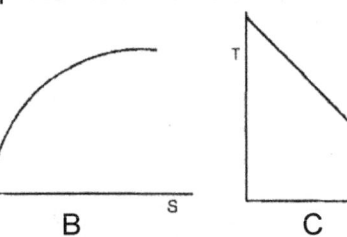
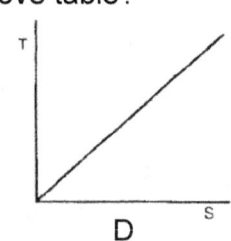

A   B   C   D

12. If 3(x+5y) = 24, find y when x = 3.
    A. 1   B. 3   C. 33/5   D. 7

13. The payroll of a grocery store for its 23 clerks is $395,421. Which expression below shows the average salary of a clerk?
    A. 395,421 × 23
    B. 23 ÷ 395,421
    C. (395,421 × 23
    D. 395,421 ÷ 23

14. If 12.8 pounds of coffee cost $50.80, what is the APPROXIMATE price per pound?
    A. $2.00   B. $3.00   C. $4.00   D. $5.00

15. A road map has a scale where 1 inch corresponds to 150 miles. A distance of 3 3/4 inches on the map corresponds to what actual distance? _____ miles.
    A. 153.75   B. 375   C. 525   D. 562.5

16. How many square feet of plywood are needed to construct the back and 4 adjacent sides of the box shown at the right?
    A. 63
    B. 90
    C. 96
    D. 126

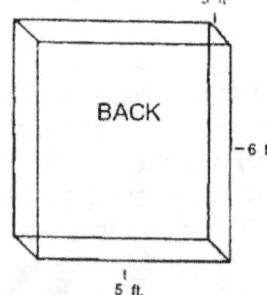

17. One thirty-pound bag of lawn fertilizer costs $20.00 and will cover 600 square feet of lawn. Terry's lawn is a 96 foot by 75 foot rectangle. How much will it cost Terry to buy enough bags of fertilizer for her lawn?
    Which of the following do you NOT need in order to solve this problem? The
    A. product of 96 and 75
    B. fact that one bag weighs 30 pounds
    C. fact that one bag covers 600 square feet
    D. fact that one bag costs $20.00

17.____

18. On the graph shown at the right, between which hours was the drop in temperature GREATEST?
    A. 11:00 – Noon
    B. Noon – 1:00
    C. 1:00 – 2:00
    D. 2:00 – 3:00

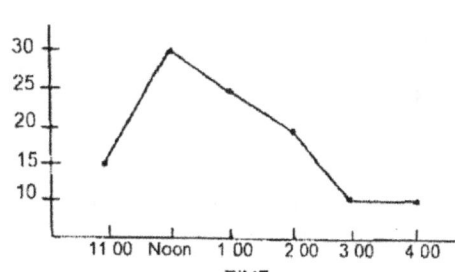

18.____

19. If on a typical railroad track the distance from the center of one railroad tie to the next is 30 inches, approximately how many ties would be needed for one mile of track?
    A. 180   B. 2,110   C. 6,340   D. 63,360

19.____

20. Which of the following is MOST likely to be the volume of a wine bottle?
    A. 750 milliliters   B. 7 kilograms
    C. 7 milligrams   D. 7 liters

20.____

21. What is the reading on the gauge shown at the right?
    A. -7
    B. -3
    C. 1
    D. 3

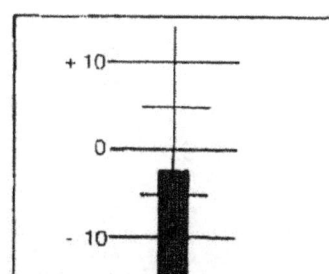

21.____

22. Which statement below disproves the assertion, *All students in Mrs. Marino's 10th grade geometry class are planning to go to college?*
    A. Albert is in Mrs. Marino's class, but he is not planning to take mathematics next year.
    B. Jorge is not in Mrs. Marino's class, but he is still planning to go to college.
    C. Pierre is in Mrs. Marino's class but says he will not be attending school anymore after this year.
    D. Crystal is in Mrs. Marino's class and plans to attend Yale University when she graduates.

22.____

23. A store advertisement reads, *Buy not while our prices are low. There will never be a better time to buy.*
    The customer reading this advertisement should assume that
    A. the prices at the store will probably never be lower
    B. right now, this store has the best prices in town
    C. prices are higher at other stores
    D. prices are always lowest at this store

24. Given any positive integer, there is always a positive number B such that A × B is less than 1.
    Which statement below supports this generalization?
    A. 8 × 1/16 = 1/2
    B. 8 × 1/2 = 4
    C. 5/2 × 1/10 = 1/4
    D. 1/2 × 1/2 = 1/2

25. Of the following expressions, which is equivalent to 4C + D = 12E?
    A. C = 4(12E-D)
    B. 4 + D = 12E − C
    C. 4C + 12E = -D
    D. $C = \frac{12E-D}{4}$

KEY (CORRECT ANSWERS)

1.	D		11.	A
2.	C		12.	A
3.	B		13.	D
4.	B		14.	C
5.	B		15.	D
6.	D		16.	C
7.	C		17.	B
8.	B		18.	D
9.	A		19.	B
10.	C		20.	A

21. B
22. C
23. A
24. A
25. D

SOLUTIONS TO PROBLEMS

1. Converting to decimals, we get $.\overline{6}$, $.8$, $.714$ (approx..), $\overline{45}$. The smallest is $.\overline{45}$ corresponding to 5/11.

2. 40% = 40/100 = 2/5

3. 10,000 ÷ 100 = 100

4. $\frac{6}{7} + \frac{11}{12}$ = (72+77) ÷ 84 = $\frac{149}{84}$ ≈ 1.77 ≈ 2

5. Let x = required minutes. Then, 12/1 ½ = x². This reduces to 1 1/2x = 24. Solving, x = 16.

6. New cost is C + .25C = 1.25C

7. For PV = nRT, V = nRT/P

8. C = 5/9 (104-32) = 5/9(72) = 40

9. Since 40% is less than 50% (or half), we conclude that less than half of the class plans to go to work directly after graduation.

10. The probability of guessing right is 1/5 or 20%

11. Curve A is most accurate since as S increases, we see that T decreases. Note, however, that the relationship is NOT linear. Although S increases in equal amounts, the decrease in T is NOT in equal amounts.

12. 3(3+5y) = 24. This simplifies to 9 + 15y = 24. Solving, y = 1

13. The average salary is $395,421 ÷ 23

14. The price per pound is $50.80 ÷ 12.8 = $3,96875 or approximately $4.

15. Actual distance is (3 3/4)(150) = 562.5 miles.

16. The area of the back = (6)(5) = 30 sq. ft. The combined area of the two vertical sides is (2)(6)(3) = 36 sq. ft. The combined area of the horizontal sides is (2)(5)(3) = 30 sq. ft. Total area = 30 + 36 30 = 96 square feet.

17. Choice B is not relevant to solving the problem since the cost will be [(96)(75)/600][$20] = $240. So, the weight per bag is not needed.

18. For the graph, the largest temperature drop was from 2:00 P.M. to 3:00 P.M. The temperature dropped 20 − 10 = 10 degrees.

19. 1 mile = 5280 feet = 63,360 inches. Then, 63,360 ÷ 30 = 2112 or about 2110 ties are needed.

20. Since 1 liter = 1.06 quarts, 750 milliliters = (750/1000)(1.06) = .795 quarts. This is a reasonable volume for a wine bottle.

21. The reading is -3.

22. Statement C contradicts the given information, since Pierre is in Mrs. Marino's class. Then he should plan to go to college.

23. Since there will never be a better time to buy at this particular store, the customer can assume the current prices will probably never be lower.

24. Statement A illustrates this concept. Note that in general, if n is a positive integer. then $(n)(\frac{1}{n-1}) < 1$

25. ———

TEST 2

DIRECTIONS: Each question or incomplete statement is followed by several suggested answers or completions. Select the one that BEST answers the question or completes the statement. *PRINT THE LETTER OF THE CORRECT ANSWER IN THE SPACE AT THE RIGHT.*

1. Which of the following lists numbers in INCREASING order?
   A. 0.4, 0.04, 0.004
   B. 2.71, 3.15, 2.996
   C. 0.7, 0.77, 0.777
   D. 0.06, 0.5, 0.073
   1.____

2. $\frac{4}{10}+\frac{7}{100}+\frac{5}{1000} =$
   A. 4.75   B. 0.475   C. 0.0475   D. 0.00475
   2.____

3. 700 times what number equals 7?
   A. 10   B. 0.1   C. 0.01   D. 0.001
   3.____

4. 943-251 is approximately
   A. 600   B. 650   C. 700   D. 1200
   4.____

5. The time needed to set up a complicated piece of machinery is inversely proportional to the number of years' experience of the worker.
   If a worker with 10 years' experience needs 6 hours to do the job, how long will it take a worker with 15 years' experience?
   A. 4   B. 5   C. 9   D. 25
   5.____

6. Let W represent the number of waiters and D, the number of diners in a particular restaurant.
   Identify the expression which represents the statement: There are 10 times as many diners as waiters.
   A. 10W = D   B. 10D = W   C. 10D + 10W   D. 10 = D + W
   6.____

7. Which of the following is equivalent to the formula F = XC + Y?
   A. F − C = X + Y
   B. Y = F + XC
   C. $C = \frac{FY}{X}$
   D. $C = \frac{FX}{Y}$
   7.____

8. Given the formula A = BC/D, if A = 12, B = 6, and D = 3, what is the value of C?
   A. 2/3   B. 6   C. 18   D. 24
   8.____

9. 5 is to 7 as X is to 35. X =
   A. 7   B. 12   C. 24   D. 49
   9.____

10. Kramer Middle School has 5 seventh grade mathematics teachers: two of the math teachers are women and three are men.
    If you are assigned a teacher at random, what is the probability of getting a female teacher?
    A. 0.2   B. 0.4   C. 0.6   D. 0.8
    10.____

227

11. Which statement BEST describes the graph shown at the right?
    Temperature
    A. and time decrease at the same rate
    B. and time increase at the same rate
    C. increases over time
    D. decreases over time

12. If 3x + 4 = 22y, find y when x =2.
    A. 0   B. 3   C. 4 1/2   D. 5

13. A car goes 243 miles on 8.7 gallons of gas.
    Which numeric expression should be used to determine the car's miles per gallon?
    A. 243 × 87   B. 8.7 ÷ 243   C. 243 ÷ 8.7   D. 243 − 8.7

14. What is the average cost per book if you buy six books at $4.00 each and four books at $5.00 each?
    A. $4.40   B. $4.50   C. $4.60   D. $5.40

15. A publisher's sale offers a 15% discount to anyone buying more than 100 workbooks.
    What will be the discount on 200 workbooks selling at $2.25 each?
    A. $15.00   B. $30.00   C. $33.75   D. $67.50

16. A road crew erects 125 meters of fencing in one workday.
    How many workdays are required to erect a kilometer of fencing?
    A. 0.8   B. 8   C. 80   D. 800

17. Last month Kim made several telephone calls to New York City totaling 45 minutes in all.
    What does Kim need in order to calculate the average duration of her New York City calls?
    The
    A. total number of calls she made to New York City
    B. cost per minute of a call to New York City
    C. total cost of her telephone bill last month
    D. days of the week on which the calls are made

18.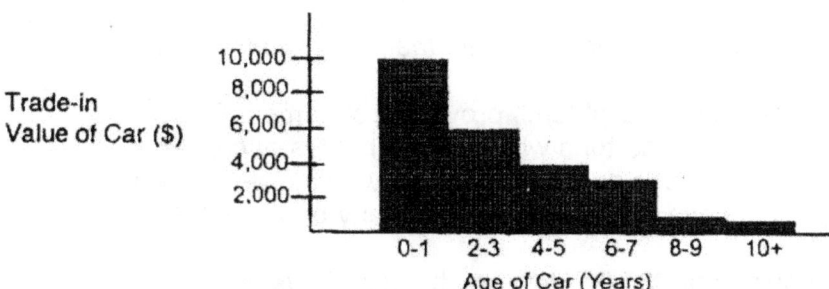

The above chart relates a car's age to its trade-in value.
Based on the chart, which of the following is TRUE?
  A. A 4- to 5-year old car has a trade-in value of about $2,000
  B. The trade-in vale of an 8- to 9-year old car is about 1/3 that of a 2- to 3-year old car.
  C. A 6- to 7-year old car has no trade-in value.
  D. A 4- to 5-year old car's trade-in value is about $2,000 less than that of a 2- to 3-year old car.

19. Which of the following expressions could be used to determine how many seconds are in a 24-hour day?
  A. 60 × 60 × 24
  B. 60 × 12 × 24
  C. 60 × 2 × 24
  D. 60 × 24

20. For measuring milk, we could use each of the following EXCEPT
  A. liters
  B. kilograms
  C. millimeters
  D. cubic centimeters

21. What is the reading on the gauge shown at the right?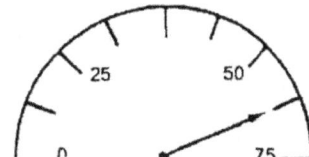
  A. 51
  B. 60
  C. 62.5
  D. 70

22. Bill is taller than Yvonne. Yvonne is shorter than Sue. Sue is 5' tall.
Which of the following conclusions must be TRUE?
  A. Bill is taller than Sue.
  B. Yvonne is taller than 5'4".
  C. Sue is taller than Bill.
  D. Yvonne is the shortest.

23. The Bass family traveled 268 miles during the first day of their vacation and another 300 miles on the next day. Maria Bass said they were 568 miles from home.
Which of the following facts did Maria assume?
  A. They traveled faster on the first day and slower on the second.
  B. If she plotted the vacation route on a map, it would be a straight line.
  C. Their car used more gasoline on the second day.
  D. They traveled faster on the second day than they did on the first day.

24. *The word LEFT in a mathematics problem indicate that it is a subtraction problem.*
    Which of the following mathematics problems prove this statement FALSE?
    A. I want to put 150 bottles into cartons which hold 8 bottles each. After I completely fill as many cartons as I can, how many bottles will be left?
    B. Sarah has 5 books but gave one to John. How many books did Sarah have left?
    C. Carlos had $4.25 but spent $3.75. How much did he have left?
    D. We had 38 models in stock but after yesterday's sale, only 12 are left. How many did we sell?

25. Let Q represent the number of miles Dave can jog in 15 minutes.
    Identify the expression which represents the number of miles Dave can jog between 3:00 P.M. and 4:45 P.M.
    A. 1 3/4 Q   B. 7Q   C. 15 × 1 3/4 xQ   D. Q/7

KEY (CORRECT ANSWERS)

1. C
2. B
3. C
4. C
5. A

6. A
7. C
8. B
9. C
10. B

11. D
12. D
13. C
14. A
15. D

16. B
17. A
18. D
19. A
20. C

21. C
22. D
23. B
24. A
25. B

SOLUTIONS TO PROBLEMS

1. Choice C is in ascending order since .y < .77 < .777

2. Rewrite in decimal form: .4 + .07 + .005 = .475

3. Let x = missing number. Then, 700x = 7. Solving, x = 7/700 = .01

4. 943 − 251 = 692 ≈ 700

5. Let x = hours needed. Then, 10/15 = x/6. Solving, x = 4

6. The number of diners (D) is 10 times as many waiters (10W). So, D = 10W, or 10W = D

7. Given F = XC + Y, subtract Y from each side to get F − Y = XC. Finally, dividing by X, we get (F-Y)/X = C

8. 12 = 6C/3. Then, 12 = 2C, so C = 6

9. 5/7 = x/35. Then, 7x = 175, so x = 25

10. Probability of a female teacher = 2/5 = .4

11. Statement D is best, since as time increases, the temperature decreases.

12. (3)(2) + 4 = 2y. Then, 10 = 2y, so y = 5.

13. Miles per gallon = 243/8.7

14. Total purchase is (6)($4) + (4)($5) = $44. The average cost per book is $44 ÷ 10 = $4.40

15. (220)($2.25) = $450. The discount is (.15))($450) = $67.50

16. The number of workdays is 1000 ÷ 125 = 8

17. Choice A is correct because the average duration of the phone calls = total time ÷ total number of calls.

18. Statement D is correct since a 4-5 year old car's value is $4,000, whereas a 2-3 year-old car's value is $6000.

19. 60 seconds = 1 minute and 60 minutes = 1 hour. Thus, 24 hours = (24)(60)(60) or (60)(60)(24) seconds.

20. We can't use millimeters in measuring milk since millimeters is a linear measurement.

21. The reading shows the average of 50 and 75 = 62.5

22. Since Yvonne is shorter than both Bill and Sue, Yvonne is the shortest.

23. Statement B is assumed correct since 568 = 269 + 300 could only be true if the mileage traveled represents a straight line.

24. To find the number of bottles left, we look only for the remainder when 150 is divided b 8 (which happens to be 6).

25. 3:00 P.M. to 4:45 P.M. = 1 hour and 45 minutes = 105 minutes
Let Q = 15 minutes
105 / 15 = 7
7(15) = 105 = 7Q

EXAMINATION SECTION
TEST 1

DIRECTIONS: Each question or incomplete statement is followed by several suggested answers or completions. Select the one that BEST answers the question or completes the statement. *PRINT THE LETTER OF THE CORRECT ANSWER IN THE SPACE AT THE RIGHT.*

1. x is what percent of 10?
   A. 10x   B. x10   C. 100x   D. 50x   E. 10/x

2. Write 1/4 percent as a fraction.
   A. 25/100   B. 1/400   C. 25/1000   D. 1/4   E. 1/40

3. The number of students in a school increased from 100 to 300. What is the percent increase?
   A. 150   B. 200   C. 250   D. 300   E. 450

4. $\sqrt{.005}$ is what percent of $\sqrt{2}$?
   A. 5   B. 10   C. 15   D. 20   E. 25

5. What is 2/5 percent as a decimal?
   A. .4   B. .04   C. .004   D. .0004   E. .00004

6. One worker picks 25 percent as many bushels as all the other workers combined. This worker picks 20 bushels.
   How many bushels were picked by all the workers?
   A. 100   B. 90   C. 80   D. 75   E. 70

7. A man bought a suit for $45 during a 10-percent-discount sale. How much money did he save?
   A. $14   B. $3.50   C. $5   D. $4.50   E. $7

8. A factory turns out 400 cars each month. This is an increase of 25 percent over the previous months.
   How many cars were turned out the previous months?
   A. 300   B. 320   C. 330   D. 350   E. 400

9. 2/5 of 14 is what percent of 7?
   A. 5 3/5   B. 125   C. 80   D. 87 1/2   E. 90

10. What is 1/2 percent written as a decimal?
    A. .5   B. .05   C. .005   D. .0005   E. .50

11. In triangle ABC, angle A is 150 percent as large as angle B, and angle B is 50 percent of angle C.
   How many degrees are there in angle C?
   A. 30   B. 40   C. 60   D. 80   E. 160

12. If each side of a square is increased by 50 percent, by what percent is the area increased?
   A. 50   B. 100   C. 125   D. 150   E. 200

13. 1/3 is what percent of 3?
   A. 33 1/3   B. 66 2/3   C. 11 1/9   D. 12 1/2   E. 16 2/3

14. In one class 30 percent are boys, and in another class 1/2 as large, 40 percent are boys.
   Find the percentage of boys in both classes combined.
   A. 12 1/2   B. 15   C. 25   D. 33 1/3   E. 50

15. x/250 = 2.4 percent. Find x.
   A. 3   B. 5   C. 6   D. 1-4 1/6   E. 600

KEY (CORRECT ANSWERS)

1.	A	6.	A	11.	D
2.	B	7.	C	12.	C
3.	B	8.	B	13.	C
4.	A	9.	C	14.	D
5.	C	10.	C	15.	C

3 (#1)

SOLUTIONS TO PROBLEMS

1. Let P = required percent. Then, x/10 = P/100. Solving, P = 10x.

2. 1/4% = 1/4 ÷ 100 = 1/400

3. Actual increase is 200. The percent increase = (20/100)(100) = 200

4. Let x = required percent. $\sqrt{.005}/\sqrt{2}$ = x/100. Then, x = 100$\sqrt{.0025}$ = 5

5. 2/5% = 2/5 ÷ 100 = .004

6. Let x = number of bushels picked by all the other workers. Then, 20 = .25x, so x = 80. Now the number of bushels picked by all workers is 80 + 20 = 100.

7. Let x = original price. Then, $45 = .90x, so x = $50. The amount saved is $50 - $45 = $5

8. Let x = number of cars produced in previous months. Then, 400 = 1.25x, so x = 320

9. (2/5)(14) = 5.6. Let x = required percent. Then, 5.6/7 = x/100. Solving, x = 80

10. 1/2% = 12 ÷ 100 = 1/200 = .005

11. Let x = ∠B, 2x = ∠C, 1.5x = ∠A. Then, x + 2x + 1. 5x = 180°.
    Solving, x = 40°, so ∠C = 2x = 80°

12. Let x = original side of the square, so that 1.5x = enlarged side of the square. Then, x^2 = original area and $2.25x^2$ = enlarged area. The increase is $1.25x^2$, which is 125%.

13. Let x = required percent. 1/3/3 = x/100, so x = 100/9 = 11 1/9

14. Let 2x = size of 1st class, x = size of 2nd class. The number of boys in the 1st class is (.30)(2x) = .60x, whereas the number of boys in the 2nd class is .40x. The ratio of boys to the total enrollment in both classes combined is x/3x, which is 33 1/3%.

15. x/250 = 2.4% = .024. Then, x = (250)(.024) = 6.

TEST 2

DIRECTIONS: Each question or incomplete statement is followed by several suggested answers or completions. Select the one that BEST answers the question or completes the statement. *PRINT THE LETTER OF THE CORRECT ANSWER IN THE SPACE AT THE RIGHT.*

1. If 3 men can do a job in 6 days, how long will it take 9 men to do the same job?
   A. 2 days   B. 54 days   C. 8 days   D. 27 days   E. 6 days

   1.____

2. It takes one minute to fill a tank 3/5 full.
   How much longer will it take to fill up the tank? _____ seconds.
   A. 5   B. 10   C. 20   D. 30   E. 40

   2.____

3. The ratio of the legs of a right triangle is 1:3.
   If the area is 6, what is the length of the hypotenuse?
   A. 8   B. $\sqrt{40}$ C. $\sqrt{12}$
   D. 30   E. None of the above

   3.____

4. If 3 pencils cost x cents, how many pencils can be bought for 30 cents?
   A. 90/x   B. x/90   C. 30/x   D. x/30   E. 90x

   4.____

5. If one kilometer equals 5/8 of a mile, how many kilometers are there in 40 miles?
   A. 25   B. 30   C. 35   D. 40   E. 64

   5.____

6. If it takes 3 minutes to fill a pool 4/5 full, how much longer (in seconds) will it take to fill up the tank?
   A. 12   B. 15   C. 30   D. 45   E. 50

   6.____

7. If one inch equals 2.54 centimeters, then 8 centimeters equals approximately how many inches?
   A. 2.7   B. 2.9   C. 3.1   D. 3.3   E. 3.5

   7.____

8. A 100-yard dash is run in 10 seconds.
   What is the approximate speed in miles per hour?
   A. 7   B. 9   C. 20   D. 25   E. 30

   8.____

9. 8 men can complete a job in 24 days.
   How long will it take 12 men working at the same rate to do the job?
   A. 10 days   B. 12 days   C. 14 days   D. 16 days   E. 20 days

   9.____

10. If a map is drawn to the scale of 1 inch to 75 miles, what is the distance between 2 cities that are 4 3/4 inches apart on the map?
    A. 340 1/3   B. 375 2/3   C. 370
    D. 344   E. 356 1/4

    10.____

2 (#2)

11. If a apples cost b cents, find the cost of c apples. 11.____
    A. bc/a B. ac/b C. ab/c D. b/ac E. c/ab

12. Find the ratio of a yard to a foot. 12.____
    A. 1:3 B. 3:1 C. 1:1 D. 12:1 E. 2:1

13. Two girls buy a radio for $15, contributing amounts in the ratio of 5:4. 13.____
    How much was the smaller amount?
    A. 1 2/3 B. 4 C. 5 D. 6 2/3 E. 12

14. A gear with 48 teeth, rotating at 360 revolutions per minute, meshes with 14.____
    a gear of 72 teeth.
    How many revolutions per minute does the second gear make?
    A. 180 B. 240 C. 277 D. 530 E. 432

15. A troop of 75 men have enough rations to last 4 days if the troop is increased 15.____
    by 25 men.
    Then, how long, in days, will the same rations last?
    A. 4/3 B. 3/4 C. 12 D. 3 E. 2

KEY (CORRECT ANSWERS)

1.	A	6.	D	11.	A
2.	E	7.	C	12.	B
3.	B	8.	C	13.	D
4.	A	9.	D	14.	B
5.	E	10.	E	15.	D

SOLUTIONS TO PROBLEMS

1. The number of men is inversely proportional to the number of days. Let x = required number of days. Then, 3/9 = x/6. Solving, x = 2

2. 1 min./$\frac{3}{5}$ = x min./$\frac{2}{3}$. Solving, x = $\frac{2}{3}$ min. = 40 seconds.

3. Let x, 3x = lengths of the two. (1/2)(x)(3x) = 6, so $3x^2$ = 12 and x = 2. The two legs are 2 and 6. Thus, the hypotenuse = $\sqrt{2^2 + 6^2} = \sqrt{40}$

4. Let p = number of pencils. 3/x = p/30, px = 90, so p = 90/x

5. 40 miles = 40 ÷ 5/8 = 64 kilometers

6. 3 min./$\frac{4}{5}$ = x min./$\frac{1}{5}$. Solving, x = $\frac{2}{3}$ min. = 45 seconds

7. 8 centimeters = 8 ÷ 2.54 ≈ 3.1 inches

8. 100 yards in 10 seconds means 36,000 yards per hour. Then, 36,000 yards = 36,000/1760 ≈ 20 miles. Thus, the speed is 20 mi./hr.

9. The number of men is inversely proportional to the number of days. Let x = required number of days. Then, 8/12 = x/24. Solving, x = 16.

10. 4 3/4 inches corresponds to (75)(4 3/4) = 356 1/4 miles.

11. Let P = cost of c apples. a/b = c/p. Solving, p = bc/a

12. 1 yard : 1 foot = 3 feet : 1 foot = 3:1

13. Let 5x, 4x represent their respective contributions. Then, 5x + 4x = $15. Solving, x = $1 2/3. The smaller amount is ($1 2/3)(4) = $6 2/3

14. The number of teeth is inversely proportional to the number of revolutions per minute. Let x = required revolutions per minute. 48/72 = x/360. Solving, x = 240

15. The number of men is inversely proportional to the number of days. Let x = required number of days. 75/100 = x/4, so x = 3.

TEST 3

DIRECTIONS: Each question or incomplete statement is followed by several suggested answers or completions. Select the one that BEST answers the question or completes the statement. *PRINT THE LETTER OF THE CORRECT ANSWER IN THE SPACE AT THE RIGHT.*

1. A club goes on a boat ride for which the fare is 80 cents per adult and 60 cents per child.
   If there are 70 people on the ride and the total cost is $47, what fractional part of the group is adults?
   A. 2/35 B. 5/14 C. 4/7 D. 9/14 E. 3/4

   1.____

2. A camping tent can be put up by 3 scout masters in 2 hours or by 5 boy scouts in 4 hours.
   How many hours will it take them to put up the tent if they all work together?
   A. 1 B. 1 1/3 C. 2 1/3 D. 3 D. 3 1/2

   2.____

3. A grocer has 60 baskets of peaches of which y baskets are spoiled.
   If he sells 3/4 of the remainder, how many baskets does he have left of the good peaches?
   A. $\frac{15-y}{4}$ B. 15 - y C. $15 - \frac{y}{4}$ D. $\frac{y-15}{4}$ E. $\frac{y}{4} - 15$

   3.____

4. A motorist drives 60 miles to his destination at 40 mph and returns at 30 mph. Find his average speed in mph for the entire trip.
   A. 28 B. 32 C. 34 2/7 D. 36 1/2 E. 43 1/4

   4.____

5. The afternoon classes in a school begin at 1 P.M. and end at 3:52 P.M. There are 4 class-periods with 4 minutes between classes.
   How many minutes are there in each period?
   A. 39 B. 40 C. 49 D. 59 E. 60

   5.____

6. If a man paid $60 for a suit after receiving a discount of 10%, how much did he save?
   A. $6 B. $6.50 C. $6.67 D. $6.75 E. $10

   6.____

7. A high school football squad consists of 40 players. They arrange to play a 60-minute practice game with another team.
   If only 11 out of the 40 players participate at one time, and each is to play the same length of time, how many minutes would each play?
   A. 12 B. 16 1/2 C. 18 D. 20 ¾ E. 22

   7.____

8. If the base of a rectangle is increased by 30% and the altitude decreased by 20%, by what percent is the area increased?
   A. 4 B. 5 C. 10 D. 25 E. 50

   8.____

2 (#3)

9. If a flexible wire 220-feet long goes around a circle 5 times, approximately how many times will the same wire go around the square in which the circle is inscribed?
   A. 2 3/4   B. 3 1/2   C. 4   D. 5 1/2   E. 6 1/4

10. A passenger ship traveling b miles an hour passes a freighter traveling c miles per hour. Fifteen minutes later the passenger ship reaches port. How many hours after this will the freighter reach port?
    A. $\frac{4(b-c)}{c}$ B. $\frac{4(b-c)}{b}$ C. $\frac{b-c}{4c}$ D. $\frac{b-c}{b}$ E. $\frac{c}{4(b-c)}$

11. If a − b = 5 and a + c = 6, what is the value of b in terms of c?
    A. c−1   B. c+1   C. 1−c   D. c−11   E. 11−c

12. Twenty-five boys in a class have an average grade of 80. Fifteen girls in the same class have an average grade of 72.
    What is the average grade for the entire class?
    A. 75   B. 76   C. 76.5   D. 77   E. 77.5

13. A line divides a square board into 2 equal triangles, each 200 square feet in area.
    How many feet are there in the length of the line?
    A. $10\sqrt{2}$ B. $10\sqrt{3}$ C. $20\sqrt{2}$ D. $20\sqrt{3}$ E. 100

14. A 20-ounce solution of salt and water contains 3 ounces of salt.
    If 5 ounces of water are evaporated, what is the percent of salt in the new solution?
    A. 12   B. 15   C. 20   D. 25   E. 33 1/3

15. If meat loses 20% of its weight when cooked, how many pounds of raw meat should be cooked to produce 2 lbs. of cooked meat?
    A. 2.25   B. 2.3   C. 2.5   D. 2.75   E. 3

16. What percent of 2 gallons is 6 pints?
    A. 30   B. 33 1/3   C. 37 1/2   D. 137 1/2   E. 300

17. How many inches are there in y yards?
    A. $\frac{y}{36}$ B. $\frac{y}{12}$ C. 3y   D. 12y   E. 36y

18. The missing number in the series is: 2, 6, 12, 20, ?, 42, 56, 72, is:
    A. 30   B. 32   C. 36   D. 38   E. 40

19. If a car travels at 50 miles per hour, how long does it take at this rate to travel 1 mile?
    A. 50 seconds   B. 70 seconds   C. 72 seconds
    D. 1 min. 15 sec.   E. 1 min. 20 sec.

20. If m − x = m, what does x equal?
    a. o   B. m   C. m/2   D. 2m   E. 2/o

KEY (CORRECT ANSWERS)

1.	B	11.	C
2.	B	12.	D
3.	C	13.	C
4.	C	14.	C
5.	B	15.	C
6.	C	16.	C
7.	B	17.	E
8.	A	18.	A
9.	C	19.	C
10.	C	20.	A

SOLUTIONS TO PROBLEMS

1. Let x = number of adults, 30 − x = number of children. .80x = .60(30-x) = $47. Solving, x = 25 adults, so there are 45 children. Now, 25/70 = 5/14.

2. The rate for the scout masters is 1/2 of the work in 1 hour. For the scouts, their rate is 1/4 of the work in 1 hour. Let x = number of hours required working together. 1/2x + 1/3x = 1. Solving, x = 1 1/3

3. The grocer will sell (3/4)(60-y) = 45 − 3/4y, where y = number of baskets with spoiled peaches. The number of baskets of good peaches left is 60 − y − (4-3/4y) = 15 y/4.

4. Average speed = total distance ÷ total time = (60+60)/(60/40+60/30) = 120/3 1/2 = 34 2/7

5. With 4 class-periods, there are three 4-minute breaks between classes, which is 12 minutes. From 1 P.M. to 3:52 P.M. represents 172 minutes. The actual number of minutes for each class period is (172 − 12)/4 = 40

6. Let x = original price. Then, x − .10x = $60, so x = $66.67 − $60 = $6.67

7. Total player-minutes = (11)(60) = 660. Then, the number of minutes per player = 660 ÷ 40 = 16 1/2

8. Let x, y represent the original base and height, so that 1.30x and .80y represent the new base and height. The original area = xy and the new area = (1.30)(.80)xy = 1.04xy. This is a 4% increase.

9. 220 ÷ 5 = 44 feet = circumference of circle. Then, the radius = 44 ÷ 2π = 7 feet. This implies that the side of the circumscribed square is 14 feet and its perimeter is 56 feet. Finally, 220 ÷ 56 ≈ 4.

10. In 15 minutes (= 1/4 hour), the passenger ship travels b/4 miles to reach port. The freighter would need b/4 ÷ c = b/4c hours to travel 6/4 miles. Thus, the extra time the freighter needs to reach port is b/4c − 1/4 = b − c/4c.

11. Subtracting a − b = 5 from a + c = 6 yields c + b = 1. Thus, b = 1 − c

12. Average grade of entire class [(25)(80) + (15)(72)]/(25=15) = 3080/40 = 77

13. The area of the entire square is 400, and the line in question is a diagonal. Let x = length of this diagonal. Thus, 1/2x² = 400, so x = √800 = 20√2

14. The original solution had 17 ounces of water. The new solution will have 12 ounces of water and (still) 3 ounces of salt. The percent of salt is (3/(3+12)(100) = 20

15. Let x = number of pounds of raw meat. Then, x − .20x = 2. Solving, x = 2.5

16. 2 gallons = (2)(8) = 16 pints. Then, 6/16 = 37 1/2%.

5 (#3)

17. Since 1 yard = 36 inches, y yards = 36y inches.

18. The difference between consecutive terms are 4, 6, 8, -, -, 14, 16. Then the difference between the 4h and 5th terms must be 10. Since the 4th term is 20, the 5th term must be 30. (Note: As a check, the difference between 30 and the 6th term should be 12. The 6th term is 42.

19. At 50 mi/hour, the car requires 1/50 hour to travel 1 mile. Now, 1/50 hour = 1 1/5 minute = 72 seconds.

20. m –x = m. Then, x = m – m = 0

TEST 4

DIRECTIONS: Each question or incomplete statement is followed by several suggested answers or completions. Select the one that BEST answers the question or completes the statement. *PRINT THE LETTER OF THE CORRECT ANSWER IN THE SPACE AT THE RIGHT.*

1. A part-time worker earns 3 times as much in September as in each of the other months.
   What part of his entire year's earnings does he earn in September?
   A. 1/5   B. 3/14   C. 1/4   D. 3/11   E. 1/3

   1.____

2. All the faces of a 4-inch cube have been painted. This is now cut into 1-inch cubes.
   The number of cubes that will show *no* paint at all is
   A. 20   B. 8   C. 1   D. 4   E. 12

   2.____

3. A 12-quart solution of alcohol and water is 10% alcohol.
   If 4 quarts of water are added, the solution becomes
   A. 50%   B. 40%   C. 33-1/3%   D. 7.5%   E. 75%

   3.____

4. It cost $3.60 for 2 adults and their child to attend the circus.
   If a child's ticket is half the price of an adult's ticket, what is the price of an adult's ticket?
   A. $0.72   B. $0.90   C. $1.20   D. $1.44   E. $1.80

   4.____

5. If the sides of a square are increased 100%, the increase in area is
   A. 400%   B. 200%   C. 300%   D. 100%   E. 500%

   5.____

6. A 100-yard dash run in 10 seconds is the same average speed in miles per hour approximately as
   A. 5   B. 10   C. 20   D. 30   E. 40

   6.____

7. A man bought 3 books for $1.50 and 2 books for $1.00 each.
   What was the average price per book?
   A. $1.00   B. $1.10   C. $1.20   D. $1.25   E. $1.30

   7.____

8. The missing number in the series: 2, 5, 10, 17, ?, 37, 50, 65 is
   A. 22   B. 24   C. 26   D. 27   E. 29

   8.____

9. If $y\sqrt{.04} = 1$, what is the value of y?
   A. .05   B. .5   C. 5   D. 6.25   E. 50

   9.____

10. The minimum temperatures for each day of one week were as follows:
    7, 13, 5, -4, -8, 0, 3.
    What was the average minimum temperature for the week?
    A. -2 2/3   B. -2 2/7   C. -2   D. 2 2/7   E. 2 2/3

    10.____

244

2 (#4)

11. A man sold a piece of land for $1,500. 11._____
If his profit was 200% of his cost, how much had the land cost him?
   A. $500   B. $750   C. $1,000   D. $1,200   E. $1,250

12. What is the area, in square feet, of a rectangular garden which is twice as 12._____
long as it is wide if the fence around it is 240 feet long?
   A. 2,400   B. 3,200   C. 4,800   D. 7,200   E. 12,800

13. Which of these quantities is the SMALLEST? 13._____
   A. 7/9   B. 9/11   C. 4/5   D. 5/7   E. .74

14. A baseball team has won 50 games out of 75 played. 14._____
How many more games must the team win in succession to raise its record to 80%?
   A. 10   B. 20   C. 22   D. 25   E. 50

15. A tank contains 500 gallons of gasoline. 15._____
If the gasoline is withdrawn at the rate of x quarts a minute for 12 minutes, how many gallons of gasoline will remain?
   A. 500-12x   B. 500-6x   C. 500-3x   D. 12x   E. 125x

KEY (CORRECT ANSWERS)

1.	B	6.	C	11.	A
2.	B	7.	E	12.	B
3.	D	8.	C	13.	D
4.	D	9.	C	14.	E
5.	C	10.	D	15.	C

3 (#4)

SOLUTIONS TO PROBLEMS

1. Let 3x = earnings in September, x = earnings in each of the other 11 months. Then, 11x + 3x = 14x = earnings for 1 year. Ratio of September's earnings to entire year's earnings = 3x/14x = 3/14.

2. There will be a total of 64 1-inch cubes of which the innermost 8 cubes will have no paint.

3. The amount of alcohol is still (.10)(12) = 1.2 quarts. Then, 1.2/16 = 7.5%.

4. Let x = price for each adult ticket, 1/2x = price for each child's ticket. x + x + 1/2x = $3.60. 2.5x = $3.60. Solving, x = $1.44.

5. Let x = original side and 2x = new side. Original area = x^2 and new area = $4x^2$. The increase is $3x^2$, which means 300%.

6. 100 yards in 10 seconds means 36,000 yards per hour.
   Then, 36,000 yards = 36,000/1760 ≈ 20 miles. Thus, the speed is 20 mi/hour.

7. The average price per book = [(3)($1.50) + 2($1.00)]/(3+2) = $1.30.

8. The differences between consecutive terms are 3, 5, 7, _, _, 13. The two blanks must be 9 and 11. Since the difference between the 4th and 5th terms is 9 and the 4th term is 17, the 5th term is 17 + 9 = 26.

9. $y\sqrt{.04}$ = 1. Then, .2y = 1, so y = 5.

10. (7+13+5-4-8+0)/7 = 16/7 = 2 2/7.

11. Let x = cost. Profit = $1,500 – x = 2x. Solving, x = $500.

12. Let x = width, 2x = length. x + x + 2x + 2x = 240. Solving, x = 40 and 2x = 80. Area = (40)(80) = 3,200 square feet.

13. Converting to decimals, answers A thru E appear as $.\overline{7}, .\overline{81}$, .8, .714, .74. Since .714 is the smallest, this corresponds to 5/7.

14. Let x = required number of wins. Then, (50+x)/(75+x) = .80. this leads to 50 + x = 60 + .80x. Solving, x = 50.

15. x quarts per minute means x gallons in 4 minutes. After 12 minutes, 3x gallons have been withdrawn from the tank. The number of gallons remaining is 500 – 3x.

TEST 5

DIRECTIONS: Each question or incomplete statement is followed by several suggested answers or completions. Select the one that BEST answers the question or completes the statement. *PRINT THE LETTER OF THE CORRECT ANSWER IN THE SPACE AT THE RIGHT.*

1. A pool which holds 300 gallons of water can be filled by one pipe in 6 hours and emptied by another in 8 hours.
   How many hours will it take to fill it if both pipes are opened together?
   A. 4   B. 7   C. 12   D. 14   E. 24

   1.____

2. The floor of a kitchen 9 feet wide by 12 feet long is to be covered with linoleum which comes in a roll 27 inches wide.
   The number of yards of linoleum needed is
   A. 16   B. 24   C. 36   D. 48   E. 54

   2.____

3. Four posts are set 15 feet apart along the edge of a field.
   How many feet is the first post from the last?
   A. 30   B. 35   C. 45   D. 55   E. 60

   3.____

4. During the second year of work a girl earned 5/4 as much as she did her first year.
   If she earned $3,600 in the two years, how much did she earn the first year?
   A. $1,440   B. $1,600   C. $1,800   D. $2,000   E. $2,880

   4.____

5. What fraction of 5 gallons is 3 quarts?
   A. 3/20   B. 1/4   C. 4/15   D. 5/12   E. 3/5

   5.____

6. A man gets 20 miles per gallon with grade X gasoline, which costs $1.00 per gallon; he gets 25 miles per gallon with grade Y, which costs $1.20 per gallon. How much does he save on a 1,000-mile trip by using grade Y instead of grade X?
   A. $1.25   B. $1.50   C. $1.75   D. $1.00   E. $2.25

   6.____

7. How many twelfths are there in 83 1/3% of a pound?
   A. 5   B. 10   C. 12   D. 14   E. 16

   7.____

8. If there is 2.2 pounds in one kilogram and one kilogram equals 1,000 grams, how many more grams are there in 8 1/2 pounds than in 3 kilograms?
   A. 824   B. 864   C. 164   D. 1728   E. 4502

   8.____

9. If, after receiving a discount of 12%, you pay $175 for a television set, the original price was
   A. $187.50   B. $192.50   C. $198.86   D. $200   E. $225

   9.____

10. The 90 members of a certain organization contributed an average of 60 cents each toward a fund.
    If 2 of the members contributed $5.00 each, how many cents was the average contribution of the other 88 members?
    A. 50   B. 56   C. 60   D. 61   E. 70

11. A person spent exactly one dollar in the purchase of 3-cent and 5-cent stamps. The number of 5-cent stamps he could NOT have bought is
    A. 7   B. 14   C. 11   D. 8   E. 5

12. In the series 3, 7, 12, 18, 25,...., the 10th term is
    A. 88   B. 75   C. 63   D. 50   E. 86

13. 3/5, 5/8, 2/3, 7/12. The fraction which is out of order is
    A. 3/5   B. 5/8   C. 2/3
    D. 7/12   E. None of the above

14. At 3:20 P.M., how many degrees has the hour hand moved since noon?
    A. 200   B. 20   C. 10   D. 100   E. 120

15. (3/8)(1/8) = (?)(1/16)
    A. 1/8   B. 3/16   C. 3/8   D. 4/3   E. 3/4

KEY (CORRECT ANSWERS)

1. E	6. D	11. A
2. A	7. B	12. B
3. C	8. B	13. D
4. B	9. C	14. D
5. A	10. A	15. E

SOLUTIONS TO PROBLEMS

1. Let x = number of hours needed to fill the pool.
   x/6 − x/8 = 1. Then, 4x − 3x = 24, so x = 24.

2. 9 feet ÷ 27 inches = 108 inches ÷ 27 inches = 4. Thus, 4 rolls of linoleum will be needed, each of which must extend to 12 feet = 4 yards. Total number of yards needed = (4)(4) = 16.

3. The distance from first post to last post is (15)(3) = 45 feet.

4. Let x and 5/4 x represent her earnings in each of the first 2 years.
   Then, x + 5/4 x = $3,600. Solving, x = $1,600

5. 3 quarts/5 gallons = 3 quarts/20 quarts = 3/20

6. Using grade X, a trip of 1,000 miles costs (1000/20)($1.00) = $50. Using grade Y, this same trip costs (1000/25)($1.20) = $48. The savings is $2.00.

7. 83 1/3% of a pound = (5/6)(16) = 13 1/3 ounces, 1/12 of a pound = 1 1/3 ounces.
   Now, 13 1/3 1 ÷ 1/3 = 10.

8. 8.5 ÷ 2.2 = 3.$\overline{863}$ kgms = 3863.$\overline{63}$ gms, whereas 3 kgms = 3,000 gms. The difference is about 864 gms.

9. Let x = original price. Then, x − .12x = $175. Solving, x = $198.86.

10. (90)(.60) = $54.00. $54.00 − (2)($5) = $44. Finally, $44 ÷ 8 = $0.50.

11. He could NOT have bought 75-cent stamps since $1.00 − (7)(.05) = .65 and .65 is not divisible by 3 cents.

12. The difference between successive terms increases by 1, with the difference between the first two terms being 4. Since the fifth term is 25, the 10th term will be 25 + + 9 + 10 + 11 + 12 = 75.

13. Since the first 3 fractions are in increasing order, 7/12 is out of order because 7/12 < 2/3.

14. The hour hand has moved 3 1/3 numbers = (3 1/3/12)(360°) = 100.

15. (3/8)(1/8) = 3/64. Then, 3/64 ÷ 1/16 = 3/4.

TEST 6

DIRECTIONS: Each question or incomplete statement is followed by several suggested answers or completions. Select the one that BEST answers the question or completes the statement. *PRINT THE LETTER OF THE CORRECT ANSWER IN THE SPACE AT THE RIGHT.*

1. One end of a ladder 26 feet long is placed 10 feet from the outer wall of a building.
   How many feet up the ladder will the ladder reach?
   A. 14   B. 20   C. 22   D. 23   E. 24

2. A quart of ice cream will serve 6 adults or 8 children.
   If 39 adults have been served from a 10-quart container, how many children may then be served?
   A. 28   B. 50   C. 29   D. 41   E. 43

3. Fifty students had an average of 80%. Thirty other students had an average of 86%.
   Find the average of ALL the students.
   A. 81   B. 81 1/2   C. 82   D. 82 1/4   E. 83

4. A dealer paid 72¢ for a fountain pen listed at 90¢.
   What rate of discount did he receive?
   A. 2%   B. 5%   C. 18%   D. 20%   E. 25%

5. A man makes a trip of 600 miles. He averages 40 m.p.h. for the first 200 miles.
   At what rate, in m.p.h., must he complete the trip to average 45 m.p.h. for the entire trip?
   A. 47 1/2   B. 50   C. 47   D. 48 1/2   E. 48

6. The water which is 7" high in a fish tank 1 1/4 ft. by 8", is poured into a tank 13" x 4.6".
   What height will it reach in the larger tank?
   A. .27"   B. .31"   C. 1.7"   D. 3.2"   E. 4.6"

7. .3% = ?
   A. 3/1000   B. 3/100   C. 1/300   D. 3/10   E. 1/3

8. In one section of a test, the first question is numbered 112 and the last 200.
   How many questions are there in this section of the test?
   A. 88   B. 89   C. 87
   D. 86   E. None of the above

9. A block of wood 8" x 4" x 12" is to be cut into cubes.
   If the cubes are the largest that can be cut from this block, how many of them will there be?
   A. 2   B. 4   C. 6   D. 8   E. 12

10. A 5-quart solution of sulphuric acid and water is 60% acid.
    If a gallon of water is added, what percent of the resulting solution is acid?
    A. 20   B. 33 1/3   C. 40   D. 48   E. 50

11. A baseball team has won 50 games out of 75 played. It has 45 games still to play.
    How many of these must the team win to make its record for the season 60%?
    A. 20
    B. 22
    C. 25
    D. 30
    E. None of the above

12. If in any two-digit numbers, the tens-digit is represented by x and the units-digit by y, the number is represented by
    A. x+y   B. xy   C. 10x + y   D. 10y + x   E. yx

13. How many pieces of cardboard 3" x 5" can be cut from a sheet 17" x 22" with the minimum amount of waste?
    A. 20
    B. 21
    C. 24
    D. 25
    E. None of the above

14. If p pencils cost c cents, n pencils at the same rate will cost
    A. pc/n cents
    B. cn/p cents
    C. npc cents
    D. np/c cents
    E. p/nc cents

15. If the population of a village was 300 before the war and is now 1,200, what is the percentage of increase in population?
    A. 25%   B. 75%   C. 300%   D. 400%   E. 3%

KEY (CORRECT ANSWERS)

1.	E	6.	D	11.	B
2.	A	7.	A	12.	C
3.	D	8.	B	13.	B
4.	D	9.	C	14.	B
5.	E	10.	B	15.	C

SOLUTIONS TO PROBLEMS

1. Let x = number of feet up the wall. Then, $x^2 + 10^2 = 26^2$. Solving, x = 24.

2. 10 quarts will serve 60 adults. Since 30 adults have been served, 21 more adults could be still served. Realizing that for every 6 adults, 8 children could be served, the equivalent of 21 adults is $21 \div \frac{6}{8}$ = 28 children.

3. Average of all students = [(50)(80) + (30)(86)]/(50+30) = 82 1/4

4. Discount = .90 - .72 = .18. Rate of discount = .18/.90 = 20%

5. Let x = rate for the remaining 400 miles. The time for this portion of the trip is 400/x hours. Then, 45 = average rate = 600/[200/40+40/x]. Simplifying, 5 + 400/x = 13 1/3. Solving, x = 48 mph.

6. Volume in first tank = (7")(15")(8") = 840 cu. in. Let x = height in second tank. Then, 840 = (13)(20)(x). Solving, x = 3.2.

7. .3% = .3/100 = 3/1000

8. Number of questions = 200 – 111 = 89.

9. (8)(4)(12) = 384 cubic inches. The largest possible side for each cube is 4 in. Each of these cubes has a volume of $(4)^3$ = 64 cu. in. Now, 384 ÷ 64 = 6

10. Amount of acid is (5)(.60) = 3 quarts. By adding a gallon of water, the new solution will contain 9 quarts. Finally, 3/9 = 33 1/3%

11. Let x = number of additional games won. Then, (50+x)/120 = .60. Solving, x = 22.

12. The number is represented as 10x + y. For example, 56 = (10)(5) + 6

13. 22 ÷ 3 = 7, with 1 in. left over and 17 ÷ 5 = 3, with 2 in. left over. Number of pieces = (7)(3) = 21. The waste is only (1)(2) = 2 sq. in.

14. Let x = cost of n pencils. Then, p/c = n/x. px = cn,

15. The increase in population is 1200 – 300 = 900. Then, 900/300 = 3 = 300%.

TEST 7

DIRECTIONS: Each question or incomplete statement is followed by several suggested answers or completions. Select the one that BEST answers the question or completes the statement. *PRINT THE LETTER OF THE CORRECT ANSWER IN THE SPACE AT THE RIGHT.*

1. If a merchant makes a 20% profit based on the selling price of an article, what percent profit does he make on the cost?
   A. 15%   B. 25%   C. 75%   D. 300%   E. 400%

    1._____

2. The dial of a meter is divided into equal divisions from 0 to 60. When the needle points to 48, the meter registers 80 amperes.
   What is the MAXIMUM number of amperes that the meter will register?
   A. 60   B. 92   C. 100   D. 102   E. 120

    2._____

3. The scale of a certain map is 3/4 inch equals 12 miles. Find, in square miles, the actual area of a park represented on the map by a square whose side is 5/8 inch.
   A. 7 1/2   B. 10   C. 40
   D. 100   E. None of the above

    3._____

4. Two boys buy a radio for $15 contributing amounts in the ratio of 5:4. Find the SMALLER amount.
   A. 4   B. 5   C. 12   D. 6 2/3   E. 1 2/3

    4._____

5. There are 25 equally placed poles in a row.
   If the distance from the first to the sixth is 30 feet, find the distance from the first to the twenty-fifth.
   A. 120   B. 125   C. 144   D. 150   E. 127 1/2

    5._____

6. A rectangular room 15' x 19' has a 10' x 10' rug in it.
   What percent of the room is covered?
   A. 25   B. 35   C. 45   D. 55   E. 65

    6._____

7. .8% is the same as one out of
   A. 20   B. 40   C. 80   D. 100   E. 125

    7._____

8. A painted wooden cube whose edge is 3 inches is cut into 27 one-inch cubes. How many of these have just two painted sides?
   A. 12   B. 18   C. 8
   D. 9   E. None of the above

    8._____

9. Four tractors working together can plow a field in 12 hours.
   How many hours will it take 6 tractors to plow the field?
   A. 6   B. 9   C. 10
   D. 18   E. None of the above

    9._____

10. A company offers a gas range for $63 cash or for $5 down and 10 months payments of $6.50 each.
    The installment price is approximately what percent greater than the cash price?
    A. 7%   B. 9%   C. 10%
    D. 11%   E. None of the above

    10.____

11. A seesaw 12 feet long is balanced at the middle by a support 3 feet high.
    If one end of the seesaw is on the ground, how many feet above the ground is the other end?
    A. 3   B. 6   C. 9   D. 14   E. 18

    11.____

12. A baseball team won W games and lost L games.
    What fractional part of its games did it win?
    A. $\dfrac{L}{W}$ B. $\dfrac{W}{L}$ C. $\dfrac{W-L}{W}$ D. $\dfrac{W+L}{W}$ E. $\dfrac{W}{W+L}$

    12.____

13. A train left A for B, a distance of 290 miles, at 10:10 A.M. The train was scheduled to reach B at 3:45 P.M.
    If the average rate of the train was 50, it arrived in B
    A. 5 minutes early   B. on time
    C. 5 minutes late   D. 13 minutes late
    E. more than 15 minutes late

    13.____

14. How many dollars would it cost to carpet a room r yards long and w feet wide at x cents a square foot?
    A. wrx   B. .03wrx   C. 100 wrx/3
    D. 100 wr/3x   E. 3wr/100x

    14.____

15. Find the number of degrees between the hands of a clock at 7:20.
    A. 90   B. 100   C. 97 1/2   D. 108   E. 33 1/3

    15.____

KEY (CORRECT ANSWERS)

1.	B	6.	B	11.	B
2.	C	7.	E	12.	E
3.	D	8.	A	13.	D
4.	D	9.	E	14.	B
5.	C	10.	D	15.	B

3 (#7)

SOLUTIONS TO PROBLEMS

1. Let x = selling price so that .20x = profit. Then, x - .20x = .80x = cost. Percent profit on cost is (.20x/.80x)(100) = 25%.

2. Let x = maximum number of amperes. 48/80 = 60/x. Solving, x = 100.

3. Let the actual length (or width) of the park = x. Then, 3/4 / 5/8 = 12/x. Solving, x = 10. The actual area of the park is 10^2 = 100 square miles.

4. Let 5x and 4x represent the respective amounts. Then, 5x + 4x = 15, so x = 1 2/3. The smaller amount = (4)(1 2/3) = 6 2/3 dollars.

5. From the first pole to the 25th pole represents 24 spaces, so the number of spaces from the first pole to the sixth pole is 5. 30 ft. ÷ 5 = 6 ft. = distance between successive poles. Thus, the distance from the first pole to the 25th pole is (6)(24) = 144 ft.

6. 10 × 10 = 100 and 15 × 19 = 285. Then, $\frac{100}{285}$ ≈ .351 ≈ 35%

7. .8% = .008 = 8/1000 = 1/125 = 1 out of 125.

8. The 12 cubes occupying center positions would have only 2 painted sides.

9. The number of tractors is inversely proportional to the number of hours. Let x = required time. 4/6 = x/12, so x = 8 hours.

10. Paying on the installment plan, the cost is 5 + (10)(6.50) = $70. This represents (70-63)/63 × 100 = 11% more than the cash price.

11. Let CD = 3' support. AC = CB = 6'. Now, AE = 3', so point A must be 6' above the ground.

12. Games played = W + L. Fractional part of games won = $\frac{W}{W+L}$

13. Time of travel was 290/50 = 5.8 hours 48 minutes. Since the train left point A at 10:10 A.M., it arrived at point B at 3:58 P.M. Thus, it was 13 minutes late.

14. x cents per square foot means 9x cents per square yard = 9x/100 dollars per square yard. The area of the room = (r yards) × (w/3 yards) = rw/3 square yards Total cost to carpet the room = (9x/100)(rw/3) = 3/100 xrw = .03 wrx dollars.

15. At 7:20, the minute hand is exactly on the numeral 4 and the hour hand lies 1/3 of the way between the numerals 7 and 8. The distance of 7 1/3 – 4 = 3 1/3 numerals on the clock is equivalent to (3 1/3/12)(360°) = 100°.

TEST 8

DIRECTIONS: Each question or incomplete statement is followed by several suggested answers or completions. Select the one that BEST answers the question or completes the statement. *PRINT THE LETTER OF THE CORRECT ANSWER IN THE SPACE AT THE RIGHT.*

1. If both the filling and emptying pipes of a pool are open, the pool fills in 10 hours. If just the filling pipes are open, the pool fills in 4 hours.
   How many hours does it take to empty the pool if only the emptying pipes are open?
   A. Less than 5
   B. More than 5
   C. Exactly 5
   D. More than 6
   E. Exactly 6

   1.____

2. A cylindrical pail 14 inches in diameter and 7 inches high is full of water. The water is poured into a rectangular aquarium 22" long, 21" wide, and 14" high. To what depth does the water rise in the aquarium?
   A. 2 1/3
   B. 9 1/3
   C. 5 2/3
   D. 7 ¼
   E. None of the above

   2.____

3. A poster is cut down by 10% of its height and 30% of its width.
   What percent of the original area remains?
   A. 3   B. 37   C. 70   D. 57   E. 63

   3.____

4. BOC is q quadrant of a circle. AD = 3 and AE = 4.
   Find the length of arc BC.
   A. 5π
   B. 5π/2
   C. 10π
   D. 12
   E. Cannot be determined from the information given

   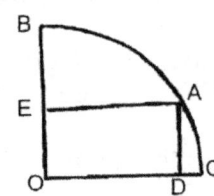

   4.____

5. A commuter runs from his house to the station, a distance of 132 feet. It takes him 9 seconds. What is his speed in miles per hour?
   A. 12   B. 9   C. 8   D. 11   E. 10

   5.____

6. A swimming pool is 4 yards deep, 6 yards wide, and 8 yards long.
   If it is filled to one foot from the top, what is the volume of water in cubic feet?
   A. 24 • 18 • 11
   B. 24 • 18 • 12 – 1
   C. 24 • 18 • 12
   D. 24 • 18 • 12-3
   E. None of the above

   6.____

7. A typist uses lengthwise a sheet of paper 9" x 12". She leaves a 1" margin on each side and a 1 ½" margin on top and bottom.
   What fractional part of the page is used for typing?
   A. 63/66
   B. 7 1/2
   C. 5/9
   D. 3/4
   E. None of the above

   7.____

256

2 (#8)

8. Eight blocks on one side of a scale balance two blocks and a one-pound weight on the other side.
   What is the weight, in pounds, of all ten blocks?
   A. 1   B. 1 1/2   C. 1 2/3
   D. 2   E. None of the above

   8._____

9. How many numbers between 131 and 259 are divisible by 3?
   A. 41   B. 42   C. 43
   D. 44   E. None of the above

   9._____

10. The consecutive angles of a quadrilateral are 60, 120, 60, and 120 degrees.
    If one side is 6 and another is 12, what is the perimeter?
    A. 18
    B. 36
    C. $24 + 6\sqrt{3}$
    D.
    E. Cannot be determined from the information given

    10._____

11. Admission tickets for children are 1/3 the price for adults. The price for 3 children and 3 adults is $10.80.
    How much is the price for one adult?
    A. $.90   B. $1.20   C. $1.80   D. $2.70   E. $3.00

    11._____

12. A man walks 10- feet north, 150 feet west, and 100 feet north again.
    How many feet is the distance from where he started to where he finished in a straight line?
    A. 350   B. 300   C. 250
    D. 200   E. None of the above

    12._____

13. A ferris wheel has a diameter of 60 feet. It makes 3 revolutions per minute. Find the distance, in miles, that the occupant of one of the cars travels in 5 minutes ($\pi = \frac{22}{7}$).
    A. 30/28   B. 15/28   C. 4/7   D. 3/5   E. 2 1/4

    13._____

14. A box contains 2 red balls, 3 blue balls, and 4 white.
    What is the LEAST number of balls a blindfolded person must draw to be sure of getting two of the same kind?
    A. 2   B. 3   C. 4   D. 5   E. 6

    14._____

15. If an apple weighs 4/5 of its weight plus 4/5 of an ounce, what is its weight in ounces?
    A. 3 1/2   B. 1 3/5   C. 4   D. 4 4/5   E. 5

    15._____

KEY (CORRECT ANSWERS)

1.	D	6.	A	11.	D
2.	A	7.	B	12.	C
3.	E	8.	C	13.	B
4.	B	9.	C	14.	C
5.	E	10.	B	15.	C

4 (#8)

SOLUTIONS TO PROBLEMS

1. Let x = time required to empty the pool using only the emptying pipes. Then, 10/4 − 10/4 = 1. Simplifying, 10x − 40 = 4x. Solving, x = 6 2/3 hours, which corresponds to more than 6.

2. Volume of pail = $(\pi)(7^2)(7)$ ≈ 1078 cu. in. Let x = height to which water will rise in aquarium. Then, 1078 = (22)(21)(x), so x = 2 1/3 in.

3. Let x = original height, y = original width, xy = original area. New height = .9x, new width = .7y, new area = .63xy, which is 63% of the original area.

4. Radius of circle = OA = $\sqrt{3^2 + 4^2}$ = 5. Length of arc BC = $(1/4)(2\pi)(5) = 5\pi/2$.

5. 132 ft. in 9 sec. means 14 2/3 ft. per sec. Since 88 ft. per sec. is equivalent to 60 mph, the commuter's speed in mph = (60)(14 2/3)/88 = 10.

6. 6 yds. = 18 ft., 8 yds. = 24 ft., 4 yds. − 1 ft. = 11 ft. The volume, in cubic feet, is 24.18.11.

7. The typing section has an area of (9-2)(12-3) = 63 sq. in. The entire sheet of paper has an area of (9)(12) = 108 sq. in. Finally, 63/108 = 7/12.

8. Let x = weight of each block. Then, 8x = 2x + 1, so x = 1/6 lbs.
   The weight of all ten blocks = (10)(1/6) = 1 2/3 lbs.

9. The numbers divisible by 3 begin with 132 and end with 258. The total number of these numbers − (258-132)/3 + 1 = 43.

10. Since opposite angles are equal, the given figure must be a parallelogram, wherein opposite sides are also equal. The perimeter = (2)(6) + (2)(12) = 36.

11. Let x = admission price per adult, 1/3x = admission price per child.
    (3)(1/3x) + 3x = 10.80. Solving, x = $2.70.

12. We are seeking the value of DA. Now, ED = BC = 150 and AE = AB + CD = 200. Since AED forms a right triangle, DA = $\sqrt{150^2 + 200^2}$ = 250.

13. In 1 min., each car of the ferris wheel travels (22/7)(60)(3) = 5 min.; this distance = 19,800/7 ft. Since 5280 ft. = 1 mi., the distance traveled in 5 min. becomes (19,800/7) ÷ 5280 = 15/28 mi.

14. By drawing only 3 balls, the person might get exactly one of each color. However, by drawing 4 balls, at least 2 of them will be the same color.

15. Let x = weight in ounces. Then, x = 4/5x + 4/5. Solving, x = 4.

WRITING EXAMINATION SECTION

INTRODUCTION

DIRECTIONS: This is a test to find out how well you write. The test has three parts: a letter, a report, and a composition. In answering each part, you must take the following steps:
1. Read ALL the information.
2. Plan carefully what you are going to write.
3. Write your first draft on scrap paper.
4. Read carefully what you have written.
5. Make any changes that will improve your first draft.
6. Check your paragraphing, sentence structure, spelling, punctuation, capitalization, and usage, and make any necessary corrections.
7. Write your final copy on the special answer paper given to you by the teacher. Be sure that the yellow paper is always underneath the white paper as you write.

You will be given as much time as you need to answer the three parts. You may answer the three parts of the test in any order you choose. Work carefully. Double check everything you have written on your final copy. You must hand in the scrap paper along with the white and yellow copies of your answer paper for each part of the test.

TEST 1
BUSINESS LETTERS

DIRECTIONS: Write a business letter about the situation described below. Read ALL the information carefully before you start to write.

The Situation: Your Corny Popcorn Popper needed repair. The popper was still under warranty. On May 26, 2020, you mailed it back to the manufacturer, Star Appliance Company, to have it repaired without cost. Today you received the popper in the mail. You tried it, but it still does not work.

Your Task: Write a business letter concerning this situation to: Star Appliance Company, 614 River Road, Fargo, North Dakota 58102.

In your letter, be sure to:
Explain the situation and explain what you want the company to do for you.
Give complete and correct information.
Use an acceptable business letter form.

OTHER BUSINESS LETTER TOPICS

Given a problem, the student writes a business letter of complaint stating the problem and explaining how he/she wishes the problem to be corrected.

Corrective action is requested because of:

1. False advertising of an item that is on sale

2. Rudeness of a salesclerk or security guard

3. Refusal of a store to refund money for a defective product

4. Incorrect printing of lettering ordered for an item

5. Defective processing of film

6. Receipt of a series of requests for payment of a bill already paid

7. Substitution of a less expensive model for an item actually ordered

8. Unsatisfactory emergency care at a local hospital

9. Unsatisfactory repair of an item mailed to a company for repair

10. Unsatisfactory action concerning a public smoking area

11. Delivery of damaged merchandise sent through the mail

12. Delivery of the wrong item from a company

2 (#1)

13. Failure to remedy unsafe conditions on neighborhood streets

14. Failure of a store to have advertised merchandise available

15. Failure to receive a product ordered by mail

16. Failure to receive a free product after sending in a coupon

17. Failure to receive copies of a magazine after a new subscription has been paid for

18. Failure to receive the free item offered for enrolling in a club

19. Failure to receive a document requested from a government office

20. Failure to receive a company's cash refund after sending in proof of purchase

21. Failure to receive a refund for a product which was returned by mail

22. Failure to provide facilities for recreational activities for young people in the neighborhood

23. Failure to receive all parts of an item which must be assembled

24. Failure to receive a satisfactory substitute for a cancelled performance

25. Failure to be notified of cancellation of services

TEST 2
REPORT WRITING

DIRECTIONS: Write a report using the situation and the set of notes given below. Read ALL the information carefully before you start to write.

The Situation: You are preparing a project on early American history for your social studies class. As part of your project, you decided to write a report about your trip this spring to Plimoth Plantation, a popular historic attraction in Massachusetts. The notes you wrote in preparing your report are in the box below.

Plimoth Plantation in Plymouth, Massachusetts
Now a *living* museum of how Pilgrims lived in 1600's
Houses of wood with stone chimneys and straw roofs
Fort, a strong building with flat roof
Windows of houses—of oiled paper instead of glass
Is a re-creation of original plantation—houses, a fort
Museum workers dress and work as Pilgrims did
Small houses with only one or two rooms
Each Pilgrim house has own vegetable and herb gardens
Museum workers: care for farm animals, build houses, cook, garden
Talked with Mr. Warren, museum worker
Mr. Warren: *We do everything exactly as it was done in 1627*
Cannons on roof of fort like ones used in 1600's
Cannons once used to protect plantation
Worthwhile trip

Your Task: Organize these notes into a written report. To help you organize and write your report, be sure to: Keep in mind that you are writing the report for your social studies class. Rearrange the notes before you start to write your first draft. Include all the information from the notes in your report.

OTHER REPORT TOPICS

Given a set of notes, the student reorganizes the notes and writes a unified report for a specific audience. The subject for the report will be:

1. A meeting on energy resources

2. A meeting of a student organization

3. An interview with a skilled worker

4. An interview with a foreign exchange student

5. An interview with a performer

6. An interview with a director of a program

2 (#2)

7. An interview with a student volunteer
8. Biographical information about a famous person
9. A sports event
10. A school event
11. A community event
12. A performance
13. An accident
14. A visit to a government agency or building
15. A visit to a health facility
16. A visit to a local industry
17. A visit to a tourist attraction
18. A visit to a city
19. A visit to a television studio
20. Research about a trip
21. Research about a consumer purchase
22. A lecture about health-related topics
23. A speech by a public figure
24. A speech by an expert in his/her field
25. A talk by a member of the school faculty

TEST 3
COMPOSITION

DIRECTIONS: Write a composition in which you try to persuade the principal of your high school to agree with your opinion about the situation described below. Read ALL the information carefully before you start to write.

The Situation: Your principal is planning to add one new physical education activity to those already offered at your school. The principal has asked students to suggest one new physical education activity that they would like to have offered.

Your Task: Write a composition of about 20 words persuading the principal to add to the physical education program the one new activity that you are suggesting. Give the principal two reasons for offering this new activity. Explain each reason.

Keep in mind that you are persuading the principal to offer the one new physical education activity that you are suggesting.
State the name of this physical education activity.
Give the principal two reasons why this activity should be offered.
Explain each of your two reasons fully.
Organize what you write.

OTHER COMPOSITION TOPICS

Given an issue, the student writes a 200-word composition to persuade a specific audience by stating his/her position and explaining two reasons for that position. The audience and the issue will be:

1. A parent concerning the need for purchasing an item

2. A parent concerning the need for lessons

3. A parent concerning the need for a particular privilege

4. A parent concerning a change in curfew regulations

5. A parent concerning the student's request to travel to a particular place

6. A parent concerning the student's plans after graduation

7. The school principal concerning ways to conserve energy at the school

8. The school principal concerning a needed change in school rules

9. The school principal asking for a change in the school calendar

10. The school principal recommending that a subject be added to the curriculum

11. The school principal requesting an improvement in the athletic or activity program

12. The school principal concerning a proposed school activity

13. The school principal requesting the institution of a *Student Administration Day*

14. The school board concerning requirements for graduation

15. Readers of the school newspaper concerning the use of money from the class treasury for a specific purpose

16. Readers of the school newspaper about closing the school cafeteria

17. Readers of the school newspaper about a problem of school discipline

18. Reader of the local newspaper about closing a local school or consolidating two school districts

19. A prospective employer to convince the employer to hire the student for a job

20. A local public official concerning a proposed neighborhood improvement

21. A local public official requesting more activities for teenagers

22. A local public official concerning the need for summer jobs

23. A local TV station concerning a change in programming

24. A member of the Legislature recommending specific legislation affecting young people

25. A manufacturer suggesting improvements in the product

TEST 4
COMPOSITION

DIRECTIONS:

A. Your favorite college basketball team has instituted a new ruling which states that all players must have tests to determine if drugs are in their system, both before they can be selected for the team and also regularly during the year.

What is your opinion of this ruling?

Write a letter to the team's coach presenting your opinion. Be sure to support your opinion with at least two (2) reasons. Your letter should be 200-250 words long. WRITE ONLY THE BODY OF THE LETTER.

B. Write a well-organized composition of 200-250 words based on ONE of the following titles. Write the title at the top of your paper.
- Dishonesty in Government
- The Best Friend I've Ever Had
- Graffiti in My Life
- If I Were Homeless
- My Walkman

TEST 5
LITERATURE ESSAY

DIRECTIONS: Give titles and authors in the essay you write. Be sure to use specific examples from the works chosen.

A. From the novels, plays, biographies, short stories, and poems you have read, select TWO. Answer the question below for EACH of the two works. You should write approximately 100 words for each work of literature.

In literature, a character frequently faces an internal struggle when a decision must be made. In some cases, the character is aware that this decision might affect someone else's life. In other cases, the decision may influence the character's future or may change the way he/she looks at life.

1. Identify a character from each work of literature you have selected.
2. Describe the events surrounding the decision which the character had to make.
3. Explain how the decision affected the life of the character, or of other people in the story. Refer to specific incidents in the story to support your explanation.

Be sure to give the title and author for each work you select.

B. From the novels, plays, biographies, short stories, and poems you have read, select TWO. Answer the question below for EACH of the two works. You should write approximately 100 words for each work of literature.

Nature sometimes plays an important role in a piece of literature. Climate, natural disasters, or settings such as the desert or the seaside may affect the mood or even the outcome of the work of literature.

1. Identify the natural element used by the author.
2. In a paragraph of at least 100 words for each work, explain how the author has used nature to set the mood or to affect the outcome of his story or poem.

Be sure to give the title and author for each work you select.

ESSAY WRITING

THE WRITING PROCESS

Under ideal conditions, writing involves a series of steps:

1. Pre-writing activities which facilitate understanding the purpose and the audience for a particular piece of writing and which might include generating ideas through brainstorming, notes, reflection, research, or discussion;

2. Focusing the material generated in step one by framing a thesis (controlling idea) and a direction (organization);

3. Getting the first draft on paper, using standard grammar, correct mechanics, and accurate spelling;

4. Assessing the success of the first draft by yourself or in consultation with a reliable reader;

5. Revising the draft by clarifying the thesis, topic sentences, supporting detail, and word choice; and

6. Proofreading for mistakes in grammar and spelling.

Ideal conditions do not always exist in the real world. Often you have to write under pressure and produce a clear statement. This is the case in a test situation. You must streamline the writing process to compose an acceptable essay in approximately one hour. This section will help you to practice necessary strategies by describing how you might do the following:

1. Turn the directions into a purpose statement.
2. Brainstorm for material to put in the essay.
3. Group and focus your ideas.
4. Compose your essay with clear signals for the reader.
5. Proofread for word choice, grammar, and mechanics.

TURN DIRECTIONS INTO PURPOSE STATEMENTS

For each of the following sets of essays, the directions specify a topic, an audience, and some possible ways to develop the essay. You have some choice about how to develop the essay, but you must stick to the topic given and a style appropriate to the audience. The directions consist of four sentences which give

2

1. an indication of audience,
2. a description of audience,
3. suggestions for development, and
4. a restatement of the topic.

You can distinguish the sentences that suggest development because they contain words which give options rather than commands; for example, the sentences that give you commands about the topic will look like this:

In writing, tell the panel why you are considering teaching as a career.

On the other hand, sentences that suggest development will look like this:
The reasons may include…
You might want to consider…
The experiences could be…

Your first step, then, is to sort out the essential commands in the directions and convert them into a clear purpose statement such as *I will explain my reasons for choosing teaching as a career*. The purpose statement must cover all the essential parts of the assignment.

EXERCISE B

For each of the following sets of directions, underline the sentences that give you commands about the topic and write a purpose statement, using your own words if possible.

Prompt 1
A committee of teachers and administrators is reviewing your qualifications for a scholarship. In writing, tell the committee about a special activity you engage in, either in school or outside of school. It could be a job, an organization you belong to, a hobby or sport you participate in, or something you do with your family. Tell the committee what your special activity is and explain why this activity is important to you.

Prompt 2
A superintendent of schools has reviewed your application for a teaching position. Before holding a formal interview with you, the superintendent wants you to provide a writing sample that tells what motivated you to choose teaching as a profession. You might want to discuss a special learning experience you had or your interest in a chosen field or subject. Tell the superintendent what your motivation is and explain why your learning experience or your interest in a special field or subject is important to you.

Prompt 3
Your college advisor has just notified you that the college has instituted an open curriculum. As a result, you may choose any three courses or activities you wish to take next semester. You will be given equal course credit for academic subjects and activities such as sports, cultural

activities (music, theater, art), school newspaper or literary magazine activities, fraternities, sororities, community projects, or any other activity whose importance you can justify. In writing, indicate what three courses you would select and how each one would make you a better person.

Prompt 4
You have just been given the opportunity to write a letter of application to the Director of Admissions at the college of your choice. Imagine that cost is not a concern to you; you may choose a college that offers a traditional liberal arts curriculum or one that allows you to study only those courses that relate to your field of interest. In your essay, tell the Director of Admissions the type of college you are choosing and identify the reasons for your choice.

Prompt 5
A committee of teachers is reviewing your application for admission into the teacher education program of your choice. The committee has asked you to write an essay that describes a book that made the most lasting impression on you or from which you believe you learned some valuable lesson. The book may be on any subject, fiction or nonfiction, that is meaningful to you. The book need not be something you read for a course. Explain to the committee what your impression or lesson is and why it is important to you.

BRAINSTORM FOR MATERIAL TO PUT IN THE ESSAY

The directions on the subtest often contains suggestions for areas to explore. The sample directions which ask for an essay on your reasons for choosing a teaching career suggest that you consider *examples set by other people, benefits you expect from a teaching career, or the challenges you think teaching offers.* Remember that these suggestions are only suggestions. Before you respond to them, you should think about how you would accomplish the writing task if the suggestions had not been made. To be convincing, the material in your essay must come from your own experiences and knowledge. Brainstorming can help you accomplish this.

There are different ways to brainstorm. Some people prefer to write freely for 5-10 minutes. Others like to make lists or sketches. Others mull over ideas and ask themselves questions before jotting down a few key words. If you have a method that works for you, stick with it. If you don't, try one of the three approaches just mentioned.

EXERCISE C

1. Think about your reasons for wanting to teach and jot down a list of those reasons.

2. Compare your list with the suggestions given for considering teaching as a career: (examples, benefits, and challenges).

3. Which reasons fit the category of the rewards of teaching?

4. Which reasons could be labeled challenges of teaching?

5. Which reasons are related to examples set by other people?

6. What labels or categories do your other reasons fall under?

7. Are some of your reasons related to experiences that you have had as a learner or teacher (e.g., sports, scouting, 4-H, religious classes)?

8. Are some of your reasons related to your interest in a particular subject such as mathematics or art?

9. Are some of your reasons related to particular qualities you possess such as patience, enthusiasm, or tolerance?

LISTEN TO YOUR INNER VOICE

The purpose of brainstorming is to come up with enough detail or elaboration to satisfy the evaluation requirements. You should aim to produce enough material for an introduction and at least three additional paragraphs. Once you list a few initial ideas, the best way to generate more detail is to imagine a voice saying, *Tell me more about that.* Let's suppose that your initial list of reasons for wanting to teach looked like this.

- I like kids.
- Summers off.
- Make a contribution to society.
- Encouragement from teachers.

Responding to that imaginary voice saying, *Tell me more*, might help you elaborate the first reason as follows:

I like kids…
    because they all have some undeveloped potential.
    because their responses aren't always predictable.
    because they get so excited when they learn something new.

Another way to elaborate on the first reason is through examples:

- The two boys I used to babysit.
- The girl I helped to get over her fear of water.
- The special education student who was my *little brother*.

Imagine the voice asking for more information until you believe you have enough for a satisfactory essay. Not every statement will give you as much room for development as others, but you can expand upon all of the statements. Each time you elaborate, your writing becomes more specific. Including specific detail makes your ideas concrete and your writing more convincing. Specific detail is one of the criteria for evaluating your essay.

EXERCISE D

1. Go back to the list of purpose statements that you developed in Exercise C, and brainstorm for material you might include in an essay.

2. Go back to your list of reasons for wanting to teach and elaborate as much as you can on each one.

GROUP AND FOCUS YOUR IDEAS

A good essay is unified by a controlling idea or thesis which dictates a pattern of organization. The thesis should be stated in one or two sentences. The words you choose to write the thesis statement should repeat or echo the directions for the essay. This strategy will ensure that you state the topic clearly. One way to write a thesis is to do one of the following:

1. Look at your purpose statement.
   Example 1: I must explain my reasons for choosing teaching as a career.
   Example 2: I must explain how a learning experience motivated me to go into teaching.

2. Look at the list of ideas you generated by brainstorming and try to sum up the ideas in a sentence or two:
   Sample Thesis 1: I have chosen teaching as a career because I enjoy young children, particularly those who have a learning disability. Teaching is a career that will enable me to make a contribution to society.
   Sample Thesis 2: The experience that I had as a *big brother* to a special education student helped me to realize that everyone has the potential to learn. This experience strengthened my interest in teaching as a career.

The thesis prepares the reader for what is to follow. It is a promise that you will discuss certain ideas and not others.

You will not always use all the material you generated during the brainstorming step. In the sample that we have been discussing, you might have decided not to use material related to summers off or the encouragement of teachers. However, if you decide that there is some material you want to include in the body of your essay material which is not indicated by the thesis, you need to revise the thesis. Suppose you decide to include the information about summers off and the encouragement of teachers, how could you revise the thesis? Here is one possibility:

Revised Thesis: There are many reasons why I have chosen teaching as a career. The pleasure of working with children, the opportunity to make a contribution to society, the encouragement of teachers, and time during the summer to continue my own education and interests are a few of them.

You should understand that it is not necessary or advisable to give every reason why you would like to teach. Be selective. Choose reasons on which you can elaborate and ones you feel strongly about. This will make a more convincing essay.

OUTLINING

There are different ways of grouping brainstorming ideas. The traditional format is the outline. Here is one example, based on the thesis we have been discussing.

Thesis: There are many reasons why I have chosen teaching as a career; some of them are the pleasure of working with children, the opportunity to make a contribution to society, the encouragement of teachers, and time during the summer to continue my own education and interests.

I. I enjoy working with children.
   A. All children have potential.
   B. Their responses are unpredictable.
   C. They are excited when they learn something.

II. I will make a contribution to society.
   A. Many jobs have questionable social value even if they have high salaries.
   B. Teachers can help children develop a good self-image and give them necessary skills.

III. Teachers have encouraged me.
   A. They say I can express myself clearly.
   B. They see that I am enthusiastic about learning.

IV. Summers will be time to continue my education and interests.
   A. Teachers must be lifelong learners.
   B. Intensity of teaching requires time for pursuing other interests.

CLUSTERING

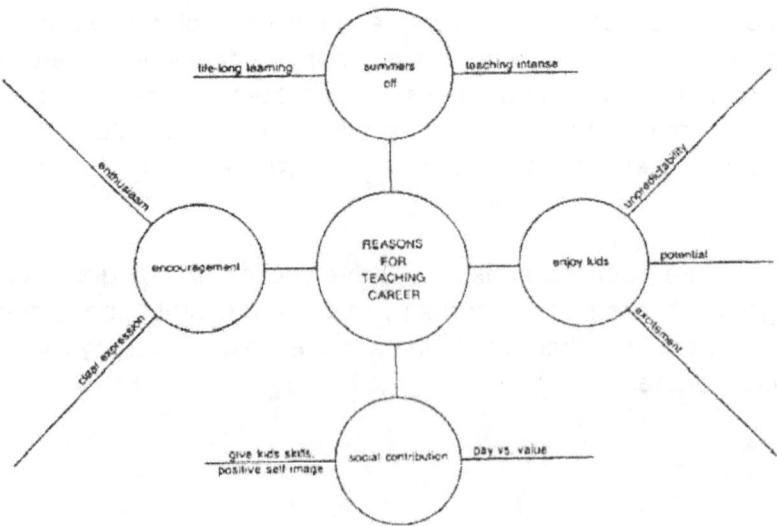

FLOW CHARTS

Still another way to map ideas is with the help of a flow chart. The main idea is placed in a box at the top, and other categories branch off below.

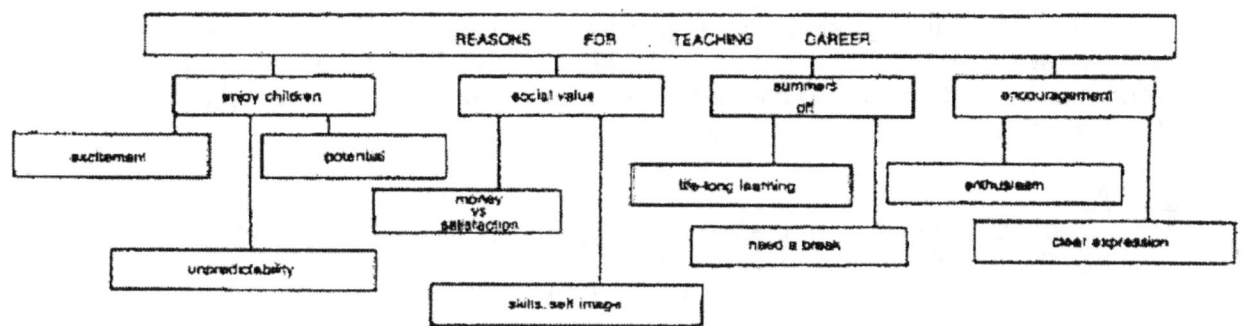

INFORMAL LISTS

An informal list is an easy way to group ideas.

My Reasons:

1. Like kids — all have potential / full of surprises / get so excited

2. Make a contribution
   - Other jobs — pay more / less satisfying
   - Teaching — skills / self-image

3. Summers off — need to keep learning / break from pressures

4. Teacher encouraged me — communication good / my enthusiasm

Regardless of which method you use to group your ideas, the goal is to pull together related bits of information and sketch the paragraph structure for your essay before you actually start writing your essay in the test booklet.

EXERCISE E

1. Go back to the material that you produced through brainstorming in Exercise D.2 and group the ideas by using one of the formulas illustrated.

2. Using one of the strategies mentioned previously, group the ideas given below in each set. For each set, read through the ideas in the set and identify or create a thesis statement; group related sentences; and find or create a sentence or phrase that will hold each group of sentences together.

   SET A.
   1. TV cartoons show characters recovering quickly from serious injury.
   2. Mr. Rogers never loses his temper.
   3. Ads associate happiness and good times with possession of a product.
   4. The ads show cereal boxes opening by themselves and dancing on the table.
   5. TV gives children a distorted sense of reality.
   6. Mr. Rogers always takes off his shoes when he comes inside.
   7. A character falls off a mountain top, shakes his head, and gets up.
   8. Positive role models, like Mr. Rogers, are unlike any real-life adult.
   9. Mr. Rogers never raises his voice.
   10. The ads are deceptive and manipulative.
   11. Characters who smash into walls are never badly hurt.

   SET B.
   1. I felt welcome when I went to see my math teacher during his office hours.
   2. The activity fair during orientation week had something to offer everyone.
   3. The counselors were helpful.
   4. Many teachers ask if students need help rather than wait for the students to get in trouble.
   5. The counselors helped with course selection.
   6. Resident advisors counsel students about adjustment problems.
   7. The counselors provided placement testing.
   8. Teachers talk to students after class rather than just rushing off.
   9. Students on campus are friendly.
   10. My experience at Winona College has been good, and I would recommend it to others.
   11. Teachers go over sample tests before you take the first test.
   12. The dorm council plans activities and projects to bring students together.
   13. The counselors offer minicourses on taking notes and tests.

   SET C.
   1. I don't belong to any organizations.
   2. I'm not involved in any special activities.
   3. I go to classes, work at the store, and see my friends on weekends.
   4. My job isn't special.
   5. I work at a supermarket.
   6. I need the job for spending money and college expenses.

7. I have learned some things from working.
8. It's not like school.
9. You have to be there to get paid.
10. The boss isn't always fair.
11. Sometimes she is impatient.
12. As a lowly clerk, you don't get any respect.
13. The boss seemed annoyed when I brought back the shopping carts.
14. There were long lines at the registers.
15. She told me to help bag groceries.
16. There's a pecking order in most companies.
17. My boss is under pressure from the manager.
18. I'm trying to stay on top of the situation rather than just reacting.
19. I ask the boss how things have been going.
20. I try to anticipate what she'll ask me to do and offer to do it first.
21. Sometimes I feel frustrated about being low on the totem pole.
22. The manager doesn't even know who I am.
23. There's not much incentive to do good work.
24. You can always be replaced by another minimum wage worker.

SET D.
1. DEATH OF A SALESMAN is a book that influenced me because of the connections between the play and my own life.
2. Each time I had a different reaction.
3. I read the play once in high school, again in college, and then saw it on TV.
4. In high school, Biff was a good-looking football hero.
5. The play is about a salesman named Willy, his wife, and two sons, Biff and Happy.
6. Happy was just an ordinary kid, living in his brother's shadow.
7. When Biff learned that his father was not perfect, he began to drift around.
8. I realized I was only hurting myself.
9. I had an older brother who was a star.
10. I was always trying to get my parents' attention.
11. I even tried to get their attention by doing poorly in school.
12. At first, I identified with Happy.
13. Biff had a big ego because of all the attention he received.
14. Biff became a bum because of all the attention he received as a teenager.
15. When I read the play in college, I sympathized with Willy.
16. He never received any respect from his boss.
17. I have been working at a supermarket.
18. Clerks are a dime a dozen, just like salespeople.
19. I want a career where a paycheck is not the only satisfaction you receive.
20. The TV version made me admire the mother.
21. She held the family together.
22. She was completely loyal to Willy.
23. We all want someone to stick by us like she did.

SET E.
1. Earning credit for my choice of courses and activities will give me a chance to integrate course work and real experience.
2. Reading Methods is a required course.
3. I'll learn how to assess a student's reading level.
4. I'll learn about various methods for teaching reading skills.
5. I plan to work as a literacy volunteer.
6. I want to know why people don't learn to read.
7. I'll learn about methods for teaching adults.
8. I'll learn how illiteracy affects a person's life.
9. I'll realize what's at stake if the education system fails.
10. I want to take either an advanced composition course or an independent study in composition.
11. I would like to keep a journal of my experience as a literacy volunteer.
12. I would like to write about the connections I see between the methods course and my tutoring experience.
13. I would like to write some feature stories about illiteracy for the college newspaper.

COMPOSE YOUR ESSAY WITH CLEAR SIGNALS FOR THE READER

Your essay is judged on how well the essay communicates a whole message. If you keep the reader in mind, your essay is likely to communicate more effectively. The most important signals to use are topic sentences to state the main idea of each paragraph and transitions to link sentences within the paragraphs. One basic pattern you might use in composing your paragraphs is the five paragraph essay. Here is one example of such an essay written in response to Prompt 1, Exercise B. Study the way in which the topic sentences give the reader a preview of what will be discussed.

<u>Paragraph I.</u>   Lead and thesis statement.

Lead   Some students may have time for sports, clubs, or volunteer organizations. Unfortunately, my schedule of classes and part-time work does not give me much time to devote to other activities. However, my job has been quite a learning experience.

Thesis   <u>Although I am just a supermarket clerk, I have gained insight into the demands of a job, the behavior of supervisors, and my ability to influence a situation,</u>

<u>Paragraph II</u>   Topic sentence developed with sufficient detail.

Topic Sentence   <u>I realized that the demands of a job re not always like the demands of school.</u> Maybe that is something that other people know from the start, but it did not work that way for me. In fact, I can remember how the equation between work and pay dawned on me; if I missed an afternoon of work, I missed an equivalent amount of money in my paycheck. The connection between work and rewards is not quite so clear in school. A student can study hard for a test and do poorly. On the other hand, a student can sometimes bluff through a test and get a good grade.

Paragraph III.	Another topic sentence with supporting detail.
Topic Sentence	<u>I did not work for very long before I also realized that bosses can be difficult.</u> At first, my supervisor seemed like a nice enough person. However, I had a look at her other side one day when I returned to the store, pushing a long line of shopping carts which she had told me to gather from the parking lot. Lines had formed at all the registers, and she snapped at me to bag for one of the cashiers. It was as if it my fault that she had sent two of the cashiers out for supper just as it was getting busy in the store.
Paragraph IV.	Another topic sentence followed by detail.
Topic sentence	<u>After my initial anger at the boss's behavior, I decided to try to influence the situation rather than just reacting to it.</u> I realized this approach might work as I was bagging groceries. I saw the store manager peering down at my box from her office window. My boss had a boss who had a boss who had a boss. She was part of the pecking order just like me. Now I try to make small talk with her, ask how things have been going, and so forth. Also, I try to anticipate what she might ask me to do and then offer to do it first. This gives me the feeling that I can be an actor rather than just a puppet.
Paragraph V.	Conclusion with restatement of thesis.
Thesis Restated	Sometimes I still get frustrated at work. As a lowly clerk, I do not get much respect in a large, impersonal company. <u>However, my job has shown me that even the most ordinary parts of my life can give me an opportunity to learn something about myself and other people.</u>

Topic sentences do not always occur at the beginning of paragraphs. In fact, at times it seems stilted to put the topic sentence at the start of a paragraph. You may need a sentence or two that makes a bridge with the preceding paragraph. For example, the fourth paragraph in the sample essay above might have been written more chronologically, following the sequence of events more closely.

Example:	After my initial anger, I noticed the store manager peering down at my boss from the upstairs office window. I realized that my boss had a boss who had a boss; She was just a part of the pecking order like me. <u>I decided to try to influence the situation instead of just reacting to it.</u>
Thesis Statement	

Placing the topic sentence at the start of a paragraph gives the clearest signal to a reader, but it is not always essential to place the topic sentence at the beginning. It is important, however, to have a sentence that holds the rest of the paragraph together. It can come at the beginning, the middle, or the end of the paragraph. Here is a paragraph without a topic sentence:

Ms. Rodriquez always had a word of encouragement on each test she handed back. Furthermore, she taught me the difference between an intelligent mistake and a dumb one. An intelligent mistake occurs when a learner applies a rule or procedure to a special situation where it does not apply. For example, if a young child says, "I taked the book," she is applying the rule to use a "d" sound for a past action. Ms. Rodriguez also had a way of making math problems exciting mysteries. We watched her solve equations on the board like Sherlock Holmes in pursuit of a suspect. The work was never easy, but she always made us feel that it was possible to succeed if we put in enough time.

One way to phrase a topic sentence for the paragraph above would be:
<u>Ms. Rodriguez was one of the best teachers I ever had.</u>

Even if you think that the point of the paragraph is perfectly clear without a topic sentence, put one in. You are now writing this essay for a sophisticated magazine; you are taking a test to show that you can get an idea across clearly to a reader.

EXERCISE F.

1. Each paragraph below lacks a topic sentence. Create a topic sentence for each paragraph and decide where best to place it.

   a. I would be happy if I could make some difference in the lives of the students I will teach. It might just mean making them more curious about the world or more accepting of themselves. I realize that it is difficult to reach each student, but that does not mean that I will not try.
   b. Mr. Wright began every class by putting the homework on the board. Then he would announce what we were going to do that day. Usually, we went over the homework problems first. Students were asked to put their solutions on the board. After discussing them and making necessary corrections, Mr. Wright would turn to the new material. Using three or four pieces of colored chalk, he illustrated and commented on the examples in the book. Finally, if we finished all of the scheduled lesson, there was time at the end of class to start on the homework.
   c. Every teacher spends a minimum of 35 hours in school. In addition, teachers must often supervise activities such as the drama club or school newspaper. Conferences with parents, staff meetings, and required professional development activities also add to the total hours required. A teacher usually has three different course-related preparations, each of which may take an hour or more, depending on the teacher's experience. English teachers who have 25 to 30 students per class may assign a short piece of writing each week, and may spend 4 to 5 minutes reading each paper. This may add 13 hours of additional work per week.

2. Go back to the material that you brainstormed and organized in Exercise D. Pick at least one batch of material and turn it into an essay following the pattern of the five-paragraph essay described previously.

TRANSITIONS

Transitions are signals to your reader about how your ideas are connected. Certain words and phrases prepare the reader for what is to follow. Examples of important transitions to use in your essay are:

1. Words that indicate sequence of events or ideas: first, second (etc.), finally, last, ultimately, eventually, later, meanwhile, afterwards;

2. Words that indicate examples: for instance, for example, specifically, in particular;

3. Words that indicate addition of similar ideas: and, also, furthermore, moreover, similarly, equally important, another;

4. Words that indicate addition of contrasting ideas: however, but, on the other hand, on the contrary, still, yet, in contrast, nevertheless.

Transitions between sentences can also be achieved by repeating key words, using synonyms, or using pronouns.

1. Example of a repeated key word: *Literacy* is not just a matter of learning the ABC's, *Literacy* means having sufficient control of the language to function in one's society.

2. Example of use of a synonym: *Literacy* is not just a matter of learning the ABC's. One's ability to read and write must be equal to the demands of one's society.

3. Example use of a pronoun: *Literacy* is not just a matter of learning the ABC's. It means having sufficient control of the language to function in your society.

EXERCISE G.

1. Look at the paragraphs you wrote in Exercise F and underline all the transitions.

2. Go back to the essay you wrote in Exercise F. Underline any transitions you used. Find places where you might insert additional transitions.

PROOFREAD FOR WORD CHOICE, GRAMMAR, AND MECHANICS

Under ideal conditions, you would complete a first draft and then evaluate it for content and structure. However, a subtest, lasting approximately one hour, does not allow time for true revision. You may want to think of your brainstorming as a type of first draft and your focusing as a type of revision. As you focus and compose your essay, you will do a certain amount of revision, deciding to change the order of paragraphs, inserting or deleting details, trying out sentences in your head before you put them down on paper. Once you have completed the essay, you need to proofread to make sure you have used words correctly and avoid errors that will detract from your essay and subsequently from the score you receive for your essay.

WORD CHOICE

In choosing words to express your ideas, keep in mind that the directions on the examination writing subtest are likely to specify an audience that requires you to use a professional tone. You should avoid slang and cliches. On the other hand, don't go overboard and complicate your essay with fancy terms and inflated language. Aim for a clear and direct expression of your ideas.

Here are a few examples of the kinds of words and expressions to avoid:

1. One activity that I've really *gotten into* lately is sailing. (Substitute *became involved in, become interested in, become enthusiastic about*).

2. The person sitting behind me talked *a lot* during the class. (Try to be as specific as possible about what *a lot* means in the sentence where you are tempted to use it. Here, you might use *continuously* or *incessantly*, but at other times, you might want to substitute *a great deal* or *often*.)

3. My first class was *awful*. (General words such as *awful, perfect, beautiful*, etc. are acceptable if you are going to follow up with more specific description. However, it is almost always better to use specific language. In what respect was the experience or the person awful, perfect, or beautiful? In the example above, was the class dull, disorganized, too demanding?)

4. I was faced with a *number of alternatives*. (Strictly defined, an alternative is a choice between two things. If you mean more than two, use options *or* choices.)

5. Computers are a *new innovation* in the classroom. (Innovation means *new*; therefore, the phrase is redundant. The same would be true of expressions such as *personal friend* and *advance planning*.)

Our language is constantly changing. At any period in history, some words and expressions are considered suitable for formal writing while others are considered colloquial and appropriate only for informal settings. As you prepare for the writing subtest, you might want to use a dictionary or a glossary of usage in a handbook. These references will provide guidance in currently acceptable choices. You might also want to keep in mind that no references will be available during the test. Therefore, if you have any doubt about the appropriateness of a word or phrase, you might want to avoid using it, and choose words about which you feel more confident.

Excess words are as much a problem as inexact words. When people don't know what to write, they often try to pad the paragraphs with sentences that say the same thing in slightly different words or fill up the sentences with empty phrases. Superfluous words and sentences may bore, frustrate, or even confuse your reader. You will be spared these problems if you practice brainstorming for relevant and interesting details before you compose your essay. Here are some examples of padded writing:

Wordy: Education faces a crisis today. At the present time, a number of problems are troubling concerned citizens. Not a day goes by that you do not hear about one problem or another.

To the Point: Many problems in education call for our attention.

Wordy: Due to the fact that a problem arose concerning the time our committee should meet, we decided in the final analysis that it would be best to postpone our decision until the new chairperson took over.

To the Point: Unable to agree on a meeting time, our committee postponed the decision until the new chairperson took over.

EXERCISE H

1. Find places in your own writing where you could eliminate words without losing meaning.

2. Trim unnecessary words from the following sentences and rewrite.

   a. The aspects of teaching that I imagine I will most enjoy are the diversity of students and the freedom to organize my own classes.

   b. The problem that I foresee causing the most difficulty in the future is that a few years from now we are going to have even more non-native English speaking students than we do now and people don't understand the need for bilingual education.

   c. In conclusion, the final point that I want to make is to say that the productivity of our economic system will decline unless we do something to tackle the problem of illiteracy among the many people who can't read at all or who can barely read.

EXERCISE I

There are a number of commonly confused words. Use a dictionary or handbook to check the correct choice for each of the sentences that follow.

1. I _____ your invitation to the party. (accept, except, expect)
2. I _____ to do well on my math exam. (accept, except, expect)
3. Everyone is going _____ Susan. (accept, except, expect)
4. I went to my guidance teacher for some good _____. (advise, advice)
5. I always _____ my students to take French literature. (advise, advice)
6. The _____ of the hurricane was horrendous. (affect, effect)
7. Does this test _____ my grade? (affect, effect)
8. _____ never too late to try. (Its, It's)
9. The committee reported _____ decision. (its, it's)
10. Please place the books over _____. (there, they're, their)
11. _____ my brother's friends. (There, They're, Their)
12. The boys have lost _____ shoes. (there, they're, their)

13. Most of the students could not choose _____ the four answers. (between, among)
14. Mary is trying to decide _____ two majors: History and French. (between, among)
15. John arrived at the game, _____. (to, too, two)
16. Please place _____ books on this corner. (to, two, too)
17. David gave the ball _____ Mark. (to, two, too)
18. Peter ran the mile _____. (bad, badly)
19. I feel _____ when it rains. (bad, badly)
20. Teachers often have to _____ packaged materials to the special needs of their students. (adopt, adapt)
21. Our school would like to _____ a dress code for all students. (adopt, adapt)
22. This corner will be the _____ for the reading materials. (site, cite)
23. Students must learn how to _____ source materials in a research paper. (site, cite)
24. Individualized activities are needed to _____ group activities. (compliment, complement)
25. Teachers should _____ children often on the work that they successfully complete. (compliment, complement)

GRAMMAR AND MECHANICS

An occasional error in grammar or mechanics in an essay written without access to a dictionary will not result in failing the writing portion of the exam. However, frequent errors will detract from the effectiveness of your message and can cause failure. There are so many possible errors, that they cannot be covered in this brief guide. A discussion of the most serious errors will be followed by a set of sentences you can use to test your proofreading skills.

1. <u>Sentence Boundaries</u>: Running two or more independent clauses together without linking words or proper punctuation violates basic rules. A grammatically incomplete sentence is equally distracting.

    a. Run-on, fused sentence, or comma splice: Teaching is not an easy field, the rewards aren't always there. (A comma is not sufficient to separate two independent clauses. Substitute a period, a semi-colon, or a linking word, such as *because* for the comma.)

    b. Fragment: The best example being the difference between the way we see a character on TV and the way we visualize a character in a story. (The *ing* form of the verb creates a fragment. Substitute *is* for *being* to correct the sentence.)

2. <u>Agreement of Sentence Elements</u>: Verbs must agree with their subjects; pronouns with the nouns to which they refer. Similar elements must have parallel structure. Parts of the sentence must fit together grammatically.

    a. Lack of subject-verb agreement: The problems that young readers have seems to come partly from the environment. (*problems* calls for the verb form *seem* not *seems*. In sentences where several words come between subject and verb, it is easy to lose track of the elements.)

b. Lack of pronoun agreement: Everyone wants to achieve their potential. (*Everyone* is singular and calls for *his/her*, not *their*.)

c. Lack of parallel structure: I learned to operate the computer, write some simple programs, and the fundamentals of word processing. (*Operate* and *write* set up a pattern which calls for a similar word. Therefore, the last part of the sentence should be rephrased to include a verb; for example, *...and use the fundamentals of word processing.*)

d. Lack of grammatical fit: While taking an elective course in design my freshman year sparked my interest in art. (The introductory phrase, *While taking an elective course*, calls for a subject to come before the verb. This sentence could be revised in at least two ways:
While taking an elective course in design my freshman year, I became interested in art.
Taking an elective course in design my freshman year sparked my interest in art.

SELECTED CAPITALIZATION RULES

A few of the rules governing capitalization are reviewed below. Consult a dictionary or handbook for more complete coverage of this topic.

1. Capitalize proper nouns and adjectives.
   <u>Example:</u> Capitalize: *Judy Blume* and *Southington High School*.
   Do not capitalize *the author* or *my high school*.

2. Capitalize titles when they precede proper names, but not when they follow proper names or are used alone.
   <u>Example:</u> Professor Kent Curtis
   Kent Curtis, professor of history
   the history professor

3. Do not capitalize the names of academic years or terms.
   <u>Example:</u> spring semester
   my sophomore year

4. Capitalize the names of specific courses, but not fields of study unless they are languages.
   <u>Example:</u> Capitalize *English, Spanish,* and *Math 101*
   Do not capitalize *math, physics,* or *education*.

5. Capitalize the important words in titles of books and underline the titles.
   <u>Example:</u> <u>Catcher in the Rye</u>
   <u>Grapes of Wrath</u>

PUNCTUATION

Punctuation is another area that you should review with the help of a good handbook or dictionary. One simple rule to remember is: Do not use the dash as a substitute for the proper punctuation. Example of a punctuation error: Although I took up swimming—the doctors said it would be good exercise—but I found that I did not have the ability to make the team

(The problem with relying on dashes is that, as in the example, dependence can lead to sloppy sentence construction. The sentence above should be revised: I took up swimming because the doctors said it would be good exercise, but I found that I did not have the ability to make the team.)

EXERCISE J

1. Proofread the following essay to identify errors in grammar, mechanics, and word use. Underline or cross out all errors.

2. Rewrite the essay, using correct grammar, mechanics, and wording.

The extent of illiteracy in the Country is documented in Illiterate America—a book by Jonathan Kozol. When I read this book and realized the extent of illiteracy gave me a shock. Kozol claims that 25 million people can not red warning labels or a simple news story, another 35 million do not read well enough to survive in the Modern Age—Like being able to follow printed instructions. For someone who can't read and has to support himself or a family could be a real disadvantage.

The problem of illiteracy will be difficult to solve. There being many causes that go deep into our society. Schools have failed to halt the problem and may be contributing to it. My parents say that the problem with schools today are a lack of respect for authority. Years ago, everyone know what would happen if they disobeyed a teacher. Today, teachers must contend with students who are often bored, rarely prepared and frequently they defy the teacher. Some respect and discipline is needed to create a learning environment.

Another problem with the schools is poorly prepare teachers. Students graduating from college without being able to read or write well. During the 1960s was the decline of strict academic standards. Students failed to learn what they should of learned. The decline may be ending, new tests and requirements are in place. For example, the college of arts and sciences at Northeastern State University changed their requirements because entering students were so poorly prepared. Some of them unable to identify Sophocles or locate spain on a map.

Kozol's book interested me in the larger issues of literacy—it is more than learning the ABCs. Literacy is when you can read and write well enough to survive in a complex technology and making informed opinions about government policies. Teachers can help to create a literate America. After reading about the problems of illiteracy facing this country, I want to become one,

19

PUTTING IT ALL TOGETHER

PRACTICE TOPICS

You will not know in advance the topic on which you will be asked to write an essay for the examination. However, the topic is likely to involve your education, education in general, or your choice of a career.

The best way to prepare for the writing subtest is to practice the skills presented in this book and to write whole essays under conditions similar to those found in examinations. Below are several topics you may use for practice.

Practice Prompt 1

The Academic Standards Committee of your college is considering changes in the current grading system and they have asked you to write a statement about the impact of the letter grade system (ABCDF) on learning. You may want to consider how the letter grade system affects certain types of students, how it is viewed by students, teachers, or prospective employers, whether there is a practical alternative, or whether modifications should be made. Write a statement of your opinion of the letter grade system and the reasons for your opinion.

Practice Prompt 2

A screening committee is reviewing your application for a teaching position and has asked you to submit a statement of your strengths and weaknesses for the position. Imagine a specific teaching position for which you might apply and write a statement about how well you qualify for that particular job. You might want to consider how your educational background, work experiences, internships, or special interests make you a suitable candidate. You might also want to consider whether there is anything about the position, the type of students you might face, the location, or the responsibilities that might be a challenge to you. Describe the teaching position for which you are applying and explain why you would be a good candidate for the position.

Practice Prompt 3

The committee considering your application to enter a teacher training program wants to learn about your awareness of students' non-academic needs. They have pointed out that a teacher must often do more than teach subject matter. Consider the psychological, physical, social, and economic problems that affect a student's ability to learn. Describe your understanding of the ways in which the role of a teacher goes beyond teaching academic subjects.

Practice Prompt 4

Your college is hosting a conference for state high school teachers to address the problem of the inadequate preparation of the average student for college work. The conference is focusing on the average student because college teachers are concerned about the many students entering freshman courses who are unable to meet the demands of college. You might want to describe how serious the problem is, whose problem it is, and to what extent high schools should consider changing what they are doing. Use your experience, observations, and knowledge to write a statement which gives your perspective on the gap between the academic requirements in high school and those in college.

POST-TEST

Writing Subtest Directions

This part of the examination consists of one writing exercise. You should allow approximately 60 minutes to complete this assignment. You may NOT use a dictionary during the subtest. Make sure you have time to plan, write, review, and revise what you have written.

Before you begin to write, read the topic carefully and take some time to think about how you will organize what you plan to say. Your writing exercise will be evaluated on the basis of how effectively it communicates a whole message to the intended audience for the stated purpose. Your writing exercise will be judged on the success of its total impression by a panel of language arts experts. When evaluating your ability to communicate a whole message effectively, the scorers will also consider your ability to:

1. state and stay on the topic;
2. address all specified parts of the writing assignment;
3. present your ideas in an organized fashion;
4. include sufficient detail and elaboration to statements;
5. choose effective words;
6. employ correct grammar and usage; and
7. use correct mechanics (spelling, capitalization, paragraph form).

PROMPT

The screening committee considering your application for a teaching position is concerned about teacher stress and burn-out. They would like to learn about your awareness of this problem and your susceptibility to it. You might want to discuss how you have handled stressful situations in the past and any techniques that you use to cope with stress. Describe in writing how you would confront the problem of stress and burn-out in the teaching profession.

NOTES/OUTLINE

KEY (CORRECT ANSWERS)

In some cases where there is no one right answer, possible answers are given. If your answer is significantly different, discuss it with a teacher or tutor.

EXERCISE B

1. I must describe an activity and tell the committee why it is important to me.

2. I must explain to the superintendent why I want to teach and how an experience or subject helped me make this decision.

3. I have to select three courses or activities and justify why they would be worthwhile.

4. I have to write a letter to the director of admissions at the college of my choice and explain why I want to go there.

5. I have to describe to the committee a significant book and concentrate on what I got out of it.

EXERCISE C

Answers will vary.

EXERCISE D

Answers will vary.

EXERCISE E

1. Answers will vary.

2. A. An ideal wheel:

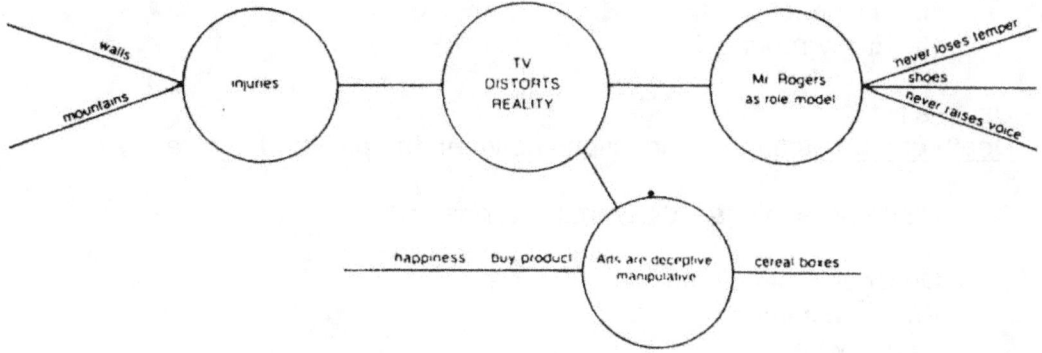

B. A flow chart:

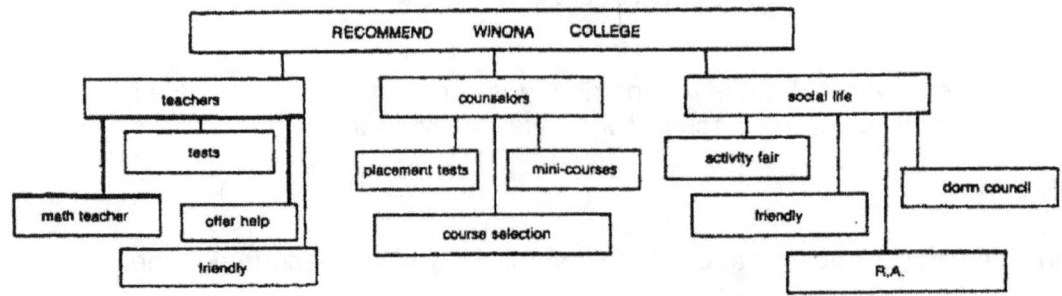

C. Using an outline:

Thesis: My job as a clerk has taught me about the reality of work and how to get along with supervisors.

I. I don't have time for special activities.
   A. School
   B. Need job
   C. Friends

II. Work is not like school because if you don't work, you don't get paid.

III. Boss is not always fair.
   A. No respect for clerks
   B. Gets impatient
   C. Got annoyed about lines

IV. I'm trying to get on top of the situation rather than just reacting.
   A. Boss is part of pecking order
   B. Make small talk
   C. Anticipate orders

V. I am still frustrated.
   A. No recognition
   B. No incentive
   C. Easily replaced

D. Using a list:
Death of a Salesman – connections between the play and my life

1. Different readings – different reactions

2. Describe characters
   Willy: salesman
   Linda: wife
   Biff: good looking, football hero breaks with Willy, drifts around
   Happy: ordinary, shadowed by Biff

3. Identified with Happy
   My older brother
   Wanted parents' attention
   School troubles
   Realized I was hurting myself
   Attention hurt Biff

4. Sympathy for Willy
   No respect from boss
   My job as a clerk, dime a dozen
   Want more than a paycheck

5. TV version – admiration for Linda
   Held family together
   Loyal to Willy
   Want someone like her

E. Another list:
   Choices: integrate courses and experiences

   1. Reading Methods Required – would choose it
      What I'll learn; assessment, skills

   2. Activity – literacy volunteer
      Why don't people learn
      How to teach skills
      Effect on a person's life
      Failure of system

   3. Course or individual study in writing
      Keep journal
      Make connections
      Write feature stories for newspaper

EXERCISE F

1. Answers will vary.

2. A. One benefit of teaching is personal satisfaction.
   B. Mr. McGrath ran a tightly structured class.
   C. Many teachers work harder than people realize.

EXERCISE G

1. Example: furthermore, for example, also, like, but
   A. but
   B. then, after, finally
   C. in addition, also, another

2. Answers will vary.

EXERCISE H

1. Answers will vary.

2. A. I will enjoy the diversity of students and the freedom to organize my own classes.

   B. The failure of people to understand the need to provide bilingual education to the increasing numbers of non-native English speaking students will be our biggest problem.

   C. Finally, failure to tackle the various forms of illiteracy will cause a decline in our economic productivity.

EXERCISE I

1. accept
2. expect
3. except
4. advice
5. advise
6. effect
7. affect
8. It's
9. its
10. there
11. they're
12. their
13. among
14. between
15. too
16. two
17. to
18. badly
19. bad
20. adapt
21. adopt
22. site
23. cite
24. complement
225. compliment

25

EXERCISE J

The extent of illiteracy in this country is documented in <u>Illiterate America</u>, a book by Jonathan Kozol. When I read this book and realized the extent of illiteracy, I was shocked. Kozol claims that 25 million people cannot read warning labels or a simple news story; because they are unable to another 35 million do not read well enough to survive in the Modern Age able to follow printed instructions. Someone who can't read and has to support himself or her or a family is at a real disadvantage.

The problem of illiteracy will be difficult to solve. Its causes go deep into our society. Schools have failed to halt the problem and may be contributing to it. My parents say that the problem with schools today is a lack of respect for authority. Years ago, students knew what would happen if they disobeyed a teacher. Today, teachers must contend with students who are often bored, rarely prepared, and frequently defiant of the teacher. Respect and discipline are needed to create a learning environment.

Another problem with the schools is poorly prepared teachers. Students graduate from college without being able to read or write well. During the 1960s strict academic standards declined. Students failed to learn what they should have learned. The decline may be ending because new tests and requirements are in place. For example, the College of Arts and Sciences at Northeastern State University changed its requirements because entering students were so poorly prepared. Some of them were unable to identify Sophocles or locate Spain on a map.

Kozol's book interested me in the larger issues of literacy, Literacy means more than learning the ABCs. It means reading and writing well enough to survive in a complex society and making informed opinions about government policies. Teachers can help to create a literate America. After reading about the problems of illiteracy facing this country, I want to become a teacher.